The Columbia Guide to
East African Literature in English
Since 1945

The Columbia Guides to Literature Since 1945

The Columbia Guides to Literature Since 1945

The Columbia Guide to
East African Literature in English
Since 1945

Simon Gikandi and Evan Mwangi

Columbia University Press
New York

Columbia University Press
Publishers Since 1893
New York   Chichester, West Sussex

Library of Congress Cataloging-in-Publication Data
Gikandi, Simon.
    The Columbia guide to East African literature in English since 1945 / Simon
Gikandi and Evan Mwangi.
        p. cm. — (The Columbia guides to literature since 1945)
    Includes bibliographical references and index.
    ISBN-10 0–231–12520–8 (cloth : alk. paper)
    ISBN-13 978–0–231–12520–8 (cloth : alk. paper)—

    ISBN-10 0–231–50064–5 (e-book)
    ISBN-13 978–0–231–50064–7 (e-book)
    1. East African literature (English)—History and criticism—Handbooks, manuals,
etc. 2. East African literature (English)—20th century—History and
criticism—Handbooks, manuals, etc. I. Mwangi, Evan. II. Title. III. Series.

    PR9340.G55 2007
    820.9′9676—dc22

                                                                2006028889

Columbia University Press books are printed on permanent and durable acid-free paper.

Printed in the United States of America

c 10 9 8 7 6 5 4 3 2 1

Contents

Preface

Simon Gikandi

Compared to other African literatures in European languages, East African writing in English is relatively new, and its presence in the major literary histories of the postcolonial world appears scanty in comparison to other regions. There are several historical and institutional explanations for what appears to be the belatedness of East African writing in English and its diminished place in Anglophone literary and cultural history. First, of all the major regions of the vast African continent, East Africa is the smallest both in terms of size and population, and thus tends to be overwhelmed by larger and more populous regions, especially West Africa and southern Africa. Second, while all the other regions of the continent have been in contact with Europe since the late sixteenth century and have thus developed traditions of culture and writing in European languages that are as old as the colonial encounter, East Africa was colonized relatively late. Indeed, except for the coastal regions of the continent, which have been in contact with Europe since the sixteenth century, large parts of East Africa did not become drawn into the drama of colonialism until the last two decades of the nineteenth century. Third, because colonial institutions were established only in the last phase of imperial expansion on the African continent, English-language literatures in East Africa did not emerge or develop until the period after World War II. East Africa has a long history of writing in African languages including Arabic, Swahili, Amharic, and Somali, but it was only after World War II that its writers turned to English as a serious medium of literary production. Finally, when a distinct East African literary tradition finally emerged in the 1960s, it was produced by writers who, unlike their West African and southern African counterparts, were still firmly located in the region in terms of their education and outlook. While other African writers turned elsewhere for their education and institutionalization, East African writers tended to develop local and regional networks.

It is thus important to begin by recognizing the regional nature of East African literature, or at least its strong sense of regionality. This sense was enabled by many circumstances, but perhaps the most important one was the region's attempt to sustain a stable political and economic culture during the 1960s, the first decade of independence. In other words, in the 1960s and 1970s, when other regions on the continent were suffering from political strife and economic crises, most of East Africa remained fairly stable. Its major writers were not forced into exile until much later, and the region had a thriving publishing industry, writers' organizations, and universities, all of which continued to privilege literary culture even in the age of science and technology.

There were, however, disadvantages to this regional focus. Writers who were published locally and became household names in East Africa (the most obvious example is the Ugandan poet Okot p'Bitek) were not well known outside the region until they were republished in Europe or the United States much later in their careers. Although East African literature in English shared the dynamism displayed by much African culture during the first two decades of independence, it was, ironically, marginalized on two fronts: (1) within the context of African literary history, it appeared new and belated in relation to English literature from southern Africa and West Africa, and (2) within the East African region itself, this literature was considered minor in relation to older and more influential literary traditions in African languages such as Somali and Swahili. Indeed, if writing in English appeared new in the period after World War II, literature in African languages was part of a canon that was several centuries old. Literature in Geez, the language of old Ethiopia, dates to the early Christian period and flourished during the Middle Ages, while writing in Amharic emerged in the middle of the nineteenth century. Along the coast of East Africa, literature written in Swahili dates back to the fifteenth century. The novels of Shaaban Robert, the leading Swahili man of letters, precede Ngugi's fiction by twelve years. The history of East African literature in English is thus marked by a paradox: it comes late on the scene of literary production on the continent, but it is fundamentally connected to older forms of literary expression in African languages. The purpose of this guide is to provide a map for understanding both this paradox and, by implication, what we consider to be the particularity of East African literature in English.

But why is a guide on East African literature after World War II important for the study of the emergence and transformation of African and world literature? There are numerous reasons for this kind of reference book: A major work of reference devoted to the English literatures of East Africa, a region that tends to occupy a minor role in existing reference works, is central to the history of world literatures in English. Since the major reference works on African literature almost instinctively tend to privilege the literatures of the other three regions of Africa, a guide devoted solely to East African literature in English will fill an important gap in the field. Furthermore, a guide to English literature in the region from the end of World War II to the present is also a major statement on the literary history of the region and its influence and effect on African literature as a whole. Arguably, because of its peculiar conditions of production, including its powerful sense of regionality, the newly emerging East African literature was able to challenge and transform established notions of what African literature was or was not. International publishers, who had fixed notions of what African literature was, did not look kindly on experimental works such as Okot p'Bitek's *Song of Lawino* and *Song of Ocol*, but local publishing houses such as the East African Literature Bureau and the East African Publishing House tended to be more attuned to the changing nature of literary culture on the continent. This was why even major West African writers such as the distinguished Ghanaian novelist Ayi Kwei Armah were willing to abandon their European and American publishers for regional East African publishers in the 1970s. When he needed to publish historical fictions whose subject and form seemed to both negate the high modernist norm that had won him international prominence and to contravene dominant ideas about colonialism, Armah turned to the East African Publishing House, which published *Two Thousand Seasons* and *The Healers*. There is thus a case to be made that a separate consideration of East African literature in English will lead to recognition of its difference, diversity, and particularity.

But there is another reason for undertaking this study. This project will be published at a unique moment in the production of knowledge about Africa, a period in which our understanding of the continent's peoples and cultures is being reevaluated in the face of changes in the nature of scholarship and the technologies that present it. African literature has become an important ingredient of scholarship and teaching about Africa. Not only is it a major subject in schools and universities in Africa itself, but it is also an integral component of the scholarship devoted to postcolonial or Third World literature. In addition, African literature is used regularly in social-science courses, in subjects ranging from history and sociology to the environment and public health. This guide will be an important reference for specialists in African literature as well as scholars and students interested in other nonliterary issues germane to the study of the continent. Together with the other proposed guides to West African and southern African writings in English, this work will be a major reference to the English-language literatures of the African continent.

One of the primary goals of this project will be to define and redefine the area covered by East African literatures in English. While the common historical and geographic definition of East Africa covers the former British colonies of Kenya, Uganda, and Tanzania, the English literature in the region is a superb example of how literary traditions can extend geographic or geopolitical boundaries. Looked at from a literary perspective, East Africa includes countries—Ethiopia and Somalia, for example—where there was no English writing before the 1960s. Eager to produce a literature in the English language to counter what they saw as a conservative literary tradition in Amharic and Somali, writers from Ethiopia and Somalia turned to the East African countries for models and institutions to support their creativity. Thus, since the 1960s, East African English-language literature has expanded from its original base in Kenya, Uganda, and Tanzania to include Ethiopia and Somalia, and writers from these latter two countries, most notably Berhane Mariam Sahle Sellassie and Nurrudin Farah, are considered major figures in the field. In addition, given the relatively fluid nature of African boundaries, writers have not been especially constrained by cartography. Writers born outside East Africa have often been important producers of literature in the region. This was the case with expatriate writers such as Karen Blixen, from Denmark, or the Malawian novelist and poet David Rubadiri, who was educated in East Africa and lived in the region for many years. At the same time, some prominent writers born in East Africa, most notably Abdurazak Gurnah and M. Vassanji, are located in other countries but still draw their historical and literary materials from East Africa. All of the aforementioned writers are included here as part of an ever-growing East African diaspora. A new English literature has evolved in southern Sudan, but as its trajectory is not yet clear, we have not covered that region in this guide.

In terms of its organization, this guide follows the format established for other guides in this series. We begin with a chronology of major historical events in the region, which gives readers a sense of the political and social processes that have affected the form and function of writing in East Africa. This is followed by a comprehensive overview of the emergence and transformation of literary culture in the region, focusing on the major writers of distinct historical moments, the institutions of literary production, and the major themes of this literature. Although we note significant developments in Ethiopia and Somalia, our emphasis is on the three East African countries that were part of the British Empire: Kenya, Tanzania, and Uganda. It was in these countries that literature in English first took root.

A notable feature of East African literature in the 1990s was the phenomenon of self-publishing and the emergence of small presses. This has opened the field of literary expression to a large body of writers, but it has meant that texts are not always easily available or accessible. We have sought to include as many writers from the region writing in English since World War II as possible, regardless of their reputation or standing in the canon. But the production of literature in the region is a dynamic, ongoing process, and we have not always been able to include writers who are just now appearing on the scene. While the nature of each of the individual author entries varies somewhat, we have sought to provide significant biographical and literary information and a description of significant works. Our goal here is to provide readers with descriptive—rather than evaluative—entries and to give them a sense of the individual author's central thematic concerns, formal innovations, and place in the tradition of East African letters. The topical entries fall into two broad categories: some present a historical, cultural, and social background to an important aspect of literary culture in the region, while others take up and amplify major themes in the tradition and compare how these themes have been treated by individual authors and how they have evolved over time. At the end of each entry, we provide bibliographic information on the authors and, in most cases, references for further reading. At the end of the book, we present a general bibliography, organized into two parts. The first part is a list of important works discussing history and culture; the second is a list of general works on literature.

Acknowledgments

In writing this project, we relied on the editorial and research assistance of several people and institutions, and we would like to take this opportunity to thank them. Initial financial support for the project was provided by the University of Michigan, through the office of the Dean of Literature, Arts, and Sciences. A humanities grant from the office of the Dean of Faculty at Princeton University enabled one of us to travel to East Africa to complete the research for the project. Valuable research assistance, including work on the bibliography, was provided by Adeline Koh, at the University of Michigan. In addition, we received invaluable help from a host of East African field scholars and Africana librarians. The following provided us with texts, information, and materials from Nairobi, Kampala, and Dar es Salaam: Pilli Kamenju, Larry Ndivo, Jennifer Muchiri, William Mkufya, Martha Wambui, Goretti Kyomuhendo, Paul Ndunguru, Mikhail Gromov, Muthoni wa Ndegwa, Elias Ng'ang'a, Tom Odhiambo, Julie Barak, Adam H. O. Korogoto, and Paul Wahiu. Loyd Mbabu, the Africana bibliographer at Ohio University, provided assistance with the acquisition of out-of-print books. We also received information on rare books and documents from the staff of the Melville J. Herskovits Library of African Studies at Northwestern University and from its director, David Easterbrook, especially. At Columbia University Press, Juree Sondker chaperoned the completion of the project with professionalism and care. Sections of the introduction have been published as "East African Literature in English," in *The Cambridge History of African and Caribbean Literature,* ed. E. Abiola Irele and Simon Gikandi (Cambridge: Cambridge University Press, 2004). They are reproduced here by permission. The chronology is adapted from "Country Profiles," BBC Monitoring Service, also with permission.

Chronology of Major Political Events

Adapted from BBC News: http://news.bbc.co.uk/go/pr/fr/-/1/hi/world/africa/country_profiles/1072611.stm.

Ethiopia

1855	Lij Kasa declares himself Emperor Tewodros II.
1868	Tewodros defeated by a British expeditionary force and commits suicide to avoid capture.
1872	Tigrayan chieftain becomes Yohannes IV.
1889	Emperor Johannes IV killed by Mahdist forces. The king of Shoa becomes Emperor Menelik II and signs a friendship treaty with Italy.
1895	Italian invasion of Ethiopia begins.
1896	Italian forces defeated by Ethiopia at the historic battle of Adwa. Italy retains control over Eritrea.
1913	Menelik dies and is succeeded by his grandson Lij Iyasu.
1916	Lij Iyasu deposed. He is succeeded by Menelik's daughter Zawditu. Ras Tafari Makonnen rules Ethiopia as regent.
1930	Zawditu dies. The Regent Ras Tafari Makonnen becomes Emperor Haile Selassie I.
1935	Second Italian invasion of Ethiopia.
1936	Italian forces capture Addis Ababa. Haile Selassie flees into exile. Ethiopia is incorporated into Italian East Africa. International outcry against the invasion and occupation of Ethiopia.
1941	Troops from Britain and its colonies defeat Italian occupiers of Ethiopia. Haile Selassie is restored to his throne.
1952	United Nations puts Eritrea under Ethiopian protectorate.
1962	Haile Selassie annexes Eritrea.
1963	Organization of African Unity meets in Addis Ababa.
1973–1974	Great Ethiopian famine. Over 200,000 people die in Wallo province. Opposition and resistance to the emperor and feudal system intensifies.

1974	Haile Selassie overthrown in military coup led by General Teferi Benti.
1975	Haile Selassie dies in custody.
1977	Benti killed in a palace coup led by junior military officers. Colonel Mengistu Haile Mariam becomes leader of the Dergue.
1977–1979	Dergue dictatorship established. Ethiopia is turned into a Soviet-style state.
1977	Somalia invades Ethiopia's Ogaden region.
1978	Somali forces defeated by Ethiopia with Soviet and Cuban assistance.
1987	Mengistu elected president under a new constitution.
1988	Ethiopia and Somalia sign a peace treaty.
1991	Ethiopian People's Revolutionary Democratic Front enters Addis Ababa. Mengistu flees into exile. Provisional government established in Eritrea.
1993	Eritrea becomes independent.
1995	Meles Zenawi becomes prime minister.
1998–1999	Ethiopian-Eritrean war over border dispute.
2000	June: Ethiopia and Eritrea sign a ceasefire.
	November: Haile Selassie buried in Addis Ababa's Trinity Cathedral.
	December: Ethiopia and Eritrea sign a peace agreement.
2004	November: Ethiopia accepts UN commission's ruling on the disputed border with Eritrea.
2005	April: First section of Axum obelisk, which was looted by Italy in 1937, is returned to Ethiopia from Rome.
	May: Third multiparty elections. Violent protests against alleged fraud leads to the deaths of forty people.

Kenya

1895	Formation of British East African Protectorate.
1900	White settlement begins. Building of Uganda Railway commences.
1902	Completion of Uganda Railway from Mombasa to Lake Victoria.
1904	Cash-crop economy initiated with establishment of sisal and tea plantations. First displacement of the Maasai from their ancestral lands.

1910	Coffee growing on a large scale begins.
1911	Second displacement of the Maasai.
1919	Settlement of white World War I veterans.
1920	Establishment of Kenya colony.
1921	Formation of Young Kavirondo and Young Kikuyu Association marks the beginning of African nationalism in Kenya.
1922	African protest against the *kipande* (identification document) system takes place outside the Norfolk Hotel. African nationalist Harry Thuku sent into exile.
1923	Devonshire White Paper clarifies colonial policy by declaring that Kenya is "a black man's country." Kikuyu Central Association formed, with Jomo Kenyatta as the secretary. Local Native Councils established.
1928	Hilton Young Committee issues its report on questions of land ownership and African representation in the colony.
1929	Conflict between the Church of Scotland Mission and Kikuyu nationalists over the issue of female circumcision breaks out at Tumu Tumu. Traditionalists set up Independent Christian churches.
1931	Kenyatta represents the case for Kikuyu land and political rights in London. Great Depression leads to collapse of economy.
1934	Conflict between Kikuyu and white settlers continues over land rights. Carter Land Commission Report issued.
1936	Introduction of income tax.
1938	Native Lands Trust Ordinance issue. Kenyatta publishes *Facing Mt. Kenya* in London.
1940–1941	Italian troops invade northern Kenya. British counteraction launched in Somalia and Ethiopia with the participation of the King African Rifles.
1943	The Reverend L. Beecher appointed to the Legislative Council to represent African interests.
1944	Kenyan African Union (KAU) formed. E. W. Mathu appointed as the first African member of legislative council.
1945	Return of disenchanted African soldiers from the war leads to the emergence of radical nationalism.
1946	Jomo Kenyatta returns to Kenya.
1947	Jomo Kenyatta becomes KAU leader.
1948	Kenya Land and Freedom Army ("Mau Mau") formed.

1952	Mau Mau begins violent campaign against white settlers and black collaborators. State of emergency declared. Kenyatta arrested.
1953	Kenyatta jailed. KAU banned. Fierce fighting between colonial and Mau Mau forces. System of villagization set up in central and eastern Kenya to contain support for Mau Mau. Detention camps set up in remote parts of the country. Nationalists and their supporters detained without trial.
1954	Mass arrest of Kikuyu in Nairobi. Capture of Mau Mau General China. Divisions within Mau Mau. Lyttleton Constitution proposes a multiracial Council of Ministers.
1956	Arrest and execution of Dedan Kimathi. Mau Mau rebellion finally put down.
1957	Eight Africans elected to Legislative Council.
1958	Lennox Boyd Constitution proposes more African representation, but Legislative Council is boycotted by members demanding the release of Jomo Kenyatta.
1959	Kenyatta is released from jail but put under house arrest.
1960	State of emergency ended. First Lancaster House Conference provides for an interim constitution. Formation of Kenya African National Union (KANU) and Kenya African Democratic Union (KADU).
1961	Kenyatta is released from detention and assumes presidency of KANU. KANU wins elections, but a coalition government is formed between KADU and the white New Kenya Party.
1962	Kenyatta becomes a member of the Legislative Council. Debate continues on the nature of an independence constitution.
1963	May: KANU wins an overall majority in new elections.
	June 1: The country becomes self-governing, with Kenyatta as prime minister.
	December 12: Kenya gains independence.
1964	Republic of Kenya formed with Kenyatta as president and Oginga Odinga as vice president.
1966	Odinga leaves KANU and forms Kenya People's Union (KPU).
1969	Assassination of popular minister Tom Mboya sparks ethnic unrest. KPU banned and Odinga arrested.

1978	Kenyatta dies in office, succeeded by Vice President Daniel arap Moi.
1982	Kenya officially declared a one-party state by the National Assembly.
	August: Attempted coup by members of the Air Force. Suppression of dissidents and students intensifies.
1987–1988	Suppression of opposition draws international criticism.
1989	Political prisoners freed.
1990–1991	Opposition against the government intensifies. Forum for the Restoration of Democracy (FORD) formed by dissidents and opposition leaders, and it is immediately outlawed and its members arrested. In response to international censure and suspension of financial aid, the government agrees to the introduction of multiparty politics.
1992	Outbreak of ethnic clashes in the Rift Valley. Government suspected of being complicit in the clashes, in which over two thousand people die. Split in opposition camp.
	December: Moi reelected in multiparty elections with a large majority.
1997	December: Moi wins further term in new elections.
1998	August: Bomb explodes at U.S. embassy in Nairobi.
2002	December: Opposition presidential candidate Mwai Kibaki wins a landslide victory over KANU rival. End of KANU rule in Kenya.
2004	Draft of new constitution completed but not enacted. Ecologist Wangari Maathai wins Nobel Peace Prize.
2005	November–December: Voters reject a proposed new constitution.

Somalia

1888	Anglo-French agreement defines the boundary between Somali territories.
1889	Italy sets up a protectorate in central and southern Somalia.
1925	Italy acquires territory east of the Jubba river.
1936	After invasion, Italy acquires Somali-speaking parts of Ethiopia.
1940	Italy occupies British Somaliland.
1941	Defeat of Italy in the East African campaign. Britain occupies Italian Somalia.

1950	Italian Somaliland becomes a UN trust territory under Italian control.
1956	Italian Somaliland (Somalia) is granted autonomy.
1960	Independence. British and Italian parts of Somalia merge to form the United Republic of Somalia, with Aden Abdullah Osman Daar as president.
1963–1964	Violent border dispute with Kenya and Ethiopia.
1967	Abdi Rashid Ali Shermarke elected president.
1969	Shermarke is assassinated. Military coup led by General Muhammad Siad Barre.
1970	Barre declares Somalia a socialist state and establishes close relations with the Soviet Union. Period of dictatorship begins.
1977–1978	Somalia invades the Ogaden region of Ethiopia and is defeated.
1981	Opposition to Barre's regime increases.
1988	Peace agreement with Ethiopia signed.
1991	Barre ousted by opposition forces and forced into exile. Former British protectorate of Somaliland declares unilateral independence.
1992	U.S. Marines land near Mogadishu to safeguard relief supplies.
1995	UN peacekeepers leave.
1996	Warlord Muhammad Aideed dies.
1998	Puntland (northern Somalia) declares unilateral independence.
2000–2003	Period of chaos and factional fighting. Collapse of Somali state.
2004	New transitional parliament formed. Abdullahi Yusuf elected president by provisional assembly meeting in Nairobi. Ali Mohammed Ghedi appointed prime minister.

Tanzania (incorporating Tanganyika and Zanzibar)

1884	German colonization begins.
1886	Britain and Germany sign an agreement on the division of Tanzania. The coastal strip is put under the authority of the Sultan of Zanzibar under British "protection." Germany has control over the rest of the country.
1903–1905	Establishment of sisal, coffee, and cotton plantations.

1905–1906	Maji Maji uprising against German rule.
1909	End of slavery in Zanzibar.
1912	Tanga Railway extended to Moshi.
1914	Central Railway reaches Kigoma. World War I begins.
1916	British, Belgian, and South African troops occupy German East Africa.
1919	League of Nations gives Britain a mandate over Tanganyika.
1922	British mandate confirmed.
1926	Legislative Council established.
1927	Clove Growers Association (CGA) is formed in Zanzibar.
1929	Tanganyika African Association (TAA) formed.
1929–1933	Great Depression leads to economic collapse.
1939–1945	World War II. German nationals detained.
1946	United Nations adopts British mandate over Tanganyika. African representation in Legislative Council.
1953	Julius Nyerere elected president of TAA.
1954	TAA transformed into the Tanganyika African National Union (TANU), with Nyerere as president. United Nations establishes a timetable for independence.
1956	United Tanganyika Party (UTP) formed.
1957	Political rivalry between Arabs and Africans intensifies.
1958	TANU wins legislative elections in a landslide.
1960	TANU wins election with large majority.
1961	May: Internal self-government begins.
	December: Full independence achieved. Political crisis in Zanzibar continues.
1963	Zanzibar becomes independent.
1964	Sultanate of Zanzibar overthrown by Afro-Shirazi Party. Tanganyika and Zanzibar merge to become Tanzania, with Nyerere as president and Abeid Amani Karume as vice president.
1967	Arusha Declaration on African socialism.
1977	TANU and Zanzibar's Afro-Shirazi Party merge to become Chama cha Mapinduzi (Revolutionary Party, or CCM). Establishment of one-party state.
1978	Uganda invades Tanzanian territory.

1979	Tanzanian forces invade Uganda and oust President Idi Amin.
1985	Nyerere retires and is replaced by Ali Mwinyi.
1992	Constitution amended to allow multiparty politics.
1995	Benjamin Mkapa chosen as president.
1999	Julius Nyerere dies.
2000	Mkapa reelected for a second term.
2001–2002	Political crisis in Zanzibar.
2004	East African Union agreement signed in Arusha.
2005	Governing CCM wins Zanzibar elections. Jakaya Kikwete, foreign minister and ruling CCM candidate, wins presidential elections, replacing Benjamin Mkapa.

Uganda

1875	Bugandan King Mutesa I allows Christian missionaries to enter the kingdom.
1877	British Missionary Society arrives in Buganda.
1879	French Roman Catholic White Fathers in Buganda.
1890	Agreement between Britain and Germany assigns Uganda to the former.
1892	Violent struggle between Protestants and Catholics in Buganda. Frederick Lugard extends the British East India Company control to southern Uganda and helps Protestant missionaries defeat their Catholic rivals.
1894	British protectorate over Uganda.
1900	Buganda Agreement. British grant the kingdom autonomy.
1904	Establishment of commercial cotton farming.
1921	Legislative council established without African representation.
1922	Makerere technical school established.
1923	Land grievances in Buganda.
1926	Financial crisis in Buganda. Resignation of Sir Apolo Kagwa, architect of the Buganda Agreement, as prime minister of Buganda.
1930	Conflict between the Kabaka (king) of Buganda and the colonial administration.
1931	Uganda Railway reaches Kampala.

1933	Conflict between the Kabaka and the Buganda legislature (the Lukiko).
1939	Mutesa II becomes Kabaka.
1941	Decision of the Namasole (the king's mother) to remarry triggers a political crisis in Buganda.
1945	Political crisis in Buganda leads to riots. Assassination of the Katikiro (prime minister).
1949	Conflict over land rights leads to more riots in Buganda.
1950	Buganda boycott of Legislative Council.
1953	Legislative reforms agreed on, but Buganda demands special status. The Kabaka is deported.
1955	Buganda constitutional crisis is briefly settled.
1961	Constitutional conference in London establishes special status for Buganda.
1962	Uganda becomes independent, with Milton Obote as prime minister.
1963	Uganda becomes a republic, with Kabaka Mutesa as president.
1966	Obote ends Buganda's special autonomy. The Kabaka is sent into exile.
1967	New constitution consolidates Obote's power and divides Buganda.
1971	Obote is overthrown in coup led by General Idi Amin.
1972–1976	Amin dictatorship. Uganda gripped by a reign of terror and destruction. Over 400,000 Ugandans killed.
1978	Uganda invades Tanzania, with a view to annexing Kagera region.
1979	Tanzania, with the help of anti-Amin forces, invades Uganda. Amin flees into exile. Yusufu Lule is installed as president, but is soon replaced by Godfrey Binaisa.
1980	Binaisa overthrown by the army. Milton Obote becomes president after elections.
1985	Obote deposed in military coup and is replaced by Tito Okello.
1986	National Resistance Army rebels take Kampala and install Yoweri Museveni as president.
1993	Museveni restores the traditional kingdoms and their rulers, but with limited power.

1996	Museveni returned to office in Uganda's first direct presidential election.
2000	Ugandans vote to reject multiparty politics in favor of continuing Museveni's "no-party" system.
2002–2004	Rebellion Lord's Resistance Army (LRA) grows in the north, leading to massive loss of lives and destruction of institutions.
2005	Parliament approves a constitutional amendment scrapping presidential term limits. Voters back a return to multiparty politics in a referendum.
2006	Yoweri Museveni is reelected president for a third term.

*The Columbia Guide to
East African Literature in English
Since 1945*

Introduction
East African Literature in English from 1945 to the Present

Simon Gikandi

Historical Context

There is a close relation between the major historical developments in East Africa during the period covered by this guide and the nature of the literary tradition that has emerged, often in response to major historical and cultural events, in the region. But in providing a context for the emergence of East African literature in English from World War II to the present day, it is important to refer to events further back in time, especially to the period from the late nineteenth century to what has come to be known as the late colonial period, because it was during this time that the institutions that would come to determine the production and interpretation of East African writing were established. It was also during this period that the events that would become central themes in East African writing acquired their distinctive and compelling character. Until recently, East African literature lived under the shadow of the region's colonial past. For this reason, the historical context crucial to the emergence of East African literature stretches from the establishment and consolidation of colonial rule in the region in the 1890s to the restoration of democratic institutions in almost all the East African countries after the tumultuous decades that followed decolonization, a period now remembered for the failure of the nationalist project and the emergence of both military and civilian dictatorships.

The drama of East African history and culture in the long century beginning with the consolidation of colonial rule in the 1890s and ending at the resurgence of democracy in the 1990s can be defined as the dialectic between colonialism and nationalism, of the forceful desire by European powers to reshape the region to serve imperial interests and the equally powerful need of colonized Africans to secure their autonomy. This dialectic is what motivated an African elite, produced and nurtured by colonial institutions, to produce a literature of their own in the language of the colonizer. In the circumstances, it is fair to say that in all of its manifestations, East African literature after World War II has been the primary medium through which the nationalist project was imagined and witnessed, briefly celebrated in the 1960s, and harshly diagnosed and deconstructed in the 1970s and after. But however we look at it, the roots of East African society—and thus the central themes in the region's literary culture—can be traced to that period in the 1890s when Europe met Africa, a confrontation captured in some memorable lines by David Rubadiri in "Stanley Meets Mutesa":

> The reed gate is flung open
> The crowd watches in silence
> But only a moment's silence
> A silence of assessment—
> The tall dark tyrant steps forward
> He towers over the thin bearded whiteman
> Then grabbing his lean white hand
> Manages to whisper
> "Mtu mweupe karibu"
> White man you are welcome,
> The gate of reeds closes behind them
> And the west is let in.   (in Cook and Rubadiri, *Origin in East Africa*, 80)

For those readers seeking beginnings and transformations, this moment of encounter has become a defining moment in East African cultural and political history.

There are, of course, important aspects of history that predate the colonial encounter. Indeed, the regional history of East Africa is one shaped by various forms of globalization even before formal European colonialism. Christianity in East Africa, introduced to Ethiopia from the Near East in the fourth century, is older than the European Christian church. And it is important to note that while in later centuries Christianity was to be associated with European colonialism, it first arrived in East Africa directly from the Middle East and was thus always associated with values and practices that were more Eastern than Western. Islam, the other great religion of the world, has been a major feature of coastal East Africa since the year 1000, with a geographic reach stretching from the horn of Africa to the Comoro islands. Much more than a religion, Islam has been associated with the rise of the Swahili civilization of the East African coast, which is clearly one of the most important examples of cultural hybridity in the premodern period.

The mercantile civilizations that arose on the East African coast from 1000 to 1500 were built on an elaborate pattern of trade across the Indian Ocean, to India and the Arabian gulf states. Between 1300 and 1500, the Swahili culture of the East African coast, built around major urban centers such as Kilwa, Mombasa, Malindi, and Zanzibar, was associated with trade and learning. This civilization was at its peak when the three-masted ships led by the Portuguese explorer Vasco da Gama were sighted off the coast of Mozambique, on March 1, 1498. A few weeks later, da Gama's ships set anchor at the port of Mombasa, where he sought a guide to lead him across the ocean to the west coast of India. This was perhaps the beginning of the first European colonial encounter. Over the next two centuries, the Portuguese established their control over the entire East African coast, often involving major and continuous battles with the gulf states, especially the Sultanate of Oman, or with established Afro-Arab dynasties such as the Mazruis of Mombasa. But by 1699, the Portuguese had been pushed out of the major East African towns, and the Omani Arabs had established their hegemony in the region.

While the struggle for the coast was taking place, most of the interior of the region remained isolated from, or indifferent to, these global events. Indeed, during this period some of the major East African groups were themselves involved in their own internal movements and resettlements. In the Great Lakes Region, the kingdom of Bunyoro-Kitala had broken up by 1600, but the kingdom of Buganda was expanding westward. In the north, the Lwo-speaking groups were migrating down the Nile from their ancestral home in the southern Sudan. In general, the period between 1600 and 1850 was characterized by the settlement and resettlement of East African communities. These movements were often triggered by internal conflicts or the desire for new land. While many of these conflicts and the movements they triggered took place gradually over two centuries, others were more cataclysmic. Such was the case with the conflicts caused in the eastern parts of the region when it was invaded by the Gala, who moved from the Horn of Africa in a sweep that was not contained until the 1860s. Another important conflict leading to a massive reorganization of the cultural geography of the region was the *Mfecane*, the great scattering of people triggered by the rise of the Zulu empire in the 1820s. As the Zulu empire under Shaka expanded in southern Africa, it forced large communities to move northward into southern Tanzania and sometimes as far north as Lake Victoria. However, not all movements were caused by invasion, war, or conflict. The movement of the Kikuyu and other central Bantu peoples to the East African highlands in the sixteenth century had been prompted by the desire to find new and secure farmland. Similarly, the movement of the Maasai and Kalenjin groups across the Rift Valley was generated by the need for new pastures.

However, in the early and mid-nineteenth century, the dynamics of social change in East Africa was radically altered by the rise of the East African slave trade and later by the arrival of European missionaries, adventurers, and traders. The slave trade had been an important source of commerce between East Africa, the Arabian Sea, and Asia for centuries, and African slaves had been a major presence in the markets and households of the gulf states and even India since 1000 AD. But by the 1820s, the trade in ivory and slaves had become the dominant form of trade, and this had important implications for both the political economy and the cultural transformation of the region. During the early eighteenth century, the major coastal towns came under the firm grip of powerful Omani trading families. Although these families had deep roots in the Arabian Sea area, they considered the East African coastal region so important to their power that their sultan, Sayid Said, decided in 1840 to move his headquarters from Oman to the island of Zanzibar.

The slave and ivory market at Zanzibar became the center of a new economy whose effects would be felt thousands of miles inland. A new class of merchants, the most prominent being Tippu Tippu, emerged to manage the trade in slaves and ivory, and they expanded their reach all the way to central Africa. Inland, new urban centers such as Bagamoyo emerged to facilitate the new trade. In the interior, new centers of power were constructed by communities such as the Yao, Kamba, and Nyamwezi, who became the middlemen in the new trade, often raiding the interior for slaves and ivory. Thus were new connections established between cultures and communities, in an elaborate system of exchange. By the 1860s, slave merchants from Khartoum had found their way down the Nile to join this system.

The trade in ivory and slaves demanded a new political economy, one in which one group of people was subordinated to another and where those with powerful patrons established fiefdoms while the unlucky were sent on long overland caravans to the coastal slave markets. The East African slave trade is perhaps not as well known as its Atlantic counterpart, but its longevity makes it special: slavery as an institution continued to thrive in East

Africa well into the early twentieth century, slave caravans were not banned until 1876, and slavery was not abolished in British-controlled East African territories until 1917.

But the fact that it was the British who were now abolishing slavery points to another significant change in the region over the course of the nineteenth century: the emergence of European powers as regional arbiters of political, economic, and social relationships. From 1844 to 1866, missionaries, traders, and adventurers turned their attention to East Africa, finally ushering the region into the orbit of empire. In 1844, a German missionary named J. L. Krapf traveled from Mombasa to the interior, searching for converts and a place to build a mission. In 1846, J. Rebmann, another German, established a Church Missionary Society (CMS) mission at Rabai, outside Mombasa. Between 1856 and 1859, Richard Burton and his companion John Speke started exploring the interior of East Africa in their controversial search for the source of the Nile. Other missionaries and adventurers soon followed. The Methodists founded a mission at Ribe in 1861, and the Holy Ghost fathers were established in Zanzibar in 1864 and Bagamoyo in 1868. By 1877, the CMS had a mission in Buganda. The death of David Livingstone at Ujiji in 1873 increased European zeal for evangelization, exploration, and trade. Livingstone had epitomized the conjoining of all three enterprises: Christianity, commerce, and empire. It would take many years for anyone to discern any contradictions between trade and Christianity, although the case against slavery did add an extra dimension to this relationship, since evangelists promoted empire in the name of controlling slavery and replacing it with legitimate trade.

The process of formal colonization was not far behind the initial evangelical zeal of the mid-nineteenth century. By 1878, each major European power wanted a piece of the region, and the easiest way of gaining a foothold there was to follow the Christian missions, whose denominations were associated with specific countries. The French saw themselves as the protectors of Catholic missions, the British identified the areas in which the CMS and later the Scottish missions were active as parts of their sphere of influence, and the Germans were most active in those areas with Lutherans. Still, competition among the European powers was motivated more by interests of trade rather than faith. Indeed, the major actors in the early process of colonization were not governments but private holding companies such as the British East African Company and the German East African Company. The competition between these companies was fierce, and by the 1880s it had become apparent that in order for empire to yield proper profits for its investors, the process of colonization needed to be rationalized. With this goal in mind, in 1884 the powerful German Chancellor Otto Von Bismarck summoned all the European powers to a conference in Berlin to establish rules for colonization. It was at this conference that the region was divided up: Kenya and Uganda were assigned to the British; Tanganyika was given to the Germans. At the end of the nineteenth century, then, through a variety of methods ranging from violent conquest to treaties and agreements, as well as by Christian conversion, the whole East African region had come under European domination.

Between 1900 and 1945, European colonizers set out to reorganize East African societies in unprecedented ways. The early decades of the twentieth century were focused on transforming the infrastructure of the countries of the region to fit the larger framework of colonial governance. This involved the building of both the Kenya–Uganda and central Tanganyika railways; the introduction of cash crops such as coffee, cotton, and sisal as widely as possible; and the settlement of white settlers in Kenya. It was during this period that the first institutions of colonial governance were also established. With the defeat of

Germany after World War I, the East African territories came under the orbit of British rule, although there were distinct differences in how each territory was governed. For example, Kenya was considered a colony, and thus was administered, through a governor, directly by the colonial office in London. Uganda and Zanzibar were considered protectorates and were governed "indirectly" through local chiefs and monarchs. Tanzania was held in trusteeship on behalf of the League of Nations and later the United Nations. These differences were perhaps more descriptive than real, but they did later affect the process of decolonization, since the British government was to prove less keen to grant independence to Kenya than to the other territories.

Ironically, it was during the process of colonization that African communities began to develop a proactive relation to the colonizer, either through elaborate collaboration, as in the case of Sir Apolo Kagwa, the architect of the Buganda Agreement of 1900, or through violent uprisings, such as the Maji Maji revolt against German rule in Tanganyika in 1905 through 1907. In addition, there was an important corollary between the establishment of colonial rule and the emergence of African nationalism. It is not a coincidence that it was in the 1920s, when the intentions of the colonial governments became readily apparent to Africans, that active resistance to colonial rule, often led by the products of colonial institutions such as the school and mission, first emerged. In Kenya, both the Young Kavirondo and Young Kikuyu Associations were formed in 1921. In 1922, a major demonstration by Africans demanding the abolition of the *kipande* (a metal identification document all Africans were required to carry) was held in Nairobi, and Harry Thuku, the leader of the newly formed East African Association, was arrested and deported to a remote part of Kenya.

In general, the period between the establishment of formal colonial rule and the outbreak of World War II was marked by conflicts between African and foreign interests or by objections of the governed against the governors. There were grievances over land in central Kenya and Buganda, and the British government was compelled to set up commissions to deal with African demands for either compensation or rational incorporation into the colonial order. The most prominent of these were the Hilton Young (1928) and Morris Carter (1934) land commissions in Kenya. If the conflict in Kenya was between Africans and white settlers, the political debate in Uganda was shaped by an ongoing crisis between local institutions of leadership and the colonial government. In 1930, there was a major conflict between the Kabaka (king) of Buganda and the protectorate government; in 1933, the conflict was between the Kabaka and the Lukiko (the traditional legislature). In Zanzibar, political conflict tended to be racialized, as Arabs, Africans, and Indians sought to develop the most profitable relationship with the colonizer. The economic collapse triggered by the Great Depression (1929–1933) tended to aggravate political conflict.

World War II and its aftermath had a profound influence on the character of East African politics. Most directly affected were the northern areas, namely Ethiopia and Somalia. Ethiopia had managed to retain its independence during the whole of the colonial period, while parts of Somalia were under Italian control. In a bid to fulfill his imperial ambitions, the Italian dictator Benito Mussolini invaded Ethiopia in 1936, occupied the capital Addis Ababa, and forced Emperor Haile Sellasie into exile. The Italian occupation of Ethiopia triggered international outrage, drew unprecedented condemnation, and helped consolidate Pan-African opinion against colonialism. With the outbreak of war in Europe, Italy allied with Germany, and in 1940, Italian forces occupied British-controlled Somaliland. In

1941, the British mobilized African soldiers for the counterattack, and East Africa became drawn into the war proper.

But perhaps the most important aspect of the war on African communities was not at home, or even closer to home, but abroad. In what at one time appeared to be a futile bid to defend its eastern empire, especially India, Burma, and Palestine, the colonial authorities in East Africa recruited young African men, most of them products of the missions, to fight to defend the crown. It was during their foreign sojourn that these young East Africans were first exposed to the larger world, discovering other Africans and Asians whose colonial experiences and grievances mirrored their own and, in the process, cultivating the spirit of nationalism. Returning home after the war, these young men radicalized the nature of politics in the region.

In more specific ways, the end of the war served as a catalyst to radical politics, especially in Kenya, where whites who had served in the war were rewarded handsomely with land while already disgruntled African soldiers often found themselves shut out of the postwar economic boom. Measures adopted by the colonial government to incorporate Africans into the political process were now seen as slow and ineffective, and new modes of resistance emerged. These included riots in Uganda in 1949 and the violent uprising that has come to be known as Mau Mau in Kenya in 1952. After the war, Ethiopia's emperor was reinstalled, but grievances against the feudal system were slowly emerging. It was only in Tanganyika and Somalia, both ruled by Britain under UN trusteeship, that the political process seemed more orderly, with a slow but systematic inclusion of Africans into the legislature.

In Uganda, the theater of politics was dominated by the so-called Buganda question, whose seeds had already been sown by the agreement of 1900. The issue here was how to map out a special relationship between the kingdom of Buganda, the colonial government, and the rest of Uganda. Under the terms of the Buganda Agreement of 1900, the kingdom was accorded special status in the colonial relationship; indeed, the Baganda ruling class had used the agreement as a cover to consolidate its land holdings and to expand Buganda's influence over the rest of the country. For most of the twentieth century, political grievances in Uganda revolved around confusion among the Baganda about Buganda's political identity and status. This uncertainty became more marked during the process of constitutional reform initiated in the 1950s and the crises that resulted. The most notable of these was in 1952, when the Kabaka of Uganda, Edward Mutesa, and the Lukiko demanded a separate status for Buganda in the postcolonial political order being organized by the colonial office. In 1952, the Kabaka was deported, but he returned in 1955, when a new constitution catering to Baganda interests was promulgated. At a constitutional conference held in London in 1961, it was agreed that Buganda would retain its semiautonomy in a federal system, and in 1962, Uganda became independent. But this was not the end of the conflict between Buganda and the central government. In 1966, Prime Minister Milton Obote abolished traditional kingdoms and sent the Kabaka into exile.

It was in Kenya, however, that the politics of decolonization were most tortuous and violent. As we have already noted, Kenya's relationship to Britain was different from that of its neighbors. Uganda and Tanzania were ostensibly governed in the interests of either international trusteeship or the indigenous authorities, who still maintained some say in the process of colonial governance. In contrast, Kenya was a classical colony, falling under the authority of a ministerial system headed by the governor. In addition, Kenya had the only significant white settler population in the region, one that was active in politics and was determined to use its clout to maintain European supremacy. The settler's motto was that Kenya was a white man's country. On the other side of the racial divide was a group of young Africans, many of them returning from the war, who felt strongly that Kenya was a black man's country. Frustrated by the slow pace of legislative reform, they formed nationalist parties to agitate for change. The most prominent of these was the Kenya African Union, formed in 1946. By 1950, it was apparent that the political process that was taking place in Uganda and Tanzania was being resisted by the conservative governor Sir Evelyn Baring and the settlers. It was at this time that the Mau Mau armed uprising began, with young men entering the forest and attacking white farms and institutions associated with white rule.

The colonial government responded to this new radicalism with draconian measures. In 1952, it declared a state of emergency in Kenya and arrested those it believed to be Mau Mau leaders, including Jomo Kenyatta. Detention camps for the thousands of Africans arrested in the period were established in remote parts of the country. In parts of central and eastern Kenya, in an attempt to cut off support for the guerillas, the whole population was confined to villages. There were some constitutional initiatives from the declaration of the state of emergency to its end in 1960, but African members of the Legislative Assembly, led by Oginga Odinga, opposed constitutional reforms proposed by successive secretaries for the colonies, insisting that Kenyatta and other nationalist leaders be released before a political settlement could be hammered out. In 1960, the state of emergency was ended and in 1961, Kenyatta was released from detention, paving the way for elections and independence in 1963.

In contrast, the process of political change in Tanzania was incremental and was carried out according to the UN mandate demanding increased African representation in the legislature. Regular elections in the late 1950s led to independence in 1961. On the island of Zanzibar, racial conflict continued to complicate the process of political change. Independence was granted in 1963, but a revolution in 1964 led to the overthrow of the sultan and the old Afro-Arab ruling class, paving the way for unification with the mainland. In 1964, mainland Tanganyika and the island of Zanzibar entered into a union, which was named Tanzania.

The Emergence of Literature in English

In 1962, an important conference on African writing, "Of English Expression," took place in Kampala, Uganda. As the Kenya writer Ngugi wa Thiong'o was to recall almost thirty years later, the list of participants at the conference "contained most of the names which have now become the subject of scholarly dissertations in universities all over the world" (Ngugi, *Decolonising the Mind*, 5). But among the many luminaries attending the conference at Makerere Hill—most prominent of whom were Chinua Achebe and Peter Abrahams—not one was from East Africa. And since writers in African languages had not been invited to the conference, the most important East African writers, such as the Swahili poet Sheikh Shabaan Robert, were excluded by default. Among the assembled makers of African literature, the East African region was represented only by student writers and apprentices (Ngugi, Rebeka Njau, and Grace Ogot), whose claims to literary reputation were merely a few short stories in college journals such as *Penpoint*.

The Kampala conference was, nevertheless, a remarkable event in the history of African writing in English: it raised many significant questions about the historical and cultural conditions in which African literature was produced, its relation to literatures in the African diaspora, and the epistemological and theoretical questions central to the identity of an emergent literature, including what came to be known as the "language question." The conference brought together a distinctive group of writers from Africa and its diaspora, and in doing so it had come to embody what Ngugi was later to characterize as "the energy and the hope and the dreams and the confidence . . . of a continent emerging from a colonial era" (Ngugi, *Detained*, 142). But for the young East African writers at Makerere, the conference was also a source of doubt and anxiety, an occasion to reflect on what appeared to be the literary impoverishment of the very region that was hosting the conference. For compared to its counterparts in West Africa and southern Africa, East African writing in English appeared recent and belated: it was not until the middle of the 1960s that it began to acquire a distinctive identity and to capture the attention of literary critics and historians. For this reason, it could not escape the anxiety of influence generated by the presence of an impressive gallery of writers from the rest of the continent and its diaspora.

At its very beginnings, then, East African literature in English was overshadowed by the manifest successes of African writing elsewhere and haunted by what was perceived as a cultural inferiority complex. Though not expressed openly, this inferiority complex was widely shared by writers from the region and was to provide one of the most obvious motivations for the production of a distinctly East African literature in English. Among a group of aspiring African writers and critics studying at Howard University in the United States, the Sudanese/Ugandan writer Taban Lo Liyong felt his "national pride" hurt by the display of West African and southern African literature, and was disgusted by his inability to conjure up East African literary figures to add to the emerging African aesthetic pantheon.

In 1965, out of his own sense of helplessness as a would-be East African writer, Lo Liyong wrote his seminal essay, "Can We Correct Literary Barrenness in East Africa?" In the essay, Lo Liyong lamented the absence of a solid culture of letters in East Africa, the failure of writers from the region to exploit their innumerable oral traditions and historical sources, and the inability of those writers to produce works that could demand the attention of an international audience. But if Lo Liyong's essay was to become the starting point for many accounts on the development of English-language literature in East Africa, it was not simply because it urged writers in the region to meet the challenge of the new African renaissance in culture and letters, but because beneath its overt polemical language, it had set the terms in which literary production and criticism would be carried out for most of the 1960s and early 1970s. Beyond identifying what he considered to be the lack of a literary culture in East Africa, Lo Liyong was very interested in the practical matters of literary production. He was eager to discover the reasons for "literary barrenness" in East Africa, the role of writers and artists in decolonized societies, and the measures needed to "to spark interest in literary production" (Lo Liyong, *The Last Word*, 31).

It is hard to say what direct influence the Kampala writers' conference and Lo Liyong's essay had on the emergence of East African literature in English; what is manifest, however, was the sudden bloom in creative writing in the 1960s, a period that saw the publication of Ngugi's major novels and the early works of Okot p'Bitek, which, as we shall see below, were to change the nature of African writing and put to rest the myth of literary barrenness in East Africa. Throughout the 1960s and 1970s, the region was in a state of cultural ferment, with new literary works and essays appearing in journals such as *Transition, Penpoint, Dhana*, and *Zuka*. This was the period associated with famous artistic centers such as ChemChem, established and run by Ezekiel Mphahlele, the then-exiled South African writer, and Paa ya Paa, founded by the Tanzanian artist Elimo Njau and the Kenyan writer Rebeka Njau. By the late 1960s, the East African Publishing House, which had hired as its literary editors leading writers such as Leonard Okola and Richard Ntiru, had established a Modern African Library to rival Heinemann's famed African Writers Series. As younger writers such as Ntiru, Jared Angira, and Okello Oculi were published side by side with established authors, namely Ngugi and Okot p'Bitek, there was a feeling that East Africa was no longer a literary wilderness.

Makerere English

In retrospect, however, it is clear that East Africa had not been a literary wilderness. While the region did not produce writers with international reputations until the 1960s, it had a substantial literary culture in African languages such as Swahili in Kenya and Tanzania, Somali in Somalia, and Amharic in Ethiopia. Because these literatures dated as far back as the fifteenth century, they often had a local and regional authority and reputation that writing in English could not easily match. Indeed, the existence of African-language literatures had perhaps a greater effect on the nature of writing in English than did the anxiety of influence that had driven Lo Liyong to declare East Africa a literary wilderness. Literacy in African schools in the region during the colonial period was primarily in local languages, and it was in such languages that many aspiring writers began their careers. The most notable of these was Okot p'Bitek, whose first two works, *Lak Tar* (translated as *White Teeth*) and *Wer pa Lawino* (later translated as *Song of Lawino*), were written in Acholi. Nevertheless, with the exception of Okot p'Bitek, many writers in African languages were not university educated, and what this meant, among other things, was that they did not have a voice in the debate on literature and culture in the 1950s and 1960s. In the end, the identity of East African literature was determined in university departments and literary journals, and thus reflected the interests and anxieties of a small elite. And since this elite was to manage the institutions of literary production after decolonization, their perspectives on what was—or was not—literature were going to be seminal in the shaping of literary culture in East Africa.

A history of English writing in East Africa must thus begin with an accounting of the location of the university as the primary site of literary production. As Ali Mazrui noted in 1971, the department of English at Makerere University College could claim to have produced "more creative writers in English than any other Department, at home and abroad" (Mazrui, "Aesthetic Dualism and Creative Literature in East Africa," 41–42). Indeed, the first attempts to produce an East African literature in English were made in intramural competitions at Makerere and in the English department's journal *Penpoint*, under the tutelage of British expatriates such as Hugh Dinwiddy, Margaret MacPherson, and David Cook. Work produced at Makerere by student writers including David Rubadiri, Jonathan Kariara, Elvania Zirimu, and Ngugi wa Thiong'o and collected by David Cook and David Rubadiri in *Origin East Africa: A Makerere Anthology* (1965) constitutes the foundational text of East African literature in English. But what exactly were the defining characteristics of Makerere English?

To answer this question, we must first reflect on the ideologies of literature and criticism that were taught at Makerere in the last days of colonialism in East Africa, for there is a distinct sense in which creative writing by student writers was an important counterpoint to the books they read and the methods of literary analysis they were taught. As Carol Sicherman had noted in her examination of Ngugi's colonial education, the syllabus and critical approach at Makerere, constructed along the lines Mathew Arnold and F. R. Leavis had popularized in Britain, promoted " 'universal' moral values, interiority, and individualism" (Sicherman, "Ngugi's Colonial Education," 19).

Sicherman provides a convincing list of the reasons why this kind of literary education stifled creativity by alienating African authors from their sources and traditions, but she does not adequately consider the extent to which this alienation created the ideological and linguistic tensions that made creative writing possible. For while it is true that most of the writing contained in *Origin East Africa* was self-consciously "Neo-European" in its form, it sought to discover and come to terms with a specific African context, which the curriculum at Makerere negated. In looking at work produced by student writers at Makerere, then, what strikes the reader most is not their imitation of European form but the ways in which their mastery of the Great Tradition would enable them to introduce African subjects into their poetry or prose.

Rubadiri's famous poem "Stanley Meets Mutesa" (see *Origin East Africa*, 78–80) was clearly fashioned after T. S. Eliot's "The Journey of the Magi," but it was through this self-conscious imitation of form that the poet was able to dramatize one of the most fateful colonial encounters in the history of East Africa—the meeting between the Anglo-American agent Henry Morton Stanley and the king of Buganda. The poem used the motif of the journey as it had been honed in the poetics of modernism, but its subject was a specifically East African event. Clearly, early East African literature in English was defined by the obvious tension between European forms of literary expression and local materials or topics. The central motif in early Makerere literature (Jonathan Kariara's short stories "Unto Us a Child Is Born" and "The Initiation" or Ngugi's "The Return" and "The Fig Tree," all four collected in *Origin East Africa*, are fairly representative of this tradition) was the struggle between the subjective desire promoted by the ideologies and forms of high modernism and the communal norms that were supposed to be characteristic of traditional African society (see also Ngugi's *Secret Lives* and Kariara's *The Coming of Power*).

The moral conflict common in these stories, a conflict that arose when individuals were forced to choose between their unique identities and communitarian pressures, was also an opposition between the forms of modern Englishness and the African setting of these fictions. The celebration of the individual as the arbiter of moral choice in these works was often reminiscent of the great masters of modernist fiction, most notably D. H. Lawrence and Joseph Conrad, but the worlds they represented were typically African. Because of this overt identification with high modernist moral norms and their concomitant styles, Makerere writers were later to be accused of "cultural slavery" (Sicherman, "Ngugi's Colonial Education," 20). But as David Rubadiri was to note in an influential discussion of the development of writing in East Africa, these stories, though written from "a personal point of view," were trying "in a rather vague and rather delicate manner to examine the position of the African and his community but hardly ever digging deeply into the people themselves" (Rubadiri, "The Development of Writing in East Africa," 149).

Almost all the works collected in *Origin East Africa* can be read as a vague and tentative attempt by an isolated colonial elite to recuperate a precolonial African tradition in literary discourse. The rhetoric of failure that seemed to characterize the works in this anthology was as much a product of modern writing as it was taught at Makerere as it was a reflection of the authors' attempts to reconcile their own subjectivity with the position of their communities. Many of the writers represented in *Origin East Africa* had come to the university from colonial zones in states of emergency. The university—and with it culture and the production of writing—was often seen as a sanctuary against both colonial and nationalist violence.

Nationalism and Literature

But if the writings of the university-educated elite were to capture critical attention because of their mastery of the idiom of modernist alienation, another tradition of East African writing had developed not to challenge Makerere's literary culture but to provide a deeper accounting of the communal histories that a colonial education had sought to repress. The earliest work in this tradition is Jomo Kenyatta's *Facing Mount Kenya* (1938), an anthropological account of Gikuyu culture produced for Malinowski's seminar on cultural change at the University of London. Kenyatta's text was ostensibly concerned with the representation of precolonial Gikuyu culture, but its significance on the emergence of a literary culture in East Africa can be found in its powerful articulation of some of the key themes of cultural nationalism in the 1920s and 1930s. The work was concerned with the existence of an autonomous Gikuyu culture with its own distinct traditions not at odds with modernity and modernization. As a counter to primitivist discourses of the time, it used the language of European social science to represent a version of African life organized according to rules and regulations, and it provided a local perspective on the effects of colonial policies on African families and communities.

Because of Kenyatta's imprisonment by the colonial government from 1952 to 1961, the effect of his work on East African writing was not felt until the early 1960s, but on the eve of decolonization, *Facing Mount Kenya* affected literary and cultural production in the region in two closely related ways. First, it provided a model for nationalist writers who could now draw on their own political experiences as representative of the African response to colonial rule. In works such as J. M. Kariuki's *Mau Mau Detainee* (1963), Tom Mboya's *Freedom and After* (1963), and Mugo Gatheru's *A Child of Two Worlds* (1964), previously taboo subjects such as Mau Mau could be represented by those who had witnessed the struggle for Kenyan independence from detention camps (Kariuki), the trade-union movement (Mboya), or the perspective of the squatters of the "White Highlands" (Gatheru). This writing, which came from the anticolonial front lines, provided in dramatic ways an alternative to the kind of writing produced at Makerere. As Ngugi was to note in his 1975 homage to J. M. Kariuki, the very existence of a literature produced by the witnesses of a now triumphant nationalism was an unprecedented act of transgression. On its publication in 1963, the year of Kenya's independence, *Mau Mau Detainee* was, in Ngugi's words, at the "center of a critical rage and storm": it outraged the local settler establishment "because an African, a Kenyan native, had dared to write openly and proudly about Mau Mau as a national liberation movement. . . . They did not know how to cope with Kariuki" (Ngugi, *Writers in Politics*, 95).

The most transgressive aspect of Kariuki's memoir, and indeed of all the other works in this tradition, was apparent in its tone: against the *angst* that dominated Makerere writing, *Mau Mau Detainee* was admired for "the triumphant ring of hope rising above the sober and restrained tones of its rendering" (Ngugi, 99). While university writers were trying to figure out the exact relationship between the aesthetic forms inherited from colonial modernism and the politics of nationalism, writers of nationalist memoirs had a more explicit view of their function. They were aware, as Tom Mboya was to note in his preface to

Freedom and After, that the process of decolonization engendered such radical reversals in the colonial relationship that the old paradigms could no longer account for the African experience. The speed of change was "heartening to a nationalist and a Pan-Africanist, but it is sometimes also daunting and awkward for an author" (Mboya, *Freedom and After*, v). Since the central trope in these memoirs was the making of the author as a nationalist, there was an implicit belief that the political experiences would shape the form of writing itself. These memoirs were not simply attempts to remember a colonial past; they were a celebration of individuals who had risen from colonialism to nationalist success. Almost without exception, these memoirs would open with the author's childhood experiences under the yoke of colonialism (Mboya on a sisal estate and Kariuki and Gatheru on a settler's farm) and end on the eve or day of Kenya's independence.

The second effect of the tradition of writing generated by *Facing Mount Kenya* and continued by *Mau Mau Detainee* can be garnered from Ngugi's remarks quoted above: reading nationalist memoirs allowed the Makerere writers to break out of their literary cloister and confront the culture of colonialism outside the academic institution. Indeed, if the problem with Makerere English was that it alienated students from their histories, cultures, and experiences, as many of them were to complain later, the nationalist writers had provided a discourse in which the relationship between writers and their communities was dynamic and symbiotic. If Makerere English had furnished students with a Europeanized aesthetic incapable of representing the pressures of colonial rule, nationalist memoirs provided striking models of how the contested history of colonialism in East Africa could be represented in writing, of how a painful colonial past could be mediated by the literary text.

For readers looking for evidence of the ways in which the nationalist memoirs came to affect the literature produced by the university elite, there is no better place to turn than Ngugi's first two novels, *Weep Not, Child* (1964) and *The River Between* (1965). For while these works were still cast within a familiar European framework—the romance of childhood, the *Bildungsroman*, and the individual subject's search for a moral position above collective interests—the dominant themes were drawn directly from the discourse of cultural nationalism (see Gikandi, *Ngugi wa Thiong'o*). As a result, historians of East African literature will find in Ngugi's first two novels an intriguing tension between modernist angst and nationalist self-assertion: the main characters in both novels (Njoroge and Waiyaki) are archetypal subjects of the bourgeois novel, characters striving to acquire self-consciousness against the political demands of their families and communities.

But it is through these modernist narrative forms that Ngugi would try to understand and valorize the key tropes of Gikuyu cultural nationalism since the 1920s, namely questions of land tenure, religion, and education. And thus, if Ngugi's early works are not marked by the triumphant tone of the nationalist memoirs, as Jacqueline Bardolph has argued (see Bardolph, "The Literature of Kenya," 37), it is because, like many members of the university elite, he was ambivalent about the violent history of colonialism in Kenya that he had chosen as a subject for his novels. What made Ngugi's works important for the development of literature in Kenya, however, was his ability to use the subjective language of the modern novel to represent political movements from which he was isolated or alienated. In this respect, his early writings provided a model for a younger generation of university-educated writers seeking a form to represent the ambivalent narrative of decolonization.

However, although Ngugi was emerging as the most important East African writer in English in the 1960s, the mode of writing he was promoting in his early novels, one in which the center of a narrative was the tragic conflict between an individual and his community, was not easily accessible or attractive to writers who were not necessarily engaged with the politics of Mau Mau and decolonization. Though not entirely indifferent to African experiences under colonialism, Grace Ogot's early works focused on the tragedies that befell individuals and communities trying to negotiate the precarious line between modernity and tradition. Whether dealing with the psychological and economic problems confronting a migrant Luo family in colonial Tanganyika in *The Promised Land* (1966) or exploring the strains put on old mystical beliefs by modern institutions in the stories collected in *Land Without Thunder* (1968), Ogot's early works were marked by an element of the Gothic unusual in African writing (see Bardolph, "The Literature of Kenya," 41). But for Ogot, Gothic was more than a literary style; the supernatural and the fantastic were the vehicles through which Luo traditions, identified as mystical or mysterious, were recovered and represented to a modern readership. Ogot was one of the first East African novelists in English to represent tradition as a bulwark against modern alienation.

This concern with tradition was also a major interest of Ethiopian literature in English published in the 1960s. But there is an important difference between the sense of tradition as it was represented in the works of Kenyan writers and their Ethiopian contemporaries: while tradition was important to Kenyan writers because it enabled a discourse that could be used to resist colonial rule, in Ethiopia, which was the only East African country that had basically escaped European conquest, traditionalism was associated with the feudal system and was often attacked for retarding modernity and rationality. In works such as Tsegaye Gabre-Medhin's *Oda Oak Oracle* (1965), Sahle Sellasie's *The Afersata* (1969), and in Daniachew Worku's *The Thirteenth Sun* (1973), the authors adeptly turned to ancient Ethiopian religious and legal sources to question an imperial order that was resisting change. In these works, it was not always clear that tradition was either the cause of or the solution to Ethiopia's entanglement with modernity and modernization.

The Okot School and the Poetic Tradition

For historians of East African literature, however, the most important literary event in the region was the publication of Okot p'Bitek's *Song of Lawino* in 1966. Okot p'Bitek had originally written the poem in Acholi, but this version, known as *Wer pa Lawino*, had been rejected by numerous publishers, who did not think there could be an audience for poetry in an African language. Before the author offered the poem in translation, it was performed to audiences in northern Uganda, where it received an enthusiastic reception. On several occasions in 1965, Okot p'Bitek read a small section of his English translation to a writer's conference in Nairobi where, as Rubadiri was to recall later, it changed the "whole tone of the conference" and the nature of East African writing (Rubadiri, "The Development of Writing in East Africa," 150). Within the context of writing in African languages, *Song of Lawino* did not mark a new event, but within the tradition of East African writing in English, a tradition struggling to establish its own identity, the poem enabled writers in the region to overcome a formidable psychological barrier—the belief that African oral forms could not be the basis of refined poetry and that the theme of cultural and political conflict "was not the kind of things that a fine writer in the English tradition should be concerned with" (151). *Song of Lawino* was the first poem in East Africa to "break free from the stranglehold of British writing" (Nazareth, "Waiting for Amin," 10) and assert the centrality of oral forms in literary production (see Lindfors, "The Songs of Okot p'Bitek and Heron").

Though a university man himself, Okot p'Bitek had nothing but contempt for the great tradition of European writing. He argued that literature was not epistemological by nature—the object of analysis and interpretation—but was about "communication and the sharing of deeply felt emotions"; it was an expressive activity "between the singer and the audience, between the story teller and his hearers" (*Africa's Cultural Revolution*, 22). Under the circumstances, literature could not "meaningfully be a subject for an examination," but was part of a "festival": "Let the people sing and dance, let them exchange stories and attend theatres for the joy of it," he urged (23). It is this idea of literature as performance that made Okot p'Bitek's songs unique experiences in East Africa. For what Okot p'Bitek had done in his construction of *Song of Lawino* and its sequel, *Song of Ocol*, was not simply make token gestures to orality, but make Acholi notions of performance (especially dance, idioms, and songs) the center of his poetic project. In the process, he redefined the idea of literature itself and its terms. Through his songs, Okot p'Bitek made the question of cultural conflict the central theme of East African writing in the late 1960s and 1970s and provided a new generation of writers with an alternative to the great tradition of European writing. In the wake of *Song of Lawino* and *Song of Ocol* and their unprecedented popular appeal, long poems in what came to be known as the Okot School included p'Bitek's own *Two Songs* (1971); Okello Oculi's *Prostitute* (1968), *Orphan* (1968), and *Malak* (1976); and Joseph Buruga's *The Abandoned Hut* (1969). These poems were characterized by two main features: their concern with what Okot p'Bitek had already popularized as the "African cultural revolution"— how could African culture be rescued from the domination of European institutions?—and a self-conscious negation of the European poetic tradition and celebration of oral culture. For reasons that are not yet clear, most of the successful poems in the Okot p'Bitek tradition were drawn from the Lwo cultures of northern Uganda.

Although the songs were the talking points of East African cultural and literary debates during the late 1960s and the early 1970s, the majority of the poetry published during this period continued to follow an older poetic tradition, in which established European forms were fine-tuned to represent local subjects. A significant development on the poetic front, however, was that even poets trained in the European tradition were now using their verse to intervene in the cultural wars, and, for this reason, they were also appropriating oral poetic forms as a distinctive aspect of their works. In the 1970s, then, even the most subjective and lyrical East African poets—Jared Angira (*Juices*, 1970; and *Silent Voices*, 1972) and Richard Ntiru (*Tensions*, 1971)—were using their poetry to comment on public issues such as corruption and urbanization, rather than working in a lyrical mode of retreat from the politics of everyday life. Here was an East African poetry that was unashamedly modernist in form (Angira's preferred form was the Poundian canto; Ntiru was partial to the dramatic monologue) but emotively concerned with the violent politics of decolonization.

In "Canto for the Rain," for example, Angira opens with three verses invoking the generalized experience of rain and the images and symbols it conjures in the poet's mind; in the second half of the poem, however, the universalizing language of nature provides the dramatic backdrop for subtle political commentary:

And I say
How can I ever
Bury all these meanings
All these symbols

And these persistent images
Of Kwame and Fanon
Shiver my jaws, tremble my hands

> Wanting to raise the image
> In a mirage of the dream
> It is me to be raised   (Angira, *Cascades*, 30)

It was not by accident that Christopher Okigbo was the figure that motivated and haunted young poets in East Africa during the late 1960s. His verse presented young writers with a model of how the rich abstract language of modernism could be Africanized; his death at the Biafran front was a frightening example of the uneasy relationship between literature and politics (see also Okola, *Drum Beat*).

Something else was apparent in the East African poetry of this period: beneath its homage to modern masters, it was being influenced just as much by local events and writers within the tradition of African and diaspora literature. From the first two lines of Ntiru's poem "Ojukwu's Prayer"—"If we must live, let it not be like dogs, / To Whom a bone is flung after the meat has been shaved / away" (Ntiru, *Tensions*, 57)—readers could simultaneously be transported to the Nigerian civil war (or its painful images and headlines) and Claude McKay's poem "If We Must Die," which Winston Churchill had used as a clarion to rally his troops against Nazi Germany. Still, as Rubadiri, the old master of European form, was to note, Okot p'Bitek's songs started a new trend in East African writing because they were boldly examining "the very kind of conflicts and problems that we had been frightened of trying to examine before. . . . We found we had been brainwashed to think that these were not the kind of things that a fine writer in the English tradition should be concerned with" (Rubadiri, "The Development of Writing in East Africa," 151). Even an irreverent poet like Taban Lo Liyong (*Frantz Fanon's Uneven Limbs*, 1971), who sought to parody the Okot p'Bitek tradition in his works, was also using oral forms to comment on the ironic complexities of postcolonial life.

The Crisis of Decolonization

One of the most distinctive aspects of East African literature in the 1960s and 1970s was its adoption of a regional character: the majority of the writers from the region had been educated at one of the three colleges of the University of East Africa, and it was not unusual for writers from one country to live and work in another; publishing houses such as the East African Literature Bureau and the East African Publishing House were regional institutions; and local newspapers and literary magazines circulated across borders. By the late 1960s, however, it was clear that the various East African countries were developing in different political directions, and long before the collapse of the East African Community, divergent cultural policies were affecting both the character of the literature being produced in the region and its centers of concern. With the Arusha Declaration of 1967, Tanzania had embarked on a policy of socialist development, in which Swahili was to play a key role in what was supposed to be a cultural partnership between the nation's government and its writers. In Kenya, on the other hand, English continued to flourish with the encouragement of the postcolonial government, but writers were increasingly finding themselves at odds with the state regarding political and cultural issues. Meanwhile, in Uganda, Somalia, and Ethiopia, military coups and the emergence of dictatorships restricted literary expression considerably.

Even with these divergences in political culture, however, the period from 1967 to 1977 was to witness the production of major works concerned with what has come to be known as the "politics of disillusionment." The signature work of this period is perhaps *Not Yet*

Uhuru (1967), the memoir of Oginga Odinga, a leading Kenyan nationalist and opposition figure. Unlike earlier narratives in this tradition, *Not Yet Uhuru* plotted the path of nationalism from the vantage point of its unfulfilled promise and ultimate failure. Ngugi's *A Grain of Wheat* (1967), perhaps the most prominent novel in the tradition of disillusionment, used modernist techniques—split temporality, interior monologue, and dialogic narration—to retell the struggle for independence in Kenya as a drama of betrayal and ironic reversal. Clearly, as the major East African writers tried to fashion literary forms for representing the crisis of decolonization, they seemed to have discovered a crucial affinity between the theme of postcolonial failure and the techniques of modernism. It is notable that novels concerned with what Frantz Fanon in *The Wretched of the Earth* called "the pitfalls of national consciousness" were simultaneously adopting and undermining the established conventions of realist representation.

Indeed, the majority of novels written at the end of the 1960s located themselves squarely within an African avant-garde tradition made famous by foundational novels by Wole Soyinka (*The Interpreters*, 1965) and Ayi Kwei Armah (*The Beautyful Ones Are Not Yet Born*, 1968) in West Africa. The most prominent East African novels in this tradition were Rubadiri's *No Bride Price* (1967), Robert Serumaga's *Return to the Shadows* (1969), Peter Palangyo's *Dying in the Sun* (1968), Leonard Kibera's *Voices in the Dark* (1970), and Ali Mazrui's *The Trial of Christopher Okigbo* (1971). Novels of disillusionment in East Africa were an important mark of the parting of ideological paths between writers and nationalist politicians; going against the rhetoric of nation building promoted by the political class, they echoed a familiar rhetoric of modernistic failure, in which intellectuals (the heroes of these novels) were shown to be uncompromising critics of the dominant political culture but, at the same time, incapable of affecting the process of social change in their respective countries (See Gikandi, "The Growth of the East African Novel," 240). The narrative energy driving these novels—especially the conflict between high philosophical ideals and the constraints of real politics—was derived from what Georg Lukacs, writing in a different context, has called the "romanticism of disillusionment": a certain imaginative retreat from the public sphere was seen as the only way that the intellectual class could give meaning to its life in an age of postcolonial disillusionment (Lukacs, *The Theory of the Novel*, 112–113).

But not all novelists from this period posited their works as modes of subjective retreat from the public sphere and nationalist politics. Indeed, in the works of Meja Mwangi and Nurrudin Farah, the most prolific novelists to come out of East Africa in the 1970s and 1980s, we have evidence of a new kind of writing, which fuses the best of both modernist and realist techniques in order to simultaneously represent and transcend the politics of everyday life. Meja Mwangi's fame rests on a series of award-winning novels (*Kill Me Quick*, 1973; *Going Down River Road*, 1976; and *The Cockroach Dance*, 1979) admired for their uncompromising representation of harsh life and what Angus Calder has called "the unselfconscious deployment of the techniques of 'popular' fiction" (Calder, "Meja Mwangi's Novels," 177). In contrast, Nurrudin Farah's novels, from *From a Crooked Rib* (1970) to the "dictatorship trilogy" (*A Naked Needle*, 1976; *Sweet and Sour Milk*, 1979; and *Sardines*, 1981) were notable for their self-conscious intertextual relationship to other modernist texts in Africa. If Mwangi's power as a novelist was his acute sense of urban life and a disregard of literary conventions, Farah's work was built around a self-conscious attempt to bring the techniques of modernism and especially the avant-garde to bear on the violent politics of the Somali dictatorship. Farah's fiction was thus highly intellectual in character. Except in his first novel, *From a Crooked Rib*, where the main character was an illiterate peasant woman, the subjects of Farah's novels were intellectuals with a profound knowledge of Somali and African politics and literary culture; their self-conscious and often introspective narratives were driven by the search for an experimental language that might be able to encapsulate the truer-than-fiction events surrounding the dictatorship.

From the 1970s and the end of the 1980s, then, three threads could be detected in East African writing. The first thread involved a series of works in which disillusionment with the politics of independence continued to generate important works. In different forms and genres, East African writers continued to produce works in which individual subjects and communities tried to figure out their relationship to pressing political problems such as the individual's alienation in urban space, corruption in the public sphere, and political repression. Writers such as Charles Mangua (*Son of Woman*, 1971) and Mwangi Ruheni (*The Future Leaders*, 1973) reached out to a reading public nourished on Western popular literature, fusing entertainment with social commentary. Other writers, most notably Rebeka Njau (*Ripples in the Pool*, 1976) and Grace Ogot (*The Other Woman*, 1976), used the experiences of their heroines to probe a culture of silence and violence in which the repression of women was often synonymous with the consolidation of political oligarchies.

A second discernable thread during this period was one in which writers responded directly to social and political crises in individual East African countries. The few English works produced in Tanzania during this period were, significantly, concerned with rewriting real historical events as a contribution to an ongoing debate on the role of culture in national development. Gabriel Ruhumbika's *Village in Uhuru* (1969) traced the development of one community from its creation, through German and British colonialism, and finally to the consolidation of its independence under the leadership of TANU. Ebrahim Hussein's play *Kinjekitile* (1970) was a dramatic reworking of the 1904 Maji Maji rebellion against German rule in Tanzania, while Ismael Mbise's *Blood on Our Land* (1974) was based on an actual land case brought before the United Nations by the Meru people of northern Tanzania.

As the genre that was "closer to life as men actually live it than any other form of artistic expression," (de Graft, "Roots in African Drama and Theatre," 3) drama was especially attuned to the political and social crises in the region during this period. While indebted to the established conventions of modern drama, the early plays of John Ruganda (*The Burdens*, 1972), Robert Serumaga (*The Elephants*, 1974; and *Majangwa*, 1974), Elvania Zirimu (*When the Hunchback Made Rain*, 1975), and Francis Imbuga (*Betrayal in the City*, 1976) favored plots and themes that addressed the questions that were troubling their middle-class audiences: What had led to the failure of decolonization? What was the role of the African elite in the politics of national failure and decay? What was the place of the individual—and civil rights—in the corrupt politics of the postcolony?

A third thread in East African literature in the 1970s can be located in a set of imaginative works that sought to intervene in the debate revolving around the culture and politics of underdevelopment, a debate that had been initiated in the region by the publication of Walter Rodney's *How Europe Underdeveloped Africa* (1972) and Colin Leys' *Underdevelopment in Kenya* (1975) and had spread among the intellectual elite like wildfire. The major works in this tradition were *Muntu* (1976), a play by the Ghanaian expatriate Joe de Graft, and *Petals of Blood* (1977), Ngugi's great novel on the politics of neocolonialism in Kenya. While de Graft and Ngugi came from opposing political directions and worked in different genres, their works were remarkably similar in their imaginative ambition and temporal dimension: they both sought to present a panoramic view of African history from precolonial times to the age of neocolonialism, they adopted a multiplicity of voices to capture the conflicting histories and visions of the continent as it struggled with its destiny, and they were both driven by an aesthetic belief in the capacity of language to capture the totality of reality and the capacity of literature to provide a resolution to the great problems of the age. The scope and optimism of these two works was unmatched in East African writing in English.

Writing in an Age of Globalization

In retrospect, however, *Muntu* and *Petals of Blood* marked the end of an era in East African writing in English, for from the beginning of the 1980s onward, writers and critics in the region were to find themselves in an unprecedented state of political, cultural, and economic crisis, one totally unexpected in the age of decolonization. This period will be remembered for the collapse of modern institutions, such as the schools, universities, and publishing houses that had been constructed during the first two decades of independence; the failure of political experiments in Kenya and Tanzania; the destructive rule of Idi Amin in Uganda; the Ethiopian revolution; and the rise and fall of the military dictatorship in Somalia. Despite the difficulties facing writers in all these countries, each of these historic events generated important literary works. During Idi Amin's regime in the 1970s, some important Ugandan writers (Pio Zirimu and Byron Kadadwa being the most prominent) died under mysterious circumstances, and the country's major writers were sent into exile. But the Idi Amin phenomenon had also generated a new kind of writing (see Nazareth, "Waiting for Amin"), as authors tried to respond to the challenge of writing about—and in—a state of political siege.

In exile in Kenya, John Ruganda wrote and produced *The Floods* (1979), a political drama matched in the dictatorship genre in Africa only by Wole Soyinka's *A Play of Giants*. While Ruganda's play mesmerized audiences with its allegory of violence and murder and its vivid invocation of Idi Amin's killing fields when it was first produced in Nairobi, his compatriot, Robert Serumaga, who had stayed in Uganda during those difficult years, had come up with an even more novel response to the culture of silence imposed by the dictatorship. In remarkable experimental plays such as *Renga Moi* (1979), Serumaga chose to dispense with spoken language altogether, using mime, dance, and bodily movements to recreate the story of political terror in Uganda. In the absence of spoken language, however, Serumaga's works relied on his audience's ability to decipher such floating movements and connect them to Ugandan politics. *Renga Moi* was a powerful indictment of the Ugandan military dictatorship—and it was said that Idi Amin, unable to unravel the hidden meaning of Serumaga's play when it was performed at the National Theater in Kampala, enjoyed it tremendously.

Political novels directed at military dictatorship also emerged in Ethiopia and Somalia at about the same time. Sahle Sellassie's novel *The Firebrands* (1979) presented readers with a detailed portrait of imperial Ethiopia on the eve of the 1974 revolution, and the political and cultural challenge of responding to military rule in Somalia was the theme of Nurrudin Farah's dictatorship trilogy mentioned above. In *Maps* (1986), Farah brought the turmoil of the Ethiopian revolution and Somali dictatorships to a work that sought to represent the minute details of life across national boundaries and to question the economies of gender, race, and nation, which had become an unfortunate rationale for the political turmoil in the horn of Africa. The stories collected in Hama Tuma's *The Case of the Socialist Witchdoctor*

(1993) were satirical representations of the nervous politics of revolution and dictatorship in Ethiopia.

The dire political and economic conditions in the East African countries made it particularly difficult for new writers to emerge and establish reputations comparable to those of the canonical figures in the region. Established writers continued to produce new works in the 1980s and 1990s: Grace Ogot's two novels *The Graduate* (1980) and *Island of Tears* (1980) were notable for their examination of the effects of politics on the private life of women. At the same time, playwrights and poets such as Ruganda (*Echoes of Silence*, 1986) and Angira (*Tides of Time*, 1996) brought a deep psychological understanding to their investigation of the effect of the culture of decay and decline on individual subjects. Because Ngugi's new fictions (*Devil on the Cross*, 1980; *Matigari*, 1987) were originally written in Gikuyu, their success in translation excludes them from the corpus of East African writing in English, but it is worth noting that these novels won critical acclaim for their incorporation of oral forms and popular culture as a way of representing—and coming to terms with—the contested realities of postcolonial life.

Matigari was also a novel produced in exile. This point is important because it points to an unexpected development in the development of East African literature in the late 1980s and the 1990s—the political and cultural crisis in the region had forced its creative energies to relocate elsewhere. The most important works from old and new East African writers were now being produced in Europe or North America. In this category belongs Farah's later novels *Gifts* (1993), *Secrets* (1998), and *Links* (2004); Abdulrazak Gurnah's *Memory of Departure* (1987), *Pilgrim's Way* (1988), *Dottie* (1990), and *Paradise* (1994); and M. G. Vassanji's *The Gunny Sack* (1989), *No New Land* (1991), and *Uhuru Street* (1991). Drawing mainly on their childhood experiences in East Africa, these writers produced texts focused on prominent themes of home, migration, and departure, works set in the specific countries in the region but produced by an awareness of the authors' separation from their natal spaces. In contrast, works produced by writers still based in the region, including the Anglo-Kenyan writer Marjorie Oludhe Macgoye (*Coming to Birth*, 1986) and Margaret Ogola (*The River and the Source*, 1994) were attempting, like earlier African literature, to place the African subject within specific histories and traditions denoted by concepts such as the family, the home, the region, and the nation.

In all these instances, creative writing in East African literature, which in the 1960s had come of age haunted by its inadequacy to other regional literatures of Africa, had been able within a space of forty years to establish its unique identity in the world of Pan-African letters. Despite the regional characteristics of this literature, East African writers were, like their counterparts elsewhere on the continent, concerned with three questions: What was African literature? What was its language? Who were its readers? At the end of the 1990s, these questions were perhaps not as pressing as they had been forty years earlier, but they had become more complicated, because in an age of globalization and multiculturalism, one was as likely to find an East African writer in London, New York, Johannesburg, or Toronto as in Nairobi, Kampala, Dar es Salaam, Addis Ababa, or Mogadishu.

REFERENCES
Primary Sources

Angira, Jared. *Juices.* Nairobi: East African Publishing House, 1970.
——. *Silent Voices.* London: Heinemann, 1972.

——. *Cascades*. London: Longman, 1979.

——. *Tides of Time: Selected Poems*. Nairobi: East African Educational Publishers, 1996.

p'Bitek, Okot. *Lak Tar*. Nairobi: East African Literature Bureau, 1953. Translated by the author as *White Teeth*. Nairobi: East African Educational Publishers, 1989.

——. *Song of Lawino*. Nairobi: East African Publishing House, 1966.

——. *Wer pa Lawino*. Nairobi: East African Publishing House, 1969.

——. *Song of Ocol*. Nairobi: East African Publishing House, 1970.

——. *Song of Prisoner*. New York: Third Press, 1971.

——. *Two Songs*. Nairobi: East African Publishing House, 1971.

Buruga, Joseph. *The Abandoned Hut*. Nairobi: East African Publishing House, 1969.

Cook, David, and David Rubadiri, eds. *Origin East Africa: A Makerere Anthology*. London: Heinemann, 1965.

De Graft, Joe. *Muntu*. Nairobi: East African Educational Publishers, 1977.

Farah, Nurrudin. *From a Crooked Rib*. London: Heinemann, 1970.

——. *A Naked Needle*. London: Heinemann, 1976.

——. *Sweet and Sour Milk*. London: Allison and Busby, 1979.

——. *Sardines*. London: Allison and Busby, 1981.

——. *Close Sesame*. London: Allison and Busby, 1983.

——. *Maps*. New York: Pantheon, 1986.

——. *Gifts*. London: Serif, 1993.

——. *Secrets*. London: Serif, 1998.

Gabre-Medhin, Tsegare. *Oda Oak Oracle*. London: Oxford University Press, 1965.

——. *The Collision of Atlas*. London: Rex Collings, 1977.

Gatheru, Mugo. *A Child of Two Worlds*. London: Routledge, 1964.

Gurnah, Abdulrazak. *Memory of Departure*. London: Cape, 1987.

——. *Pilgrim's Way*. London: Cape, 1987.

——. *Dottie*. London: Cape, 1990.

——. *Paradise*. London: Cape, 1994.

Hussein, Ibrahim. *Kinjekitile*. Dar es Salaam: Oxford University Press, 1974.

Imbuga, Francis. *Betrayal in the City*. Nairobi: East African Publishing House, 1976.

Lo Liyong, Taban. *Frantz Fanon's Uneven Limbs*. London: Heinemann, 1971.

Kariara, Jonathan. *The Coming of Power*. Nairobi: Oxford University Press, 1986.

Kariuki, J. M. *Mau Mau Detainee*. Oxford: Oxford University Press, 1963.

Kenyatta, Jomo. *Facing Mount Kenya*. New York: Vintage, 1965.

Kibera, Leonard. *Voices in the Dark*. Nairobi: East African Publishing House, 1970.

Macgoye, Marjorie O. *Coming to Birth*. Nairobi: East African Educational Publishers, 1986.

Mang'ua, Charles. *Son of Woman*. Nairobi: East African Educational Publishers, 1971.

Mazrui, Ali. *The Trial of Christopher Okigbo*. London: Heinemann, 1971.

Mbise, Ishmael. *Blood on Our Land*. Dar es Salaam: Tanzania Publishing House, 1974.

Mboya, Tom. *Freedom and After*. Boston: Little, Brown, 1963.

Mwangi, Meja. *Kill Me Quick*. London: Heinemann, 1973.

——. *Going Down River Road*. London: Heinemann, 1976.

——. *The Cockroach Dance*. London: Heinemann, 1979.

Ngugi wa Thiong'o. *Weep Not, Child*. London: Heinemann, 1964.

——. *The River Between*. London: Heinemann, 1965.

——. *A Grain of Wheat*. London: Heinemann, 1967.

——. *The Black Hermit*. London: Heinemann, 1968.

——. *Secret Lives*. London: Heinemann, 1975.

——. *Petals of Blood*. London: Heinemann, 1977.

——. *Detained: A Writer's Prison Diary*. London: Heinemann, 1981.

Ngugi wa Thiong'o, and Micere Githae Mugo. *The Trial of Dedan Kimathi*. London: Heinemann, 1976.

Njau, Rebeka. *Ripples in the Pool*. London: Heinemann, 1976.

Ntiru, R. C. *Tensions*. Nairobi: East African Publishing House, 1971.

Oculi, Okello. *Orphan*. Nairobi: East African Publishing House, 1968.

——. *Prostitute*. Nairobi: East African Publishing House, 1968.

——. *Malak*. Nairobi: East African Publishing House, 1976.

Odinga, Oginga. *Not Yet Uhuru*. London: Heinemann, 1967.

Ogola, Margaret. *The River and the Source*. Nairobi: Focus Publications, 1994.

Ogot, Grace. *Land Without Thunder*. Nairobi: East African Publishing House, 1967.

——. *The Promised Land*. Nairobi: East African Publishing House, 1967.

——. *The Graduate*. Nairobi: Uzima Press, 1980.

——. *Island of Tears*. Nairobi: Uzima Press, 1980.

——. *The Other Woman*. Nairobi: East African Educational Publishers, 1992.

Okola, Leonard. *East African Poems*. Nairobi: East African Publishing House, 1967.

Palangyo, Peter. *Dying in the Sun*. London: Heinemann, 1968.

Rubadiri, David. *No Bride Price*. Nairobi: East African Publishing House, 1967.

Ruganda, John. *The Burdens*. Nairobi: Oxford University Press, 1972.

——. *The Floods*. Nairobi: East African Publishing House, 1980.

——. *Echoes of Silence*. Nairobi: Heinemann, 1986.

Ruheni, Mwangi. *The Future Leaders*. London: Heinemann, 1973.

——. *The Minister's Daughter*. London: Heinemann, 1975.

Sellasie, Sahle. *The Afersata: An Ethiopian Novel*. London: Heinemann, 1969.

——. *Warrior King*. London: Heinemann, 1974.

——. *The Firebrands*. London: Longman, 1979.

Serumaga, Robert. *Return to the Shadows*. London: Heinemann, 1969.

——. *The Elephants*. Nairobi: Oxford University Press, 1974.

——. *Majangwa and a Play*. Nairobi: East African Publishing House, 1974.

——. *Renga Moi*. Unpublished.

Tuma, Hama. *The Case of the Socialist Witchdoctor*. London: Heinemann, 1993.

Vassanji, M. G. *The Gunnysack*. Oxford: Heinemann, 1989.

——. *No New Land*. Toronto: McClelland, 1991.

——. *Uhuru Street*. Oxford: Heinemann, 1991.

Worku, Danichew. *The Thirteenth Sun*. London: Heinemann, 1973.

Zirimu, Elvania. *When the Hunchback Made Rain*. Nairobi: East African Publishing House, 1975.

Secondary Sources

Bardolph, Jacqueline. "The Literature of Kenya." In *The Writing of East and Central Africa*, edited by G. D. Killam, 36–53. London: Heinemann, 1984.

p'Bitek, Okot. *Africa's Cultural Revolution*. Nairobi: Macmillan, 1973.

Fanon, Frantz. *The Wretched of the Earth.* Translated by Constance Farrington. New York: Grove Press, 1968.

Gikandi, Simon. "The Growth of the East African Novel." In *The Writing of East and Central Africa,* edited by G. D. Killam, 231–246. London: Heinemann, 1984.

——. *Ngugi wa Thiong'o.* Cambridge: Cambridge University Press, 2000.

Heron, G. A. *The Poetry of Okot p'Bitek.* London: Heinemann, 1976.

Killam, G. D., ed. *The Writing of East and Central Africa.* London: Heinemann, 1984.

Leys, Colin. *Underdevelopment in Kenya.* Berkeley: University of California Press, 1975.

Lindfors, Bernth. "The Songs of Okot p'Bitek." In *The Writing of East and Central Africa,* edited by G. D. Killam, 144–158. London: Heinemann, 1984.

Lo Liyong, Taban. *The Last Word.* Nairobi: East African Publishing House, 1969.

Lukacs, Georg. *The Theory of the Novel.* Translated by Anna Bostock. Cambridge, Mass.: MIT Press, 1971.

Mazrui, Ali. "Aesthetic Dualism and Creative Literature in East Africa." In *Black Aesthetics,* edited by Andrew Gurr and Pio Zirimu, 32–51. Nairobi: East African Literature Bureau, 1973.

Nazareth, Peter. "Waiting for Amin: Two Decades of Ugandan Literature." In *The Writing of East and Central Africa,* edited by G. D. Killam, 7–35. London: Heinemann, 1984.

Ngugi wa Thiong'o. *Decolonising the Mind: The Politics of Language in African Literature.* London: James Currey, 1981.

——. *Writers in Politics.* London: Heinemann, 1981.

Rubadiri, David. "The Development of Writing in East Africa." In *Perspectives on African Literature,* edited by Christopher Heywood, 148–156. New York: Africana Publishing, 1971.

Rodney, Walter. *How Europe Underdeveloped Africa.* Dar es Salaam: Tanzania Publishing House, 1972.

Sicherman, Carol. "Ngugi's Colonial Education: 'The Subversion of the African Mind.'" *African Studies Review* 38, no. 3 (1993): 11–42.

Authors and Topics A–Z

AIDS/HIV Sub-Saharan Africa is the area of the world worst hit by the HIV/AIDS pandemic. By 2001, 15 percent of Kenya's population was HIV-positive, Tanzania had a 7.8 percent infection rate, and the prevalence in Uganda was 5 percent. Eastern African literature has changed in response to the AIDS scourge, even if it at times uses the disease merely as a metaphor for what is wrong with postcolonial society. The toll of the pandemic on the general population and the mystery surrounding the disease have been the subjects of plays, novels, poetry, and oral literature from the region. AIDS has also been used as a metaphor for the various social and economic problems facing East Africa. In addition, the AIDS/HIV motif has been employed, especially in the early 1990s, to inject sensation into literary texts: the infection has been ascribed to negative characters as a form of punishment in the texts' moral scheme. Yusuf Dawood's *Water Under the Bridge* (1991) is one of the earliest novels to allude to the emergence of AIDS. In Dawood's novel, Hugh, the main character, becomes a lecher because he is "very old-fashioned and thought that the only danger from sex was pregnancy," but he ends up infected by the virus, which he uses to try to kill his rival. Wamugunda Geteria's *Nice People* (1992) portrays AIDS as a punishment for the nurses that the promiscuous Dr. Joseph Munguti has been having a "nice time" with but who remain too faithful to him. Margaret Ogola's *The River and the Source* (1994) presents the physically beautiful but morally empty Becky finally dying of AIDS, but its sequel *I Swear by Apollo* (2002) is more sympathetic to the victims of the infection. Sympathetic, too, is Ugandan Namige Kayondo's *Vanishing Shadows*, a love story that uses AIDS to force the denouement of a romance that cannot be fulfilled. Several stories in the collection *Reversed Dreams*, edited by Nana Wilson Tagoe and Wanjira Muthoni, have AIDS as a specific theme.

The AIDS condition has also inspired full-length novels by new writers. Joseph Situma's *The Mysterious Killer* (2001) depicts a traditional society fighting to defend itself against death by AIDS. Set in the village of Randi (Thunder), where people are dying of a strange epidemic, the novel revolves around Cecilia's encounter with a strange disease that traditional treatments, including sacrifices, fail to cure. The novel presents the conflict between modern science and traditional beliefs and the tragedy the tension poses in the era of AIDS.

As it has become more prevalent as a literary theme, AIDS/HIV has attracted the works of popular writers. David Maillu's *Broken Drum* (1991) depicts a European visitor who believes Africans are infected with AIDS simply because they are African. In the second edition of his controversial *My Dear Bottle* (1973), Maillu represents AIDS as the new scourge of the African urban class. The text provides racialized and ideological theories about the origin of AIDS— "I hear it was manufactured / in America /

to wipe away Niggers / and the Soviets / during Cold War times"—and cynically thanks the scourge for killing certain politicians: "My country is invaded / by parasite politicians / thanks Aids / for killing some of them." A little more textured is Meja Mwangi's *The Last Plague* (2001), which documents the near annihilation of a village tellingly named Crossroads. Despite the high rates of death in the village, the people do not want to use the free condoms handed out by Janet Juma, and the village government is not keen to assist her. At one point, the village chief wants to sleep with her and dismisses vehemently the idea of using a condom: "I can't use *kodom* . . . I'm the Chief. . . . Why do you want to waste your life telling people shameful things. . . . To live all your life begging people to use *kodom*?" In a society where AIDS victims are stigmatized because of the association of the disease with sexual promiscuity, Mwangi's novel uses plot and character relationship to demystify the infection. In the novel, Janet's HIV-positive husband, Broker, changes his sexual behavior and joins the war against the disease, giving confidence to other people with the infection: "You see what most people don't understand about Aids is that it is possible to live a normal and reasonably active sex life with Aids. But one has to take the necessary precautions not to infect others with the Aids virus."

Women writers have often used the AIDS issue to expose gender problems in East Africa, where women have little control over their sexuality. Violet Barungi's "The Last One to Know" (in Barungi and Okurut's *Woman's Voice*) laments the disempowerment of women who end up as the victims of the virus. Carolyne Adalla's *Confessions of an AIDS Victim* offers an in-depth analysis of the vulnerability of women to AIDS. When she finds that she is HIV-positive, Catherine Njeri is seized by fear and panic and confesses about her past as a strategy for regaining her agency. Written as a long letter to her confidante Maryanne, this epistolary novel analyzes the gendered conditions that led Catherine to her present condition. Mary Okurut's *The Invisible Weevil* (1998) uses AIDS as a metaphor for the political and social problems of postindependence Uganda, such as military dictatorship, widespread corruption, gender discrimination, and other forms of inequality. While symbolizing the problems eating into the vitals of the nation, the weevil in the story is figured as the AIDS-causing virus. The novel ends on an optimistic note, with the main character hearing a didactic song about AIDS being played on the radio: "But now in openness we live / The guns demystified / And AIDS no longer a mystery / It too shall be conquered."

In the same vein but in a more complicated way, in that it interweaves the AIDS condition with the state of postindependence East Africa, Marjorie Oludhe Macgoye's *Chira* documents the shortcomings of postcolonial Kenyan society in a way that parallels the issues it presents about AIDS/HIV. The novel examines the Luo concept of *chira* ("wasting disease"), a term applied to AIDS although it predates the AIDS phenomenon. The novel depicts a society that still mystifies AIDS as a curse instead of seeing it as a condition produced by sexual interactions. AIDS/HIV is certainly not the central theme in *Chira* and the narrative rarely depicts HIV-infected characters, but the brute fact of AIDS pervades the text as part of the cultural landscape in which the story is set. The characters find themselves thinking about AIDS even when their minds are on other issues, such as the possibility of a marriage in a morally rotten city. The main character, Gabriel Otieno, has many friends who have *chira*. However, his society is in denial. Haunting all aspects of his society, AIDS is presented as a metaphor of the problems of the whole nation:

So when an Assistant Minister is declared bankrupt—the declaration itself being more potent than the amount of money in play—his immune system becomes deficient, he is unable to retain the wealth that he still eats: it dribbles away obscenely, his intimate touch becomes infectious and his substance dwindles. . . . Repentance can change things for the individual but not avert the creeping corruption.

Finally, as it has become central to political discourse, AIDS has appeared as a major theme in many popular songs from East Africa and is also the most prevalent subject in oral literature, popular theater, and drama in the region. In fact, plays such as David Mulwa's *Clean Hands* were some of the earliest texts to depict the issue at a time when it was considered taboo in East Africa.

PRIMARY TEXTS

Adalla, Carolyne. *Confessions of an Aids Victim*. Nairobi: East African Educational Publishers, 1993.

Barungi, Violet, and Mary Karooro Okurut, eds. *A Woman's Voice: An Anthology of Short Stories by Uganda Women*. Kampala: Femrite, 1999.

Dawood, Yusuf. *Water Under the Bridge*. Nairobi: Longman, 1991.

Geteria, Wamagunda. *Nice People*. Nairobi: East African Educational Publishers, 1992.

Kayondo, Namige. *Vanishing Shadows*. London: Macmillan, 1995.

Macgoye, Marjorie Oludhe. *Chira*. Nairobi: East African Educational Publishers, 1997.

Maillu, David. *My Dear Bottle*. Nairobi: Comb Books, 1973.

——. *Broken Drum*. Nairobi: Jomo Kenyatta Foundation and Maillu Publishing House, 1991.

Mulwa, David. *Clean Hands*. Nairobi: Oxford University Press, 2000.

Mwangi, Meja. *The Last Plague*. Nairobi: East African Educational Publishers, 2000.

Ogola, Margaret. *The River and the Source*. Nairobi: Focus, 1994.

——. *I Swear by Apollo*. Nairobi: Focus, 2002.

Okurut, Mary. *The Invisible Weevil*. Kampala: Femrite Publications, 1998.

——. *The Official Wife*. Kampala: Fountain Publishers, 2003.

Situma, Joseph. *The Mysterious Killer*. Nairobi: Africawide Network, 2001.

Wilson-Tagoe, Tagoe, and Wanjira Muthoni, eds. *Reversed Dreams and Other Stories*. Nairobi: Writers' Association of Kenya, 1996.

REFERENCES

Kruger, Marie. "Narrative in the Time of AIDS: Postcolonial Kenyan Women's Literature." *Research in African Literatures* 35, no. 1 (2004): 108–129.

[Mwangi]

Akare, Thomas (b. 1950) Kenyan writer of popular fiction. Akare's work chronicles the problems of the seedier parts of the Kenyan capital city, focusing on the lives of prostitutes and the homeless. His first novel, *The Slums* (1981), is a documentary first-person narrative in which Eddie Chura Onyango recounts his life in Nairobi. "Chura," his middle name, is a derogatory term for a lowly cleaner, especially of toilets. He and his friend Hussein make a living washing cars in the slums of Nairobi, mostly in the sprawling Majengo slum where sex is cheap and the police are corrupt and violent. The shell of a derelict car that he calls "home" is eventually towed away, along with his school certificate. He decides to rob a bank, and eventually decides that turning himself in to the police might be safer than being murdered by the mob. In the end, Eddy resorts to alcohol, drugs, and cheap sex as way of escaping from the harsh realities of life in the city. Through its colloquialisms, the novel underlines the mundane spread of crime, prostitution, unemployment, violence, and corruption in postindependence East Africa.

Similarly, *Twilight Woman* (1988) depicts life in the underbelly of Nairobi, where poverty is widespread and prostitution is one of the few ways to earn a living. It is the story of Resila, who goes to Nairobi expecting a good life with her husband. She becomes disillusioned and decides to run away with a rich man, Arthur. When Arthur abandons her, she becomes a "twilight girl," the euphemism for a hardcore prostitute. Akare's novels are episodic in structure, a style enabling him to capture the fragmentation and unsettled life of the postcolonial urban landscape.

PRIMARY TEXTS

Akare, Thomas. *The Slums*. London: Heinemann, 1981.
——. *Twilight Woman*. Nairobi: Spear Books, 1988.

[Mwangi]

Angira, Jared (b. 1947) Kenya's leading poet and one of East Africa's most talented writers. In addition to his poetry, Angira has written in English and Swahili about issues ranging from the promise and betrayal of independence to the effects of poverty. Angira studied commerce at the University of Nairobi and did graduate work at the London School of Economics, and this background explains his sharp sense of the politics of underdevelopment in Kenya. He sees his poetry, especially in its use of irony and expressive imagery, as a site for bringing economics and poetics together. In the 1970s, he declared himself a follower of Karl Marx and Pablo Neruda, who had to "confront the world without end and see how to endure all the spirit of forgetting all the present and bad things." Drawing on techniques of traditional African poetic expression and modern European traditions to fashion a hybrid genre that is experimental and deeply philosophical and realistic, his poems reflect postindependence disillusionment and the abuse of natural and human resources by an irresponsible elite.

Angira's first collection of poems, *Juices*, are built around a confrontation between, on the one hand, the process of modernity and individualism and, on the other hand, the nationalist desire to turn different ethnic communities into one nation while respecting the traditions of each group. It examines the alienation of the modern postcolonial East African, who is caught at the crossroads of cultures and not sure on which side he or she belongs. For example, his poem "Masked" uses the image of a mask to evoke estrangement and to express the uprootedness of the postcolonial Kenyan subject exposed to Western modernity. The speaking persona in the poem narrates the conflicts he encounters when he returns home from a place where he has mixed his own culture with other traditions:

> We opened our virgin palms
> and received the potent juice from
>   each other
> and synthesized with
> the beauty we had carried.

The virginal image tries to recreate an uncontaminated purity, but in the poem is also the excitement that accompanies hybrid possibilities: "and all of us went wild / with weighty rucksacks on our backs / and leather sandals / and flew like balloons in frenzy." This excitement does not last long, because the subject cannot reintegrate in his village when he returns. The metaphor of the balloon expresses the ephemeral nature of the exhilaration, an animation that is buoyant but can easily be deflated. The speaker's encounter with other cultures is at a superficial level, but he prefers this condition to that of his colleagues who were fully immersed in alien traditions, those who "went tipsy with nectar / And lost their way homewards."

Silent Voices is a collection of eighty-five poems in which Angira deploys diverse, often anguished voices to express the expectations and fears of postindependence East Africa. The poet taps into African cultural traditions without losing sight of the conditions defining contemporary society. This is underlined in the poem "Meeting," which discusses the poetic persona's influence by other writers. Angira underscores his indebtedness to Western forms but at the same time claims and registers a voice unique to his culture. The first five lines invoke canonical Western poets as imagined by the speaker:

> Milton stood on the rock
> And looked down
> To see excremental whiteness of life
> Owen emerged from Flanders
> To inspect the camp of existence.

The coinage "excremental" connotes "mental" and "extreme," signifying to the reader that the condition thematized here is more philosophical and aesthetic than physical. With this word, the writer suggests a deliberate avoidance of absolute enslavement to the Western aesthetics that he calls to his aid in the poem. He situates himself in the physical and intellectual landscape of his community: "And a blizzard blew my floating head / To float me down the Nilus water."

Angira's other collections of poems, *Soft Corals* (1973), *Cascades* (1979), and *The Years Go By* (1980), are relatively more direct in their presentation of social problems. Invoking biblical tropes and simple diction,

the poet pitches his tent with the ordinary people exploited and repressed by the postindependence leadership. The widely anthologized poem "No Grave, No Coffin" presents a politician who has been killed by insurgents and left out in the open to be eaten by scavengers:

> He was buried without a coffin
> without a grave
> the scavengers performed the post-
>   mortem
> in the open mortuary
> without sterilized knives
> in front of the nightclub.

The place that gives the poem its setting—a city nightclub—suggests the politician's immoral lifestyle. The poet also lists ways in which the politician's life contrasts with the ordinary people represented in the poem by the speaker, who uses the collective "we." The vanity of the self-aggrandizement that characterizes politics in East Africa is stressed through the disjunction between the rank reality of the politician's death and the lofty desires he has inscribed in his diary, where he says "he wished / to be buried in a golden-laden coffin / like a VIP / under the jacaranda tree beside his palace / a shelter for his grave / and much beer for the funeral party." The poem thus serves as a warning that those who live at the expense of others will soon be overthrown, pushing to oblivion their own vain desires. *Tides of Time: Selected Poems* (1996) collects many of Angira's important poems.

PRIMARY TEXTS

Angira, Jared. *Juices*. Nairobi: East African Publishing House, 1970.

——. *Silent Voices*. London: Heinemann, 1972.

——. *Soft Corals*. Nairobi: East African Publishing House, 1973.

——. *Cascades: Poems*. London: Longman, 1979.

——. *The Years Go By: Poems*. Nairobi: Bookwise, 1980.

——. *Tides of Time: Selected Poems*. Nairobi: East African Educational Publishers, 1996.

REFERENCES

Calder, Angus. "Jared Angira: A Committed Experimental Poet." In *Individual and Community in Commonwealth Literature*, edited by Daniel Massa, 36–44. Malta: University of Malta Press, 1979.

Ezenwa-Ohaeto. "The Human Angle: National Consciousness in Jared Angira's Poetry in *Cascades*." *The Journal of Commonwealth Literature* 11, no. 1 (1988): 100–106.

——. "Conscious Craft: Verbal Irony in the Poetry of Jared Angira." *African Literature Today* 20 (1996): 87–101.

Nazareth, Peter. "The Social Responsibility of the East African Writer (in African Literature)." *Callaloo* 8, no. 10 (1980): 87–105.

Ojaide, Tanure. "Modern African Literature and Cultural Identity." *African Studies Review* 35, no. 3 (1992): 43–57.

Roscoe, Adrian. *Uhuru's Fire: Literature from the East and South*. New York: Cambridge University Press, 1977.

Yesufu, Abdul R. "Jared Angira and East African Poetry of Social Testimony." *World Literature in English* 23, no. 2 (Spring 1984): 327–335.

——. "The Sympathetic Consciousness: A Study of Modern East African Poetry in English by Jared Angira, Richard Ntiru, Okot p'Bitek, and Okello Oculi." PhD thesis, Indiana University, 1983.

[*Mwangi*]

Autobiography In comparison to southern Africa and West Africa, the East African region has not produced famous literary autobiographies to equal the power of classic texts such as E'skia Mphahlele's *Down Second Avenue*, Peter Abrahams' *Tell Freedom*, Wole Soyinka's *Ake*, and Nafissatou Diallo's *A Dakar Childhood*. Nevertheless, autobiographical works and life narratives in general have been central in the literary history of the region largely because the genre was considered, during both the period of decolonization and afterward, to be an ideal medium for the exploration of a number of key themes in East African writing, including the relationship of individuals to communities and the process of education and social change.

In fact, some of the first literary texts of the region, produced in the period just prior to World War II, were autobiographical in character and were connected to a specific political program of adding an African voice and perspective to international debates about human rights and sovereignty. These early autobiographies were written by Africans in the West who sought to represent their own personal experiences and to present them as representatives of larger collective entities. The function of this kind of autobiography is echoed most vividly in *Africa Answers Back*, by the Toro Prince Akiki Nyabongo, written during his sojourn in the United States and published in 1936. In this work, Nyabongo does not focus so much on his own life as a member of Toro royalty, but rather on how his life experiences and background represented a specific African response to the colonial encounter. In this text and others, the writing self presented its life as a representative of the whole, and sought to establish a deep and profound relationship to an African culture that would be celebrated as the source of cultural authority and authenticity. Writing about oneself in a "thick" cultural context was one way by which Africans could call into question what they considered to be the distortion and slander of the African subject in the colonial text.

Early autobiography from East Africa thus tended to merge autobiography and ethnography in one of two ways: First, an African ethnography would derive its authority from the author's claim to a certain intimacy with the culture about which they were writing. This view was expressed explicitly in the preface to Jomo Kenyatta's *Facing Mount Kenya*, where the author based his authority on his personal involvement with the cultural practices he was describing, concluding that he could "speak as a representative of my people, with personal experience of many different aspects of their life" (xx). Second, early autobiographers were keen to ethnologize their own lives and present them as if they were the collective records of specific political entities. Prince Nyabongo would thus present himself as the voice of Toro. Similarly, in 1934, Kenyatta's compatriot Permenas Githendu Mockerie published the autobiographical text *An African Speaks for His People*. A distinctive feature of these autobiographies was that, unlike European texts of the genre, they eschewed the claims that the writing self was unique and that it derived its authority from a breaking away from the community. Autobiography was posited as conduit for recovering a usable African past, and writers of ethnographic autobiographies often posited themselves—and their works—as the bridge between the precolonial African past and the colonial present.

But autobiography in East Africa was also the primary genre through which the colonial encounter was narrated. In this sense, most autobiographies from the region had a close affinity to the discourse of cultural nationalism. In writing about their lives, often at the cusp of colonialism and decolonization, nationalists such as Harry Thuku (*The Autobiography of Harry Thuku*), Mugo Gatheru (*A Child of Two Worlds*), Tom Mboya (*Freedom and After*), J. M. Kariuki (*Mau Mau Detainee*), and Oginga Odinga (*Not Yet Uhuru*) presented their lives as examples of the tragic conflict between the African desire for political and economic freedom and the constraints imposed on them by colonial policies.

The political intentions of these nationalist narratives were apparent in their basic structure. Many would start with a reflection on the nature of their respective communities before colonialism; they would then present the birth of the author as an important communal event, thus symbolizing childhood as the embodiment of a certain cultural moment antecedent to colonialism. However, the focus of these autobiographies was the narration of the author's dramatic entry into the alienating world of the colonial school and the struggle to retain the integrity of the self against the deracinating and often brutal forces of the colonizing power and its institutions of government. Almost without exception, these autobiographies end with the discovery of nationalism as the site of fulfillment, the moment when the formerly alienated colonial subject discovers his or her political vocation. Indeed, most of the most dominant political autobiographies in East Africa were written from the vantage point of decolonization, positing nationalism as the fulfillment of years of struggle, disappointment, and ultimately, arrival. Kariuki would end *Mau Mau Detainee*, his powerful story of life in colonial detention camps, with the hope that his book—and "our new state"— would serve as a fitting memorial to the fighters for freedom (182).

In both its ethnographic and nationalist manifestations, autobiography was an important instrument for imagining African subjectivities during and after colonialism, a process through which African identities could be rethought during moments of political crisis and transition. In fact, many East African autobiographies were conceived by their authors as attempts to come to terms with moments of political and social crisis. Mugo Gatheru opens *A Child of*

Two Worlds with a rejection of the representation of the Kikuyu as either bloody or noble savages, professing the simple goal of showing that "to me, however, the Kikuyu are simply *my people*" (1). His point of closure was strategic, as he ends his autobiography on June 1, the day of Kenyan self-government, thus fusing self and nation:

> As I write today, the first day of June 1963, the end of my journeying is in sight after fourteen years away from my country, Kenya, and I can say that I am a happy man. On this day, I sit in London and thousands of miles away, in space if not in spirit, Jomo Kenyatta stands in Nairobi on a platform draped in scarlet and, as the very first Prime Minister of Kenya, swears "true allegiance to Her Majesty, Queen Elizabeth the Second, her heirs and successors according to law. So help me God." (215)

A similar structure of feelings was repeated in Mboya's *Freedom and After*, an autobiography that opens with the author's struggle for education in the sisal plantations of eastern Kenya and ends with the foregrounding of the significance of the sixth anniversary of Ghana's independence as "the event which gave so much encouragement to nationalists in African countries farther south" (261).

The relation between the structure of autobiography and the moment of crisis is evident in what one may call "autobiographical fiction," narratives that seek to mimic autobiography or to have a close relation to the author's life. A case in point is Ngugi's first published novel, *Weep Not, Child*, which, while not strictly autobiographical, is anchored around key moments in the author's life, or, rather, with his engagement with history, especially Mau Mau. Given the traumatic nature of the events surrounding it, Mau Mau was a discernable feature of auto-

biographical writing from Kenya in the period after decolonization. That the fiction of Mau Mau in this period contained a strong undercurrent of the autobiographical is evident in the novels and short stories of Leonard Kibera and Samuel Kahiga, Charity Waciuma, Muthoni Likimani, and Meja Mwangi. Those were writers who looked back on the immediate past and tried to see how it had been responsible for the production of their own identities and thus their making as writers. In the late 1960s and 1970s, there was a cluster of memoirs published by former members of the nationalist movement. The most notable of these were *Mau Mau General*, by Waruhiu Itote (General China), and Karari Njama's *Mau Mau from Within*. In the same period, radical politicians turned to autobiography to express their own disenchantment with what came to be known as "flag independence," a euphemism for failed decolonization. The most prominent works in this tradition are Oginga Odinga's *Not Yet Uhuru*, Bildad Kaggia's *Roots of Freedom*, and Ngugi's *Detained*, a memoir of his imprisonment by the Kenyan state in the late 1970s.

PRIMARY TEXTS

Gatheru, Mugo. *A Child of Two Worlds*. New York: Praeger, 1964.

Itote, Waruhiu. *Mau Mau General*. Nairobi: East African Institute Press, 1967.

Kaggia, Bildad. *Roots of Freedom 1921–1963: The Autobiography of Bildad Kaggia*. Nairobi: East African Publishing House, 1975.

Kariuki, Josiah Mwangi. *Mau Mau Detainee*. London: Oxford University Press, 1963.

Kenyatta, Jomo. *Facing Mount Kenya*. New York: Vintage Books, 1965. First published in London by Secker and Warburg in 1938.

Mboya, Tom. *Freedom and After*. Boston: Little Brown, 1963.

Mockerie, Permenas Githendu. *An African Speaks for His People*. London: Hogarth, 1934.

Njama, Karari, with Donald L. Barnett. *Mau Mau from Within*. New York: Monthly Review, 1966.

Nyabongo, Akiki K. *Africa Answers Back*. London: Routledge, 1936.

Odinga, Oginga Ajuma. *Not Yet Uhuru: The Autobiography of Oginga Odinga*. With a foreword by Kwame Nkrumah. London: Heinemann, 1967.

Thuku, Harry. *The Autobiography of Harry Thuku*. Nairobi: Oxford University Press, 1970.

REFERENCES

Geesey, Patricia. "Autobiography and African Literature." Special issue of *Research in African Literatures* 28, no. 2 (Summer 1997).

Olney, James. *Tell Me Africa: An Approach to African Literature*. Princeton, N.J.: Princeton University Press, 1973.

[Gikandi]

Barungi, Violet (b. 1948) Ugandan writer and editor. Barungi was born in Mbarara, in western Uganda, and went to school at Bweranyangangi Girls School, Gayaza High School, and Makerere University. Barungi's most successful work is *Cassandra* (1999), a novel about a rural girl, Cassandra Tibwa, who learns to safeguard her gender integrity in a society that believes that a woman has to sacrifice her sexuality in order to succeed. Set in the turbulence that defined Uganda in the 1980s, the novel celebrates Cassandra's determination to overcome her problems without having to be subservient to the lecherous men in town. Her play *Over My*

Dead Body won a British Council International New Playwriting Award for Africa and the Middle East Region in 1997. The novel *The Shadow and the Substance* appeared in 1998, and *Tit for Tat*, a self-published collection of short stories, appeared in 1999.

PRIMARY TEXTS

Barungi, Violet. *Cassandra*. Kampala: Femrite, 1999.

———. *Words from a Granary*. Kampala: Femrite, 2001.

EDITED WORKS

Barungi, Violet, and Ayeta Anne Wangusa. *Tears of Hope: A Collection of Short Stories by Ugandan Rural Women*. Kampala: Femrite, 2003.

Barungi, Violet, and Mary Karooro Okurut. *A Woman's Voice: An Anthology of Short Stories by Ugandan Women*. Kampala: Femrite, 1999.

[Mwangi]

p'Bitek, Okot (1931–1982) Ugandan poet, anthropologist, and cultural critic. Okot p'Bitek was one of the most important writers to emerge out of East Africa in the 1960s, and with the publication of the English version of *Song of Lawino* in 1966, he inaugurated a new genre of writing, which came to be known as the song poem. As the writer and critic Ngugi wa Thiong'o noted in 1972, *Song of Lawino* "is the one poem that has mapped out new areas and new directions in East African poetry . . . it is read everywhere arousing heated debates" (*Homecoming*, 75). Okot p'Bitek was born in Gulu in northern Uganda, in a family that represented the social and cultural forces that were shaping the region in the 1930s and 1940s. His father and uncle were prominent in the Catholic Church, one as a teacher, the other as a pastor. Although he was later to become a prominent critic of the church and its connection to colonial institutions (some of the most notorious satirical moments in *Song of Lawino* are directed at the Catholic Church and its liturgical tradition), there is a strong undercurrent of Catholicism in Okot p'Bitek's poetry and cultural criticism. But Okot p'Bitek was also heavily influenced by the traditional Lwo culture of the Acholi and Lango of northern Uganda. His mother, Lacwaa Cerina, was a renowned singer and composer.

Okot p'Bitek, who eschewed inherited notions of literature as a formal and learned process, credits his parents for having inspired him to produce works that would be built primarily on performance and oral expression. As he put it in his *Africa's Cultural Revolution*, his interest in African literature was sparked by "my mother's songs and the stories that my father performed around the evening fire" (quoted in Heron, *The Poetry of Okot p'Bitek*, 2). But if he seemed to disclaim the influence of formal literary culture on his oeuvre and insisted that his works were rooted primarily in Lwo festival traditions, dance, and song, it was also because, like other African writers of his generation, he was the ideal product of the colonial school. In fact, he was educated at two of the most prestigious schools in Uganda: Gulu High School and King's College, Budo. Between 1952 and 1954, Okot p'Bitek was trained as a teacher at the Government Teacher Training College, Kyambogo, and he later became a teacher at the Sir Samuel Baker School in Gulu. One of his students was Taban Lo Liyong.

It was during his stint as a teacher that Okot p'Bitek became heavily involved in cultural activities in northern Uganda, organizing festivals, composing songs, and even writing an opera (*Acan*) in English. It was also during this period that he published a novel, *Lak Tar*, in Acholi. He also completed *Wer per Lawino*, the Acholi version of *Song of Lawino*, but the manuscript was rejected by publishers, who considered it too vulgar. An accomplished athlete, Okot p'Bitek was a member of the Ugandan soccer team that toured Britain in 1958. After the tour, he remained in Britain to continue his higher education. Between 1958 and 1963, he acquired a diploma in education at Bristol University, a law degree from the University of Wales at Aberystwyth, and an advanced degree in social anthropology from Oxford University, where he presented a thesis on the oral literature of the Acholi and Lango.

On returning to Uganda in 1964, a year after independence, Okot p'Bitek joined the Extra-Mural division of Makerere University in Gulu, where he immediately resumed his work as a cultural activist and researcher. He was the organizer of the historic Gulu Festival of Acholi Culture in 1965. It was at this festival that he first presented a stage version of *Wer per Lawino*. In 1966, he was appointed director of the Uganda Cultural Center in Kampala, but in 1968, while he was leading a cultural delegation to Zambia, he was dismissed, for reasons that were never disclosed. Unable to continue his cultural activities in Uganda, he crossed the border into Kenya and worked for the University of Nairobi's Adult Education Center in Kisumu, where he organized a major cultural festival. During his period of exile, Okot p'Bitek taught in the sociology department of the University of Nairobi and was a guest lecturer at various institutions in Europe and the United States. At Nairobi, he was recognized as a major cultural commentator and a powerful advocate of African culture. With the overthrow of Idi Amin in 1979, Okot p'Bitek finally returned to Uganda, where he was appointed a senior fellow at the Makerere Institute of Social Research and later the first professor of creative writing at the university.

Okot p'Bitek's first important works, *Lak Tar* and *Wer per Lawino*, were first written in

Acholi, and for this reason he needs to be recognized, first and foremost, as a pioneer in African-language literature. But it was the publication of the English version of *Song of Lawino* by the East African Publishing House in 1966 that revolutionized East African writing. The impact of *Song of Lawino* was both cultural and literary. On the cultural level, it was one of the first sustained works of art to crystallize and structure the heated debates that were defining the African landscape in the aftermath of decolonization. In Lawino, the main character of the poem, and her husband Ocol, the target of her ridicule and supplication, Okot p'Bitek was able to dramatize the struggle between advocates of tradition and proponents of modernity. For at the center of the poem is Lawino's resentment over her husband's blind worship of European culture and his contempt for Acholi traditions, which he wants uprooted in the name of modernity. Lawino's poem is both a lament at this cavalier dismissal of old ways and an ethnographic commemoration of authenticity. In reading the poem in the 1960s and 1970s, African readers were able to acquire a set of metaphors and expressions they could use to comment on their own experiences as they tried to negotiate the claims of tradition and modernity. Indeed, *Song of Lawino* was, and continues to be, one of the most popular social texts in East Africa.

The poem's impact on the literary level was equally significant. By focusing on a poem as a song—a public performance—and by drawing on the forms of Acholi oral tradition, such as song, dance, and metaphor, Okot p'Bitek had freed East African poetry from the grip of the Makerere School of English and its alignment with high modernism. The success of the poem convinced other writers that African oral traditions could be effective sources of a new language for articulating the postcolonial moment. Most importantly, Okot p'Bitek

sought to produce songs that would intervene directly in the murky politics of the day, and do so through direct expression rather than the indirect and sometimes abstract language of the Makerere modernists. On a structural level, his songs were constructed as a set of debates between social protagonists discussing perhaps two of the most pressing questions of the postcolonial moment in East Africa: What would be the cultural foundation of the new African nation, its repressed African past or its inherited colonial moment? And what had been the effect of colonialism on the mentality of the African?

Having presented the case, in *Song of Lawino*, for making African cultures the basis of the new nation, Okot p'Bitek sought to present the modernist's view in *Song of Ocol*, but the sequel lacked the persuasive or rhetorical power of its predecessor. Okot p'Bitek seems to have found it difficult to marshal a language to seriously represent a position—the celebration of modernity—that he inherently disdained. The poems that he wrote in the 1970s were also overshadowed by *Song of Lawino*, but they were significant interventions in the political culture of the time. In *Song of Prisoner*, for example, Okot p'Bitek adopted a polyphonic stance to represent the experiences of intellectuals imprisoned for their political beliefs. In *Song of Malaya*, he adopted a comic tone to express the feelings and thoughts of a prostitute at home in the new urban centers of Africa. In the incomplete *Song of a Soldier*, he tried to write an epic song that would commemorate the lives of Africans living under military dictatorship.

In addition to the songs, Okot p'Bitek was involved in several other cultural projects. As an active anthropologist he was contemptuous of the discipline, but he also had a primary interest in issues of religion and culture, and out of his research came such works as *The Religion of the Central Luo* and

African Religions in Western Scholarship. An important corollary to his anthropological research were significant collections of traditional songs and folklore, collected in *Horn of My Love* and *Hare and Hornbill.* Finally, Okot p'Bitek was one of the most astute cultural critics in the region. Upon its publication in 1973, his first collection of essays, *Africa's Cultural Revolution*, was considered the ultimate manifesto of cultural nationalism in East Africa.

PRIMARY TEXTS (IN ENGLISH)

p'Bitek, Okot. *Song of Lawino: A Lament.* Nairobi: East African Publishing House, 1966.

——. *Song of Ocol.* Nairobi: East African Publishing House, 1970.

——. *Two Songs (Song of Prisoner, Song of Malaya).* Nairobi: East African Publishing House, 1971.

——. *Horn of My Love.* London: Heinemann Educational Books, 1974.

——. *Hare and Hornbill.* London: Heinemann Educational Books, 1978.

SECONDARY TEXTS

p'Bitek, Okot. *The Religion of the Central Luo.* Nairobi: East African Literature Bureau, 1971.

——. *African Religions in Western Scholarship.* Nairobi: East African Literature Bureau, 1972.

——. *Africa's Cultural Revolution.* Nairobi: Macmillan Books, 1973.

——. *Artist, the Ruler: Essays on Art, Culture, and Values.* Nairobi: Heinemann, 1986.

REFERENCES

Heron, G. A. *The Poetry of Okot p'Bitek.* London: Heinemann, 1976.

Goodwin, K. L. *Understanding African Poetry: A Study of Ten Poets.* London: Heinemann, 1982.

Mugambi, J. N. Kanyua. *Critiques of Christianity in African Literature, with Particular Reference to the East African Context.* Nairobi: East African Educational Publishers, 1992.

Ngugi wa Thiong'o. *Homecoming: Essays on African and Caribbean Literature, Culture, and Politics.* London, Heinemann, 1972.

Ojaide, Tanure. "Poetic Viewpoint: Okot p'Bitek and His Personae." *Callaloo* 27 (1986): 371–383.

Ramazani, Jahan. *The Hybrid Muse: Postcolonial Poetry in English.* Chicago: University of Chicago Press, 2001.

Wanjala, Chris. *Standpoints on African Literature: A Critical Anthology.* Nairobi: East African Literature Bureau, 1973.

[Gikandi]

Black Aesthetic A surprising development in East African literary culture from 1968 to 1973 was the emergence, as a major preoccupation of writers and critics, of the question of a black aesthetic. This development began with the circulation of a memo written by Ngugi wa Thiong'o, Henry Owuor-Anyumba, and Taban Lo Liyong, then junior members of the English department at University College, Nairobi, which was at the time a constituent college of the University of East Africa, seeking to question the nature and role of "English" in an African university. In the memo, aptly titled "On the Abolition of the English Department," Ngugi and his colleagues set out to question the basic assumption that "the English tradition and the emergence of the modern west is the central root of our consciousness and cultural heritage" (See the appendix to *Homecoming*, 146). Although the memo did not use the term "Black Aesthetic" and its overall concerns were humanistic rather than nationalistic, it was built on three assumptions that were to resonate with black cultural nationalism in other parts of Africa and its diaspora.

First, the memo made an explicit connection between writing in Africa and "sister" traditions in Caribbean and Afro-American literature:

> The Caribbean novel and poetry: the Caribbean involvement with Africa can never be over-emphasized. A lot of writers from the West Indies have often had Africa in mind. Their works have had a big impact on the African renaissance—in politics and literature. The poetry of Negritude indeed cannot be understood without studying its Caribbean roots. We must also study Afro-American literature. (149)

Second, the memo located the social energies and functions of literature within an explicitly African tradition, in what it called a "Cultural Renaissance." In this context, the function of a literature department was "to illuminate the spirit animating a people, to show how it meets its new challenges, and to investigate possible areas of development and involvement" (146). Third, the memo identified the study of oral literary forms as the locus of a nonalienated form of literary education: "By discovering and proclaiming loyalty to indigenous values, the new literature would on the one hand be set in the stream of history to which it belongs and so be better appreciated; and on the other be better able to embrace and assimilate other thoughts without losing its roots" (148).

Still, the writers of the manifesto wanted to displace the colonial tradition of letters from literary studies without giving up the idea that literature was part of a larger humanistic enterprise. Their challenge was to procure a new center of cultural values to replace the Western tradition they had denounced, without giving up altogether the idea of literature in the European sense. The idea of a black, or African, aesthetic, which began to appear in critical texts in the early 1970s, was an ideal instrument for reconciling an innate African tradition—one based on the nature of Africans and their culture—with the idea of literature as a formal and pedagogical process. What made the idea of a black aesthetic attractive was its capacity to gesture toward a set of values that could be defined as authentic even within the institution of Eurocentrism. Authenticity was what accounted for African identity, it was argued. In a 1969 lecture on "Okot p'Bitek and Writing in East Africa," for example, Ngugi asserted that *Song of Lawino* "is the one poem that has mapped new areas and new directions in East African poetry. It belongs to the soil. It is authentically East African in its tone and in its appeal" (*Homecoming*, 75). The connection between writing and a black aesthetic was promoted further in Okot p'Bitek's 1973 collection of essays, aptly named *Africa's Cultural Revolution*, and was firmly entrenched in a collection of essays published that same year, titled *Black Aesthetics*, edited by Pio Zirimu and Andrew Gurr.

In 1971, a collection of essays titled *The Black Aesthetic*, edited by Addison Gayle, was published by Doubleday in New York. This collection represented the cultural manifesto of the Black Arts Movement in the United States, and the claims it made were fairly similar to those circulating in East African culture at the time. Gayle's collection, which brought together the thoughts of some leading figures in the Black Arts Movement, was intended to establish a fundamental link between the politics of protest, embodied by the civil rights movement, and the notion of black cultural autonomy, namely, the search for norms of judgment, value, and standards of beauty not subject to the desires and interests of the dominant white culture. A black aesthetic would liberate artists from what Ron Karenga called "the madness of the Western world." To avoid this madness, what was needed was "a criteria for judging the validity and/or beauty of a work of art" (30). Behind the idea of the black aesthetic as it was evolving in the United States in the late 1960s was the belief that art had a crucial role to play in both the establishment of a black identity and in the revolution that was taking place in the streets of major American cities, as the civil rights movement reached its climax. And in order for it to intervene in the politics of everyday life, blacks needed to counterbalance the Western aesthetic project in two ways that were to find resonance in Africa and the Caribbean: First, art had to eschew individualism (the ideal of genius and subjective autonomy) and insist on its collective function. Second, the black aesthetic was a mode of rethinking or reevaluating what Larry Neal, in "The Black Arts Movement," saw as an exhausted Western aesthetic:

> It is the opinion of many Black writers, I among them, that the Western aesthetic has run its course: it is impossible to construct anything meaningful within its decaying structure. We advocate a cultural revolution in art and ideas. The cultural values inherent in western history must either be radicalized or destroyed, and we will probably find that even radicalization is impossible. In fact, what is needed is a whole new system of ideas.   (*Black Aesthetics*, 258)

Similar views were being echoed in East Africa at the same time. Indeed, the keynote speaker at the colloquium on the Black Aesthetic held at the University of Nairobi in 1971 was David Dorsey, a black American literary critic then teaching in East Africa. It was Dorsey who defined the Black Aesthetic in terms of audience perception and response, arguing that it was "a syndrome of internal factors governing a black audience's perception and appreciation of a work of art" (7). Dorsey rejected the assumption that a black aesthetic was inherently revolutionary, but insisted that East African writings had "a firm grounding in a healthy, sensible attitude toward the human body and natural functions" (15). In one of the most significant statements to come out of the colloquium, the Ugandan scholar Pio Zirimu drew direct comparisons and contrasts between black art in Africa and the diaspora, concluding that what black arts had in common, regardless of their diverse histories and geographies, was their "participatory rather than alienatory" character.

Within the black aesthetic, then, art was posited as the way out of decolonization. An African aesthetic was championed as the mark of a continuous and authentic cultural tradition that would serve, in the words of Taban Lo Liyong, as an antidote against the alienating culture of colonialism. For Lo Liyong, who had studied at Howard University at the height of the civil rights movement, "the African essence" was so potent that "it now challenges the white cultures of the Americas" (*Popular Culture of East Africa*, xi). For his compatriot Okot p'Bitek, the field of art and aesthetic judgment represented the battlefield on which the struggle for the soul of Africa was being fought. Okot p'Bitek described all his writings, from his anthropological treatises to his long poems, as "ammunition for one big battle, the battle to decide where we here in Africa are going, and what kind of society we are building" (quoted in *Artist the Ruler*, viii). Throughout the 1970s, when Ngugi and others shifted from cultural nationalism and embraced Marxism, with its more universal and materialistic notions of culture, Okot p'Bitek continued to argue for the role of art as the mark of African identity. Drawing on his research in Acholi aesthetic traditions, he argued that the aesthetic in Africa was not abstract, but rooted in the experience of everyday life: "The true African artist has his eyes firmly fixed, not to some abstract idea called beauty 'up there' as it were, but on the philosophy of life of his society" (*Artist the Ruler*, 23).

REFERENCES

p'Bitek, Okot. *Africa's Cultural Revolution*. Nairobi: Macmillan Books for Africa, 1973.

———. *Artist the Ruler: Essays on Art, Culture, and Values*. Nairobi: Heinemann Kenya, 1986.

Gayle, Addison, Jr., ed. *The Black Aesthetic*. New York: Doubleday, 1972.

Lo Liyong, Taban, ed. *Popular Culture of East Africa*. Nairobi: Longman Kenya, 1972.

Ngugi wa Thiong'o. *Homecoming: Essays in African and Caribbean Literature*. London, Heinemann, 1972.

Zirimu, Pio, and Andrew Gurr. *Black Aesthetics: Papers from a Colloquium Held at the University of Nairobi, June 1971*. Nairobi: East African Literature Bureau, 1973.

[Gikandi]

Blixen, Karen (Isak Dinesen, 1885–1962)
Like her dual names, Blixen occupies a divided place within the literary tradition. In Europe, she is regarded as one of the most innovative writers in the Gothic tradition, and her first collection of short stories, *Seven Gothic Tales* (1934), was considered a masterpiece of the genre. Her European novels and stories have often been celebrated for their masterly fantasy, keen sense of the place of women in society, and ethical concerns. In East Africa, however, Blixen has been viewed as a member of the white settler class, and *Out of Africa* (1937), the memoir that brought her international recognition, is considered to be representative of a certain European image of Africa, one that treasures the landscapes but denigrates its people.

Blixen was born in an aristocratic Danish family outside Copenhagen and was educated in private schools in Switzerland before studying art at the Danish Academy of Arts. She started writing short stories when she was in her early twenties. The turning point in her life was her marriage to Baron Bror von Blixen, a colonial settler in Africa, and her subsequent move to Kenya. *Out of Africa* is a chronicle of her life in Kenya, her involvement in coffee farming, and her tumultuous relationship with the English hunter Denys Finch Hatton. The memoir is best known in its film version, directed by Sydney Pollock and starring Robert Redford and Meryl Streep.

The qualities that have attracted Western readers to *Out of Africa* and its sequel *Shadows in the Grass* (1961) are also the ones that have made Blixen's works objectionable to African readers. European and American readers (and viewers) were attracted and enthralled by what a blurb from the 1985 Vintage edition called "her affection for and understanding of the land and its people." For African readers, however, this ostensibly intimate portrait of the Kenyan landscape was undergirded by a colonialist and racist ideology. The distinguished Kenyan novelist Ngugi wa Thiong'o considers *Out of Africa* to be "one of the most dangerous books ever written about Africa, precisely because this Danish writer was obviously gifted with words and dreams. The racism in the book is catching, because it is persuasively put forward as love. But it is the love of a man for a horse or for a pet" (*Moving the Center*, 133).

PRIMARY TEXTS

Blixen, Karen. *Out of Africa*. London: Putnam, 1937.

———. *Shadows in the Grass*. New York: Random House, 1961.

REFERENCES

JanMohammed, Abdul. *Manichean Aesthetics: The Politics of Literature in Colonial Africa*. Amherst: University of Massachusetts Press, 1983.

Ngugi wa Thiong'o. *Moving the Center: The Struggle for Cultural Freedom*. London: James Currey, 1993.

[*Gikandi*]

Bukenya, Austin (b. 1944) Ugandan novelist, poet, literary theorist, actor, and playwright. Bukenya was born in Masaka, Uganda, and educated in Uganda, Tanzania, and England. His verse play *The Bride* was first performed in 1973 and presents the conflict between a young generation of Africans who define themselves as modern and an older group that sees itself as the custodian of tradition. Bukenya uses the idiom of African languages to give the play a pan-African perspective and to critique the academic tendency to ossify African culture in anthropological studies. The play depicts young people who are becoming increasingly tired of the obsolete traditions and prejudice that govern life in their society. While criticizing some aspects of African traditions, the play brings African culture to life and shows it to be capable of tolerance, peace, and love. This is contrary to the way it is applied by the supposed guardians of tradition. Bukenya's other play, "The Secrets" (1968), also uses a local idiom, but it is not as accomplished as *The Bride* in its structure and language. Bukenya's only novel, *The People's Bachelor*, is a hilarious examination of the excesses of the African educated elites, whom it satirizes for wallowing in pleasures and convoluted theories of social change as the community around them suffers from poverty. Bukenya's poetry, which, like his other works, explores the themes of unrequited love and the place of traditions in contemporary Africa, has appeared in different journals and anthologies, including David Cook and David Rubadiri's *Poems from East Africa*.

Bukenya is also a pioneer researcher in oral literature, giving the subject a fresh disciplinary direction beyond the nationalism that prompted its inclusion in schools and universities as an area of study in the 1970s. *African Oral Literature for Schools*, cowritten with Jane Nandwa, offers the most widely accepted definitions and procedures for classification in the study of oral literature from the region. "Oracy as a Tool and Skill in African Development," cowritten with Pio Zirimu, argues that oral literature and performance have a purpose beyond the polemical rhetoric of Africanizing literary studies, in the sense that they are a mobilizing tool in developmental projects. *Understanding Oral Literature*, a collection of essays coedited with Wanjiku Mukabi Kabira and Okoth Okombo, is considered to be a seminal work on the methodology and theory of oral art. In his writings on oral literature, Bukenya has cautioned against the tendency to view oral literature as the preserve of Africans or technologically underdeveloped cultures, insisting that oral literature is a dynamic form used even in "technologically advanced" societies to represent the immediacy of art and everyday communication.

PRIMARY TEXTS

Bukenya, Austin. *The People's Bachelor*. Nairobi: East African Publishing House, 1972.

——. *The Bride*. Nairobi: East African Educational Publishers, 1987.

Bukenya, Austin, Jane Nandwa, and Muigai Gachanja. *Oral Literature*. Nairobi: Longhorn Publishers, 1998.

Bukenya, Austin, Wanjiku Mukabi Kabira, and Okoth Okombo, eds. *Understanding Oral Literature*. Nairobi: Nairobi University Press, 1994.

Nandwa, Jane, and Austin Bukenya. *Oral Literature for Schools*. Nairobi: Longman, 1983.

Zirimu, Pio, and Austin Bukenya. "Oracy as a Tool of Development." Paper presented at the Festival of African Arts and Culture (Festac '77), Lagos, Nigeria, January 15, 1977.

[Mwangi]

Buruga, Joseph (b. 1942) Ugandan scientist and poet. Born in West Nile, Uganda, in 1942, Buruga was educated at Arua; King's College, Budo; and Makerere University, where he graduated with a science degree in 1966. His long poem *The Abandoned Hut* was fashioned after Okot p'Bitek's *Song of Lawino*. Like *Song of Lawino*, Buruga's poem is an examination of the clash between African culture and European values. Unlike Okot p'Bitek, however, Buruga uses a male persona to explore the beauty and shortcomings of African precolonial cultures and practices. In symbolic terms, he presents the rejection of African traditions by the educated elites as the abandonment of the traditional African hut and the wisdom, stability, and morality it represents. Through a critique of Basia, the Westernized woman in the long poem, Buruga excoriates the unabashed imitation of the West by postindependence East Africans. Basia, the addressee in the bulk of the poem, has rejected her culture and therefore becomes the target of the speaker's laughter:

> You refuse
> To wear beads
> Of the red *muteru* seeds;
> You refuse
> To wear beads
> Made from the shells
> You say
> These things
> Are crude.   (27)

Using oral forms to evoke rural speech patterns, the speaker mocks Basia's Westernized mode of dressing, which, in a traditional context, would appear ridiculous:

> Sometimes you wear shoes
> That stand on a small peg,

> Shoes that make you walk
> As if you had just removed
> Jiggers from your toes   (28)

The poem, however, does not fully endorse the speaker's hostility to modernization, for readers are made to hear, in the poetic speaker's denunciation of Basia, the stereotypes about educated women in East Africa and the rigidity that works against development efforts in the region.

PRIMARY TEXTS

Buruga, Joseph. *The Abandoned Hut.* Nairobi: East African Publishing House, 1969.

[Mwangi]

Christianity and Christian Missions Except for Ethiopia, where the Orthodox Church has existed since the early Christian period, Christianity in the East African region dates from the era of European imperialism in the mid-nineteenth century. Thus, the processes of colonization and Christianization have been intertwined in the imagination of the people, and especially the writers, of the region. But the relationship between colonialism and Christianity goes far deeper than this historical association suggests: it was colonialism that enabled the spread of Christian missions in the region and demarcated specific functions for Christian churches in the modernization project, in areas such as education, cultural production, and the vetting of systems of belief. Conversely, Christian missions acted as an important advance guard for colonizing forces. Indeed, in the early scramble for Africa in the mid-nineteenth century, explorers in the East African region—

including important figures such as Ludwig Krapf and David Livingstone—were also missionaries, and the line dividing their evangelical mission and their imperial interests was not always distinct. The work of Livingstone in East Africa and central Africa was done in the name of both his missionary society and the British government; Krapf's "discoveries" in Kenya were made in the name of both his mission and the German Kaiser. Mission stations were quite often the first marks of a colonial presence in the region. The spread of missions mirrored the advancement of colonialism. Between 1848 and 1928, mission stations were established in the coastal regions of Kenya and Tanzania (Rabai and Zanzibar) and moved steadily inland into Kibwezi and Moshi, Kikuyu and Tabora, and eventually Buganda.

In their advancement along the lines of colonialism, missions often sought the protection of the European governments from which they originated. It is not accidental then that the great period of colonial expansion in East Africa (1850–1880) was also the time when Christian missions consolidated their presence in the region. Quite often in the nineteenth century, the line that divided the political and evangelical interests of the missions was hard to demarcate. The political rivalry between Protestants, Catholics, and Muslims in Buganda in the 1890s was also about imperial zones of influence. Catholics came to be associated with the French presence in the region, Protestants represented British interests, and the Muslims were perceived as the custodians of Egyptian designs in Buganda. The triumph of the Protestants in the religious wars of Buganda in 1890 was, in effect, the triumph of British imperialism, a fact affirmed by the signing of the Buganda Agreement of 1900.

Missionaries were not involved in the tasks of colonial governance, but their influence in the shaping of the new social order was apparent in the political, economic, and cultural spheres. In politics, missions and missionaries provided the African elite with a point of entry into the new colonial order. The most powerful political figures in the new colonies, men such as Sir Apolo Kagwa in Buganda, were also staunch members of the dominant church. It was because he was an Anglican that Sir Apolo became a major player in the network of political power spreading from Cambridge, Whitehall, and Canterbury. Later, the political influence of missionaries would play out in the emergence of nationalism, because major nationalists—and, ironically, the earliest critics of colonialism (Harry Thuku and Jomo Kenyatta, for example)—were the first products of the new Christian missions. On the economic front, the role of missionaries in the modernization of the region was immense. Missionaries were the first to plant coffee in East Africa. As Roland Oliver noted in *The Missionary Factor in East Africa*, the introduction of "material civilization" was as central to the missionary enterprise as the conversion of souls. Quite often, the reason why young Africans were attracted to missions was not so much the promise of salvation but the association of the missions with a social order, one defined by the power of literacy and access to modern amenities, which represented social mobility.

By the 1920s, however, these young Africans were beginning to question the spiritual cost of religious conversion, and this questioning led to the rise of cultural nationalism across the region. The impetus for cultural nationalism, which can be considered a direct revolt against the civilizational claims of the missionary enterprise, was the belief that beneath the veneer of a civilizing mission, Christian missionaries had systematically embarked on a project whose goal was nothing less than the destruction of African selves and the cultural foundations on which they rested. The new religion in East Africa, argued Kenyatta in a seminal chapter in *Facing Mount Kenya*, represented the greatest threat to the cultural integrity of the African; the discourse of conversion that Christianity espoused was based on the radical yet erroneous assumption that when it came to matters of belief, the African was "a clean slate on which anything could be written":

> In the early days of European colonisation many white men, especially missionaries, landed in Africa with preconceived ideas of what they would find there and how they would deal with the situation. As far as religion was concerned the African was regarded as a clean slate on which anything could be written. He was supposed to take wholeheartedly all religious dogmas of the white man and keep them sacred and unchallenged, no matter how alien to the African mode of life. The Europeans based their assumption on the conviction that everything that the African did or thought was evil. The missionaries endeavoured to rescue the depraved souls of the Africans from the "eternal fire"; they set out to uproot the African, body and soul, from his old customs and beliefs, put him a class by himself, with all his tribal traditions shattered and his institutions trampled upon. The African, after having been detached from his family and tribe, was expected to follow the white man's religion without questioning whether it was suited for his condition of life or not.   (206–207)

The irony, of course, is that the cultural nationalists who spearheaded the attack on the doctrines of Christianity and Christian conversion were themselves products of the missions. Since these nationalists were unable to break entirely from this heritage, or to give up the modern life that they associated with it, many of them tended to favor so-called African independent churches, in which Christian beliefs could be reconciled with African cultural practices such as polygamy or clidectomy, which were opposed by the missions.

Ngugi's first written novel, *The River Between*, is perhaps one of the most famous dramatizations of the conflict between missionaries and the emergent African elite and the latter's attempt to create an independent African church. The central conflict in the novel arises when a new generation of Christian missionaries, driven by evangelical fervor, condemn African cultural beliefs as barbaric and insist that in order for their African protégés to be true Christians, they had to give up their ancient beliefs and practices. The tragic moment in Ngugi's novel arises when African converts insist on being Christian while holding on to old values. Muthoni wants to be "circumsized in the tribe" and yet be a Christian, and Waiyaki wants to be the custodian of the ancient prophesy while also being modern as prescribed by the Church. Clearly, a central dilemma of cultural nationalism in the late colonial period was how to be Christian (and thus modern) while espousing a certain idiom of Africanness. Since African writers were themselves products of the colonial mission, it is not surprising that their works contain dramatic and imaginative examples of the dilemma of being Christian and African in the colonial period.

Of course, Christian missions created and controlled the institutions that were responsible for the emergence of a culture of letters in East Africa. It was at Christian missions in places such as Rabai, Kikuyu, and Mengo that the oasis of the colonial education systems first emerged; these in turn created the first colonial readers and writers. The first printed texts in the region came out of the mission presses, and the first works of creative writing were often rewritings of the Bible, religious texts, or primers. But Christianity also created a system of beliefs and a way of life that demarcated so-called traditional African worlds from modern ones, and, in the process, it generated perhaps one of the most persistent themes in African writing: the tradition/modern dialectic. This dialectic was to take two forms: First, the pioneer generation of writers in English posited their fiction as a revolt against the alienating forces of modernity (identified closely with Christian beliefs and ways) and an attempt to recover a precolonial African tradition. This theme is most evident in the works of the Makerere writers anthologized by David Cook and David Rubadiri in *Origin East Africa.*

Second, it was in their creative writing that East African writers often figured their own ambiguous location or adventure in the Christian doxa. In Ngugi's early works, for example, there is a continuous and unresolved tension between the forces of Christian civilization and the threat of so-called African barbarism as it had been adumbrated in the missionary text. Later, of course, writers could direct their anger and satire at the civilizational claims of Christianity, but it is also interesting to note that the works renowned for their uncompromising antimissionary stance (the songs of Okot p'Bitek, for example, or Ngugi's "Marxist" novels) are underwritten by a deep anxiety about the power and logic of Christianity and the Christian mission. Okot p'Bitek's most famous text, *Song of Lawino*, is rooted in the Acholi oral tradition, but its primary target—and thus content—is the poet's inescapable Catholic heritage. The mother who taught Okot p'Bitek Acholi songs was also a staunch Catholic. In Ngugi's later novels, especially *Petals of Blood* and *Devil on the Cross*, the language of class is simply a rehearsal of the *ustaarabu* (civility) promoted by the Scottish Church in central Kenya. Christianity was thus seen as the alien force that threatened African traditions even as it provided the idiom of its own critique.

REFERENCES

Kenyatta, Jomo. *Facing Mount Kenya*. New York: Vintage Books, 1965. First published in London by Secker and Warburgh in 1938.

Oliver, Roland. *The Missionary Factor in East Africa.* 2nd ed. London: Longman, 1965.

Temu, A. J. *British Protestant Missions.* London: Longman, 1972.

[Gikandi]

Colonialism   The colonization of East Africa by the major European powers, a process that began at the end of the sixteenth century and continued until the early 1960s, is one of the most monumental events in the history of the region. Colonialism is now regarded as central to the study of East African culture and society and is imperative to our understanding of the modern literature of the region for a number of reasons, many of which have been constantly debated since independence in the early 1960s. Colonialism has come to be seen as a traumatic moment, because it represented the unprecedented loss of independence and autonomy by both established polities (mostly kingdoms in the interlacustrine region) and emergent regional powers such as the Nyamwezi and Kamba peoples of central Tanzania and eastern Kenya. From the moment of initial conquest, when the Portuguese established their strongholds on the East African coast and built Fort Jesus in Mombasa in 1593, to the consolidation of European rule, initiated by the 1898 Conference of Berlin, East African communities came to discover that, under colonialism, local desires and initiatives were now subject to the larger geopolitical and economic interests of the European powers. In addition, they quickly realized that relations with outside entities, which prior to this period had been conducted on the basis of mutual reciprocity, were now uneven and unequal. Even in those cases where powerful East African kingdoms such as Buganda maintained a measure of local autonomy, their relationship with the outside world was determined by the sponsoring European power.

But colonialism was perhaps to leave its most lasting effect on East African communities in its systematic and radical transformation of local institutions and political, economic, and cultural structures and the practices they sustained. This transformation was to outlast formal European rule on the subcontinent. At the most basic level, the process of colonization meant the delegitimation and reorganization of African institutions and either their supplanting by colonial institutions or their subordination to European structures. Under colonialism, older forms of education were either declared obsolete or marginalized, ancient belief systems were labeled barbaric and suppressed, and the only political systems that survived were those that cohered with European theories about governance and tradition, such as the monarchical system in Buganda. Where local institutions threatened colonial rule, as happened during the Maji Maji rebellion against the German occupation of Tanganyika in 1917, they were ruthlessly crushed.

One of the most persistent themes in East African literature is how colonialism remade the character of local society. But on another level, colonialism has been an important theme in the literature of East Africa because of its indispensable role in the production of the modern institutions and elites that have shaped the political and cultural geography of the region. Colonialism not only created the boundaries within

which different national entities evolved, but also the infrastructure that has established a regional identity for East Africa.

The history of colonialism in East Africa is similar to that of the colonial experience elsewhere on the African continent. The first phase of European colonialism on the East African coast begins with the arrival of the Portuguese sailor Vasco da Gama, on his way to India, and the subsequent development of trade along the Indian Ocean from the 1500s to the mid-nineteenth century. A second phase begins in the mid-nineteenth century, just before the Conference of Berlin (1884–1885), when European missionaries and explorers like Ludwig Krapf, David Livingstone, Joseph Thompson, and Samuel Teleki were instrumental in establishing a beachhead for their respective missions and governments. While missionaries and explorers were either individual entrepreneurs or agents of specific religious denominations, they were often associated with imperial powers, and by the time the colonial map of East Africa took shape in the 1880s, mission stations and geographic "discoveries" were to serve as landmarks of the zones of influence of colonizing powers such as Britain, Germany, and Italy. What had appeared to be informal zones of influence in the mid-nineteenth century were instituted as fixed boundaries of imperial control at the Conference of Berlin. It was at that conference that the geography of colonialism in East Africa was formalized. Under the arrangement reached under the watchful eye of Otto Von Bismark, the German chancellor, the British were awarded what was later to become the Kenyan colony, and were granted protector status over Uganda and the Sultanate of Zanzibar. The Germans were given Tanganyika.

While the Conference of Berlin determined the overall map of colonization in Africa, there were some significant differences in the history of colonialism between

East Africa and the rest of the continent. In general, the European colonization of the East African region was, in comparison to West Africa, relatively late and scattered in time and space. Until the arrival of the Portuguese at the end of the sixteenth century, the foreign occupiers of the region were from the East, mostly Arabs from the gulf who established longstanding trade links with the East African coast. The trade between East Africa, the Persian Gulf, Arabia, and India, aided by the annual monsoon winds, had been going on for centuries prior to the arrival of the Europeans. During this time, Arab families and caliphates were established on the East African coast. In fact, the struggle for dominance of the coastal region at the beginning of the modern imperial era was not between native Africans and Europeans, but between Arabs—and Afro-Arab families such as the Mazruis, originally from Oman—and the new invaders. The East African slave trade was primarily an Arabic, not European, phenomenon. The East African coast was considered so central to the gulf trade that by the middle of the nineteenth century, the Sultanates of Muscat and Oman (in the gulf region of southwestern Asia, near the present-day Gulf of Oman and the Persian Gulf) had decided to relocate their capital to the island of Zanzibar, a major producer of valuable spices such as cloves and the leading slave market on the eastern coast of Africa.

Also, it is significant to note that when the Europeans first arrived in East Africa, they were not, like their West African counterparts, involved primarily in trade but in missionary activities. Missionaries rather than traders were the vanguard of East African colonization. As happened in Buganda in the 1890s, missionaries were often the surrogates of major European powers. In fact, the colonial map of East Africa reflected the general locations of European mission stations, for wherever the missionaries went they assumed the authority and protection of their respective governments. Imperial agents, such as the German Karl Peters, were also advocates of one Christian denomination or another. In the end, the geography of colonialism in East Africa was a patchwork of competing European interests: the British in Kenya and Uganda, the Germans in Tanganyika until the end of World War I, the Italians in parts of Somalia, and the British and French in the rest. The key exception was Ethiopia, which for several centuries had resisted European colonization vigorously, defeating the Italians at the famous battle of Adowa in 1896. It was briefly occupied by Mussolini's fascist forces in 1936.

In regard to literary production in the region, it is fair to say that up until the 1980s, when extreme political and economic crises shifted the concerns of writers and intellectuals to questions of domestic failure, colonialism and its origins, forms, and effects were the major themes in the region's literature. In fact, modern East African literature came into being in the late 1950s and early 1960s as an attempt to account for the process of colonialism and its consequences. This concern was reflected most vividly in the student works appearing Makerere University College's journal *Penpoint*, works now collected in the volume *Origin East Africa*. The poems, plays, and stories in this inaugural collection are diagnoses of the colonial encounter from several angles: the initial meeting of Africans and Europeans, the attempt to give voice to a world before colonialism (for example, in the short stories and poems of Jonathan Kariara), the tragic split in the psyche of the colonized African, and the challenge of nationhood. These were the nascent themes that were taken up in the early texts of East African literature at the moment of decolonization.

Much poetry from the period is an attempt to use European forms to give meaning to the African experience before and during colonialism. The most popular poem is perhaps David Rubadiri's "Stanley Meets Mukasa," a dramatic monologue describing the confrontation between Henry Molton Stanley, one of the most famous agents of imperialism, and the Kabaka (King) Mutesa, the last great defender of Buganda's freedom. Most of the plays produced to celebrate the coming of independence dramatize the tragedy of the new African against the forces of a resurgent tradition, and the key novels of the period, most prominently Ngugi's *The River Between* and *Weep Not, Child* center around the violence and tragedy generated by colonialism and the resistance against it on both political and cultural levels.

REFERENCES

Ogot, B. A. *Zamani: A Survey of East African History.* New ed. Nairobi: East African Publishing House/Longman Kenya, 1973.
Were, Gideon, and Derek Wilson. *East Africa Through a Thousand Years.* 3rd ed. New York: Africana Publishing Company, 1983.

[Gikandi]

Cultural Nationalism The issue of cultural nationalism in East Africa cannot be separated from questions of nationality and nationalism, and it must be considered as part of the general process of decolonization; nevertheless, it represents an important context for understanding the politics of literature and culture in the modern period. Cultural nationalism has, directly or indirectly, been one of the most persistent themes in the literature of the region. Indeed, issues of cultural nationalism represent an important point of intersection for larger questions on the relation between literature and politics, debates about the role of culture in decolonization and nation building, and the function of cultural activism in both the colonial and postcolonial periods. On another level, cultural nationalism can be seen as both an important signifier of key moments of political crisis in the region and as one of the central informing ideas of, and themes in, modern East African literature. With regard to political crisis, almost all the movements against colonialism in the region had a cultural component. The revolt of Somali Dervishes against British colonialism in the early twentieth century produced an important tradition of mystical poetry in Somalia, the 1905–1907 Maji Maji uprising against German rule in Tanganyika was led by mystics who appealed to the authority of culture to lead their followers into battle, and the so-called female circumcision conflict in central Kenya in the 1920s was expressed through songs and dances that denigrated the civilizing claims of the colonizer. Culture was also powerfully associated with nationalist movements in the 1950s and early 1960s. The Mau Mau movement in Kenya was an armed revolt against British rule that also appealed to the authority of traditional culture, producing songbooks that posited the nationalist struggle as political, economic, and cultural in nature. Similarly, the literary renaissance in East Africa in the 1960s was animated by heated debates over the relation between culture and identity, alienation and authenticity, many of them revolving around Okot p'Bitek's long poems *Song of Lawino* and *Song of Ocol*. In the 1970s and 1980s, radical intellectuals, even those invested in the Marxist idea of historical materialism, accepted that culture represented an important ground for political struggle. The most influential collections of essays in the postcolonial period, Okot p'Bitek's *Africa's Cultural Revolution* and Ngugi wa Thiong'o's *Homecoming*, were motivated by the desire to make debates about culture central to rethinking the order of decolonization.

Why did the politics of culture occupy such a central role in the modern history of East Africa? There are several reasons for the prominence of culture in the politics of nationalism. The first one was the claim, articulated most powerfully in Kenyatta's *Facing Mount Kenya*, that the idea of culture symbolized both the integrated aspect of African life and the fundamental difference between Europeans and Africans. In the conclusion to his ethnography, Kenyatta was at pains to emphasize that the various sides of Gikuyu life there described were the parts of an integrated culture: "No single part is detachable; each has its context and is fully understandable only in relation to the whole" (297). This point was echoed by Okot p'Bitek and Ngugi wa Thiong'o in the cultural essays they wrote in the 1960s and 1970s.

Second, in the colonial period, at a time when missionaries presented themselves as the active agents of the irreversible process of civilizing the African, cultural nationalists saw their defense of an African cultural system as the first and most important step in defending their rights to land, liberty, and group autonomy. It was in the field of culture that two opposing views on the future of Africa came to an unprecedented confrontation, with one group identifying with colonial modernity and the other insisting that only a return to African values could ensure the autonomous identity of East Africans. Thus, while Kenyatta argued that *Facing Mount Kenya* was an attempt to establish an alternative path to modernity, one freed of colonial political control, the missionary critics of his book, most notably Dr. H. R. A. Philp, dismissed it as a work against the "Christian Spirit": "The author glorifies in shame and parades that which is indecent, and this in the name of science" (quoted in Rosberg and Nottingham, *The Myth of "Mau Mau,"* 134). Kenyatta's point, of course, was that his ethnography was intended to reinstitute an African cultural tradition as logical, desirable, and sensible.

Third, culture appealed to nationalists because they believed that it could be marshaled, sometimes in powerful and emotive ways, to address urgent political and economic grievances. In moments of cultural crisis, new dances such as the *Beni* in the coastal region of Tanzania and the *Muthirigu* in central Kenya would emerge to galvanize the peoples' energies against colonial transgressions such as forced labor or land alienation. In its idiom and structure, the *Muthirigu* dance was considered to be such a powerful tool directed against the colonial government in central Kenya during the late 1920s that it was banned in January 1930: "Heavy penalties were imposed on the singers by the Courts, but it continued to circulate underground as an anthem of resistance" (Rosberg and Nottingham, *The Myth of "Mau Mau,"* 123).

Finally, for the intellectuals in the postcolonial state, culture represented an alternative public sphere—one that would be deployed against the institutions of the state. It is not by accident that in all the seminal essays published in the 1970s and 1980s, Ngugi would locate his literary project within a larger struggle for national culture. Debates about culture were not confined to essays and public debates, but often made their way into imaginative texts. Cultural themes associated with moments of political crisis could become the basis of important literary works. Ngugi's *The River Between* was about the "female circumcision" controversy of the 1920s and its effect on notions of Gikuyuness. Ebrahim Hussein's historical play *Kinjekitile* was a dramatization of the 1917 uprising against German rule. Okot p'Bitek's poems *Song of Lawino* and *Song of Ocol* and Ngugi's later works *Petals of Blood* and *Devil on the Cross* presented a powerful staging of the struggle for the idea of national culture between the political class and the intellectual elite.

REFERENCES

p'Bitek, Okot. *Africa's Cultural Revolution.* Nairobi: Macmillan Books for Africa, 1973.

Ngugi wa Thiong'o. *Homecoming: Essays on African and Caribbean Literature.* London: Heinemann, 1972.

Rosberg, John, and John Nottingham. *The Myth of "Mau Mau": Nationalism in Kenya.* New York: Meridian Books, 1970.

[Gikandi]

Dawood, Yusuf Kodwavwala (b. 1928) A renowned Kenyan doctor, novelist, and newspaper columnist of Asian ancestry. His writings are semiautographical and are based on cases he encountered as a surgeon. Although they seem devoid of serious content, Dawood's novels have a wide following in East Africa because of the writer's use of humor and his sense of drama and suspense. *No Strings Attached,* Dawood's first novel, tells the story of Ahmed, a doctor who sets up a medical practice in Nairobi after his training in England. *The Price of Living* depicts the social contradictions of the rich and powerful in Kenya. *Off My Chest* and *Behind the Mask* narrate the strange events that happen to families that seek the narrator-surgeon's treatment. *One Life Too Many* is an account of an expatriate surgeon's life in a multiracial society made up of distinct social classes, while *Water Under the Bridge* is a Kenyan saga spanning three decades, three generations, and three races. In *Return to Paradise,* Dawood is concerned with the expulsion of Asians from Uganda by President Idi Amin. *Yesterday, Today, and Tomorrow* narrates Dawood's life in the Muslim area of Bantwa, Pakistan, in prepartition India, where he was born and brought up, his experiences in England where he trained as a surgeon and married, and his encounter with postindependence Kenya, where he eventually settled and became a successful surgeon. *Nothing but the Truth* is also autobiographical.

PRIMARY TEXTS

Dawood, Yusuf Kodwavwala. *No Strings Attached.* Nairobi: East African Educational Publishers, 1978.

——. *The Price of Living.* Nairobi: Longhorn, 1983.

——. *Yesterday, Today, and Tomorrow.* Nairobi: Longhorn, 1985.

——. *Off My Chest.* Nairobi: Longhorn, 1988.

——. *One Life Too Many.* Nairobi: Longhorn, 1991.

——. *Water Under the Bridge.* Nairobi: Longhorn, 1991.

——. *Behind the Mask.* Nairobi: Longhorn, 1995.

——. *Return to Paradise.* Nairobi: East African Educational Publishers, 2000.

——. *Nothing but the Truth.* Nairobi: East African Educational Publishers, 2002.

[Mwangi]

Decolonization An important aspect of colonialism in East Africa was the resistance against it, a subject that was to preoccupy writers and intellectuals in the postcolonial period. Each major period of colonial conquest in East Africa generated notable resistance toward foreigners and their agents. The earliest examples are the struggles between the Portuguese and the Mazrui family on the East African coast in the sixteenth century. With the intensification of colonization in the nineteenth century, resistance came either from established traditional rulers of kingdoms such as Buganda and Bunyoro or local lords such as Waiyaki among the Gikuyu and Mekatilili among the Giriama. Such movements were often put down through military expeditions, their leaders killed or exiled. Other resistance movements took on what has come to be known as a millennial character, invoking the power of traditional religion or Islam as rallying calls against the colonizers. The most famous of such movements were the Dervish movements against British rule in Somaliland between 1899 and 1920 and the Maji Maji uprising against German rule in Tanganyika from 1905 to 1907.

In the twentieth century, resistance against colonialism came mainly from the first generation of African elites, men and women who had been educated in colonial institutions and come to aspire to the modern life, but had become disillusioned with the unfulfilled promises of colonial modernity, such as access to jobs and political representation. These Africans came together to form the first nationalist movements, such as the East African Association, formed by Harry Thuku in 1912. Other nationalist movements, such as the Buganda Association and the Kikuyu Central Association, tended to be limited to specific regions or ethnic groups, but they shared with the larger associations similar tactics and goals—the appeal for African rights through the political process. Occasionally, the struggle against colonialism took a cultural form, as was the case in the "female circumcision" controversy in central Kenya, when Gikuyu nationalists broke away from the mainstream churches, arguing that attempts to outlaw the practice threatened the foundations of their culture.

Political efforts against colonialism intensified after World War II, fuelled here, as elsewhere in the colonial world, by disenchanted soldiers who had fought for the British Empire, mostly in the Middle East and Burma. These veterans were often responsible for the radicalization of existing nationalist movements. In the last decade of empire in the 1950s, resistance against colonialism took three forms: a militant guerilla resistance (the Mau Mau movement in Kenya), a radical nationalism often embodied by the political parties that were to take the East African countries to independence (TANU, KANU, UPC), and the crystallization of cultural notions of Africanness in the works of the educated elite, who were increasingly producing literature to, in the words of Ngugi wa Thiong'o, "restore the African character to his history" (*Homecoming*, 43).

The process of decolonization in East Africa followed the same pattern as elsewhere on the continent: First, the desire of the African elite for political representation, economic rights, and social modernization without colonial control was expressed through newspapers and political rallies, but it was frustrated by the colonial government's slower, devolutionary model of transferring power—or by its outright hostility. Second, nationalist movements in the region were continuously caught between the competing interests of intellectuals with a larger pan-African vision of the future, interests that were vested in the authority and power of privileged regions, and the more moderate desire to transform the colonial state into a nation in which a plurality of interests could be unified.

But decolonization in East Africa had its own peculiarities. For one, elites in the region were more recent products of the colonial enterprise and were fewer in number, and thus did not have the political clout of their West African counterparts. In addition, the region had a powerful class of white settlers with vested interests in the thriving agricultural sector, and while their numbers were concentrated in Kenya, they were numerous enough to generate the myth of a multiracial future, which was presented as the precondition for independence. As a result, the process of decolonization in the region was characterized by continuous tensions between African nationalists and settler interests, a tension that is vividly dramatized in Ngugi's *Weep Not, Child*.

At the same time, individual countries each had their own subtle but important differences in the process of decolonization. In Kenya, the violence of decolonization and what has come to be known as the "myth of Mau Mau," in which the nationalist movement was cast as regressive and atavistic, was to shape the drama of politics and highlight the radical division between settler interests, African aspirations, conservatives, and radicals. In Tanzania, where there were no white interests as such, decolonization tended to appeal to universal nationalist desires and to revolve around the trade-union movement. In Uganda, the process of decolonization was determined by the struggle between the demands of the kingdom of Buganda for special rights and the colonial government's investment in a unified Ugandan state. In Zanzibar, the presence of a powerful Arab population, a sultanate with historical connections to the Arabian Sea, and a disenchanted African population led to a political coup a few months after independence in 1963, paving the way for unification with the Tanganyika mainland a year later. Somalia, on the other hand, was decolonized according to the dictates and practices of its three competing colonizers, Britain, France, and Italy. Ethiopia was an exception to this pattern of colonial rule, as it had managed to retain its sovereignty and independence during the era of empire, apart from its occupation by Mussolini's forces between 1936 and 1941.

Given this history, decolonization has been as much a central theme of East African literatures in English as colonialism, its great opposite. Indeed, if we locate the process of decolonization in the period between the crisis of the colonial state after World War II and the formal achievement of independence in the early 1960s, then it is possible to argue that East African literature in English was generated by both the imperative and crisis of decolonization. Most of the writers who emerged during this period were part of a generation of educated Africans who were beginning to rethink the role of culture in the process of decolonization, publishing their works at a time when dreams about a postcolonial future seemed to demand an imaginative response or when doubts were emerging about the nature of decolonization and its consequences. Ngugi's early novels and essays are ideal products of this moment, for they attempt to look back at the past and see what useful lessons could be gleaned from it, probe the meaning and place of previously repressed traditions in the national imaginary, and often represent liberal anxieties about the role of the masses—and intellectuals—in the making of the new nation.

East African literature produced during the cusp period between the end of colonialism and the beginning of postcolonialism also reflects the themes and tensions that had come to define the narrative of decolonization in the late 1950s and early 1960s. In the works collected in anthologies such as *Origin East Africa* and in the monumental song poems of Okot p'Bitek, which appeared in English in the mid-1960s, decolonization is represented as both a moment of hope, the harbinger of a new beginning, and also a process fraught with contradictions and anxieties. This commingling of hope and anxiety is vividly represented in a memorable description of the scene of independence at the end of Ngugi's *A Grain of Wheat.*

But perhaps the process of decolonization has been most influential in East African literature because it has produced some of the most powerful critiques of the aftermath of colonialism. By the mid-1960s, the belief that the end of colonialism would lead to the achievement of total political, economic, and cultural liberation was put to the test both by events and the practices of the African elite in power. The dream of modernization without colonialism had faltered. The most successful economic states, such as Kenya, were the ones in which foreign economic interests continued to be dominant. Democracy was fragile because, when faced with political opposition, the states of the region tended to want to consolidate the power of the president, the ruling party, or the state.

For writers and intellectuals, then, decolonization seemed incomplete or still-born, and there was no better analysis of this condition than the one presented by Frantz Fanon in *The Wretched of the Earth*. In the period of colonialism, nationalist parties had mobilized the people "with slogans of independence" and left the rest "to future events," argued Fanon (150). Now that independence had arrived, it had turned into a future of political corruption, party control, economic failure, and rabid ethnic nationalism, and so national consciousness, instead of being "the all-embracing crystallization of the innermost hopes of the whole people" had become "an empty shell, a crude and fragile travesty of what it might have been" (148). The great irony of the narrative of decolonization is that it was precisely at that moment of the realization that the dream of independence had perhaps been betrayed that some of the most innovative works of literature in East Africa emerged.

REFERENCES

Fanon, Frantz. *The Wretched of the Earth*. Translated by Constance Farrington. New York: Grove Press, 1963.

Ngugi wa Thiong'o. *Homecoming: Essays in African and Caribbean Literature*. London: Heinemann, 1972.

[Gikandi]

Education and Literacy   There is an intimate relation between the process of education, the acquisition of literacy, and the production and circulation of literature in East Africa. The introduction of formal education through the process of colonization transformed the character of literary culture from oral to written forms. Without doubt, the introduction of the modern school by colonial authorities and missionaries heralded a new order of culture in many communities in the region, except those which, as in the cases of Islam at the coast and the Amharic language in Ethiopia, already had an established literary tradition. It was through its system of education that colonialism set out to change the nature of culture and society in the region, creating subjects who were to become both the first writers and consumers of the written word. The readers produced at mission stations were the first to produce a literature in African languages or to translate European texts for local reading.

The first sets of texts produced in the East African colonies were primers used for the acquisition and promotion of literacy, but these primary texts were not innocent instruments of instruction. They sought to promote two competing views of the African: first, as the product of a premodern tradition, and second, of a subject in the throes of a process of social change and thus modernization. Early texts had a strong moral content and often involved translations of evangelical works such as Bunyan's *Pilgrim's Progress* or the Gospels into local African languages. The first writers and readers in East Africa were heavily involved in the act of translation. In Uganda, for example, Ham Mukasa, the secretary to the Katikiro (Prime Minister) Sir Apolo Kagwa translated the Gospel of St. Matthew into Kiganda. The first printing presses were established either at Christian missions, such as the Italian Consolata Mission in Nyeri, Kenya, or in leading schools, most prominently King's College, Budo.

In spite of the revolutionary nature of literacy in East African communities in the early twentieth century, colonial systems of education did not enable the production of much creative writing in English. There were two main reasons for this: First, colonial education, which in any case was limited to a relatively small number of people, was essentially confined to the lowest primary levels, where instruction was either in the vernacular or Swahili. Second, after the report of the Phelps Stokes Commission in 1924, a doctrine was established in which African education would be vocational in nature, modeled after Booker T. Washington's Tuskegee model. The emphasis on vocational training often precluded an education in general humanistic disciplines that might familiarize students with established models of literature in English.

Before the Stokes Commission imposed its imprint on the school system in East Africa, the cultivation of a literary culture had been accepted as an important aspect of the curriculum, especially in the few, but highly select, high schools that existed in the region, most notably Alliance in Kenya and Budo in Uganda. But the Stokes commissioners, coming from the United States, where notions of education were tied up with race, considered a literary education to be unsuitable for the African. When they visited King's College, Budo, established in 1898 initially to educate the children of Baganda chiefs, the members of the Stokes Commission criticized the school for being too academic in its orientation.

Budo and Alliance High School, established by Protestant missions in Kenya in 1926, were modeled after British grammar schools, and for this reason, among others, they considered literature (and sports) to be central to the moral education of Africans. At Alliance High School, the principal, E. Carey Francis, a missionary and mathematician, built a program of education based on a set of Victorian moral claims that might have come out of Thomas Arnold's system at Rugby. In this system, literature, especially Shakespeare, was central to the moral education of Africans. The highlight of the school year at Alliance was the production of a Shakespeare play.

The idea of literature in East Africa was intimately connected to the process of education. Literary people were those who had gone through the school system. In addition, literature was considered part and parcel of the social mission of colonialism. It was through the system of education that Africans were linked to the network of literary culture in Europe itself. Budo was not simply set up and run by Anglicans; its teachers were drawn from Cambridge, and the doctrines driving their projects in the 1920s reflect very much the debates on education and the making of moral character that were taking place at that university after World War I. Although the curriculum at Budo in the early years was in the vernacular, the founders were keen that it should contain teaching in English, "so that the boys could eventually read and enjoy English literature" (McGregor, *King's College, Budo*, 8). For Protestant missions and schools, literacy was a precondition for conversion: the Anglicans who founded Budo could not allow an African to be baptized before he or she could read. In most Protestant missions, the gifts given to Africans upon conversion were copies of the Bible and John Bunyan's *Pilgrims Progress*. The gift of literacy was the key to heaven, it seemed.

English literature was also privileged because it was considered to contain models of civility and civilization toward which the newly educated Africans were to aspire. In this sense, literary education in African "grammar" schools was geared toward pupils who could appreciate literature in order to learn the lessons of modernity and civility rather than to produce a culture of letters. While it is true that the most prominent East African writers in English went to Alliance (Ngugi wa Thiong'o and Kariara) and Budo (Okot p'Bitek and Rubadiri), it is important to note that they did not start writing when they were in those institutions. If one is looking for the institutions that enabled the production of an African literature in the crucial period of the 1950s, it was undoubtedly the university, especially Makerere University College. Started in 1922 as an institution to train paraprofessionals in fields such as agriculture and veterinary medicine, Makerere steadily expanded its vocation in the 1930s and 1940s, and by 1949 it had become a constituent college of the University of London, catering to students from the whole of East Africa.

Makerere offered a wide range of courses in the arts, sciences, and the professions, and perhaps the influence of its literary education has been exaggerated; still, it was here that the first and most prominent East African writers in English emerged. There was certainly creative writing by non-Makerere writers in African languages, but literature in English emerged at the college, and later in the 1960s and 1970s at the universities of Nairobi and Dar es Salaam.

Why did the university become the site of a new kind of literature, one modeled on the English canon and modernist writing? First, Makerere adopted the University of London model of education. The University of London had been established under liberal principles in the late nineteenth century and was unique in its emphasis on the study of English (rather than Greek and Latin) as a discipline central to the building of character. Second, the college attracted the best students from the elite "grammar" schools and provided them with a secular model of Anglophone high culture. A highlight of the Makerere academic calendar was the performance of a play by Shakespeare, whose prestige is attested to by the fact that in the first production of *Julius Caesar* in 1949, the title role was played by none other than Apollo Milton Obote, the future prime minister and president of Uganda. And, as is well known, Julius Nyerere, the future president of Tanzania, an alumni of Makerere, gained literary fame as a translator of *The Merchant of Venice* and *Julius Caesar* into Swahili.

There is a third reason why Makerere became a crucible of literary culture in the 1950s, and this has to do with the establishment of an honors program in English. The first students in this program, most notably the Kenyan writer Jonathan Kariara, were engaged in the construction of serious institutions of literary culture, conducted intramural writing competitions, and edited the departmental journal *Penpoint*, where the works of the region's most prominent writers first appeared. The editors of *Penpoint* read like a who's who of the East African literary elite: Kariara, Ngugi, Peter Nazareth, John Nagenda, John Ruganda, and N. G. Ngulukulu. Many graduates of the English Honors program went on to influence government policies as diplomats, bankers, and administrators. One of them, Ben Mkapa (English Honors 1962) rose through the ranks of the Tanzanian political system to become president.

Finally, literary culture most probably thrived at Makerere (and later at the other East African universities) because of a significant historical coincidence between the rise of English honors and the last phase of decolonization. By the late 1950s, it was obvious that the political destiny of the people of the region did not lie in any identification with Britain but in the development of autonomous national institutions. Literature became one method through which writers could take stock of their colonial past and imagine their postcolonial future. This is, indeed, the big theme in early Makerere writing published in *Penpoint* and anthologized by David Cook and David Rubadiri in *Origin East Africa*. After independence, the system of education in East Africa was freed from colonial constraints and notions. There was a massive increase in the number of students at all levels of education, and this expanded the base of readership. The optimism surrounding decolonization in its first decade was accompanied by a fervor for literature, and the three universities that developed in the region in the 1960s became centers for writing and debates about literature. Not only did the universities produce and nurture new talent, they were often the sole employers of prominent creative writers.

REFERENCES

Ajayi, J. F. Ade, et al. *The African Experience with Higher Education.* Accra: Association of African Universities; London: James Currey; Athens: Ohio University Press, 1996.

Goldthorpe, J. E. *An African Elite: Makerere College Students, 1922–1960.* Nairobi and London: Published on behalf of the East African Institute of Social Research by Oxford University Press, 1965.

Greaves, L. B. *Carey Francis of Kenya.* London: Rex Collings Ltd., 1969.

Macpherson, Margaret. *They Built for the Future: A Chronicle of Makerere University College, 1922–1962.* Cambridge: Cambridge University Press, 1964.

McGregor, G. P. *King's College, Budo: The First Sixty Years.* Nairobi: Oxford University Press, 1967.

Musisi, Nakanyike. *Makerere University in Transition, 1993–2000: Opportunities and Challenges.* Oxford: James Currey; Kampala: Fountain, 2003.

Smith, J. S. *The History of Alliance High School.* Nairobi: Heinemann, 1973.

[Gikandi]

Ethnicity and Ethnic Literatures   East Africa is extremely ethnically diverse and variegated, but different communities were lumped together as single nations during the partition of the continent at the Conference of Berlin (1884–1885). For example, Tanzania has about 130 distinctive ethnic communities, each with a different language. Although about 95 percent of Tanzanians speak a Bantu language, the languages are in most cases mutually unintelligible, leaving Swahili as the only common, national language. In Kenya, where there are over seventy divergent ethnic groups, some of the communities, such as the Kikuyu, are large, while others, such as the Ogiek, are small, marginalized, and threatened with extinction. Uganda, too, has several broad linguistic groups, each with an ethnic identity of its own. Asians and Arabs have lived in East Africa since the sixteenth century, and are the dominant nonindigenous communities. Initially confined to the coastal region, the Arab community has intermarried with local people, and some have moved inland and acquired the citizenships of the various countries. Ethnicity and ethnic identities play a key role in the arts of East Africa because they are seen, paradoxically, both as a threat to the desired idea of the nation and as positive markers of national identity.

There have been continuous debates on the relation between ethnicity, ethnic writing, and national literature. This debate was ignited by Nigerian novelist and theorist Chinua Achebe at the landmark conference of African writers of English expression held at Makerere University College, Kampala, in 1962. In his address to the conference, Achebe established a firm distinction between "national" and "ethnic" literature in the following terms:

> A national literature is one that takes the whole nation for its province and has a realized or potential audience throughout its territory. In other

words a literature that is written in the national language. An ethnic literature is one which is available to one ethnic group within the nation. If you take Nigeria as an example, the national literature, as I see it, is written in English; and the ethnic literatures are in Hausa, Ibo, Yoruba, Efik, Ijaw, etc. etc.   ("The African Writer and the English Language," 56).

If we take Achebe as a guide, a national literature is that which is written in Swahili (the national language in Kenya, Uganda, and Tanzania) and English (the official language of the East African countries). All other language literatures would be considered ethnic. But Achebe's criterion has been challenged by critics such as Kimani Gecau, who favors the use of indigenous languages; these critics argue that ethnic languages can also produce national literatures.

But what makes ethnicity central to literary production in all languages is the fact that each East African ethnic community is a rich source of folklore. A remarkable amount of folklore has been collected, transcribed, and translated into the national language, but the essence of the artistic expressions is best expressed in the ethnic languages in which it was originally created. Although there is heavy borrowing from one language to another and stories have often been changed to suit different communities, oral literature is largely ethnic in orientation, language, and idiom. Indeed, studies of oral literature in East Africa focus on ethnic communities. Examples of such collections of oral literature include Naomi Kipury's *Oral Literature of the Maasai* (1983), Ciarunji Chesaina's *Oral Literature of the Kalenjin* (1991), and Wanjiku Mukabi Kabira and Karega Mutahi's *Gikuyu Oral Literature* (1988).

The question of ethnicity is also a major feature of literature written in indigenous languages and has been prominent in the region since Ngugi wa Thiong'o stopped writing novels and plays in English in 1978. But Ngugi was not the first major writer to produce literature in an ethnic, or what he prefers to call a national, language. Other significant writers who are known for their writings in English have also written fiction in their native tongues. For example, Grace Ogot had written her major works primarily in Dholuo, the language spoken by the Luo community, before she became famous as a writer in English. Her Dholuo novel *Simbi Nyaima* (1968) is based on a flood that hit her western Kenya homeland in the 1960s, while *Miaha* (1969), which has been translated into English by Okoth-Okombo as *The Strange Bride*, is based on a Luo myth about the origins of farming in the community.

Many early texts on the history and culture of various ethnic communities were produced in local languages from the 1930s onward. In fact, it was in these texts that ethnic identities were invented or consolidated. For example, Paul Mboya published *Luo Kitgi gi Timbegi* (*Luo Customs and Culture*) in 1938. In his book, Mboya focused on the Luo community's "Fourteen Commandments" to demonstrate a synthesis between Luo culture and Christianity. Another early promoter of writing in indigenous languages was Samuel G. Ayany, a graduate of Makerere University College, who wrote *Kar Chakruok Mar Luo* (*The Origins of the Luo Community*) when he was an undergraduate. Ayany's book, which was published by the East African Literature Bureau in 1952, set out to trace the history of the Luo from their arrival in Nyanza to the colonial period. The model for these kinds of cultural histories was Sir Apolo Kagwa's *Ekitabo kya basekabaka be Buganda, na be Bunyoro, na be Koki, na be Toro, na be Nkole* (*The History of the Kings of Buganda, Bunyoro, Koki, Toro, and Ankole*), first published in 1912.

The most prominent role in the promotion of ethnic literatures was by journalists, especially those involved in the nationalist movement. In Kenya, Gakaara Wanjau (1921–2001) wrote prolifically in African languages, focusing on ethnic values and the culture of his Gikuyu community. He started the magazine *Gikuyu na Mumbi* and the monthly *Waigua Atia*, in which he published original articles, poetry, and songs. His 1946 novel *Uhoro wa Ugurani* (*Marriage Manual*) was the first major work of fiction in Gikuyu. He reissued it in 1951 as *Ngwenda Unjurage* (*I Want You to Kill Me!*). In the late 1920s, Jomo Kenyatta edited the Gikuyu paper *Muigwithania* (*The Reconciler*). In 1945, Henry Mworia Mwaniki started the weekly *Mumenyereri* (*The Guardian*). By the late 1940s, as the opposition to colonialism grew, African newspapers and magazines proliferated. These included the Kenya African Union's *Sauti ya Mwafrika* (*Voice of Africa*), Bildad Kaggia's *Inooro ria Agikuyu* (*The Whetstone of the Agikuyu*), John Cege's *Wiyathi* (*Freedom*), *Muthamaki* (*The Statesman*), *Hindi ya Agikuyu* (*Gikuyu Times*), *Mwaraniria* (*The Conversationalist*), *Wihuge* (*Emergency/Beware*), and *Muramati*.

Indigenous-language theater and journalism played an important role in the development of ethnic writing. Leading dramatists such as Ngugi wa Thiong'o, Wahome Mutahi, and Byron Kawadwa have produced masterpieces in local languages. Particularly striking is Kawadwa's Luganda-language play *Oluyimba lwa Wankoko* (*Song of Wankoko, the Cock*), a presentation of the tensions between monarchism and republicanism in Uganda in the 1960s. Ngugi wa Thiong'o and Ngugi wa Mirii's *Ngaahika Ndeenda* (*I Will Marry When I Want*) in the Gikuyu language was written and produced in collaboration with peasants in the village of Kamiriithu.

Apart from promoting a sense of ethnic awareness, literatures in indigenous languages have been used to challenge or transform the form of dominant national languages such as English and Swahili. Kithaka wa Mberia's poetry, for example, avoids the traditional rhyme and meter of Swahili verse, which would associate it with the hegemony of the Arabic classical tradition and the literature of the Swahili ethnic community of the Kenyan coastal region. The Swahili used in the poems tries to free itself from the Swahili ethnic group to carry the speech rhythms of other ethnic communities in Kenya. Okot p'Bitek uses his Acholi ethnic community to enrich his writing in English. Ngugi's and Grace Ogot's writings use the Gikuyu and Luo languages to transform the generic conventions of the novel.

While the choice of writers to use an ethnic language might limit their audience, what is often remarkable in all the cases cited above are the writers' attempts to transcend ethnic boundaries by invoking heroes and heroines of ethnic communities thought to be antagonistic to their own. Conversely, in the self-consciously urban literatures that disavow ethnicity, it is not unusual for characters to refer to other ethnic communities in a way that reveals that they are indeed conscious of their own ethnicity. A good example of such a character is Dodge Kiunyu, in Charles Mangua's *Son of Woman*.

The question of ethnicity is not limited to writing in African languages. A consciousness of being Asian or Arab is an important part of the literary tradition in the region. An ironic consequence of Idi Amin's expulsion of Uganda's Asian population in 1972 was the production of an Asian literature that was conscious of its ethnic roots. The novels of Moyez Vassanji, Yusuf Dawood, and Peter Nazareth explore the nature and location of Asian identities in East Africa. Abdulrazak Gurnah's novels are powerful chronicles of the Arabic presence in East Africa. Marjorie-Oludhe Macgoye, an English-born writer who settled in the country in 1954, has produced a remarkable body of fiction and poetry that revolves around the culture of her adopted Luo community. Finally, even writers such as Nuruddin Farah, who self-consciously reject the essentialism of ethnicity in favor of a nomadic identity, derive their sources from the cultures of a particular ethnic group, in Farah's case, the Somalis living in several East African countries.

REFERENCES

Achebe, Chinua. "The African Writer and the English Language." In *Morning Yet on Creation Day*, 55–56. London: Heinemann, 1975.

Forster, Peter G., et al. *Race and Ethnicity in East Africa*. New York: St. Martin's Press, 2000.

Gecau, Kimani. "Do Ethnic Languages Divide the Nation?" *African Perspectives* 2 (1972): 15–18.

Gerard, Albert S. *African Language Literatures*. Washington, D.C.: Three Continents Press, 1981.

Pugliese, Christiana. "Kenyan Publishers in Vernacular Languages: Gikuyu, Kikamba, and Dholuo." *Africa* 2 (1994): 250–259.

——. "The Organic Vernacular Intellectual in Kenya: Gakaara Wanjau." *Research in African Literatures* 25, no. 4 (1994): 177–187.

Somjee, Sultan. "Oral Traditions and Material Culture: An East Africa Experience." *Research in African Literatures* 31, no. 4 (2000): 97–103.

[Mwangi]

Farah, Nurrudin (b. 1945) Somali novelist and essayist. Farah is considered by many critics and literary historians to be the most important writer to have come out of East Africa since Ngugi wa Thiong'o. He was once described by the *New York Times* as the most prominent writer to have come out of Africa since the 1970s. Along with his regional reputation, Farah is also considered a central figure in the modern novel, both for the late colonial period and the end of the twentieth century, a fact attested to by the major international awards he has won, including the English Speaking Union Literary Award, for *Sweet and Sour Milk*, and the 1998 Neustadt International Prize. Located between the generation of writers who emerged during the period of decolonization in the 1950s and those who came of age in the period of postcolonial failure and crisis (the 1980s and 1990s), Farah's works constitute an important bridge in the literary history of East Africa. His works are rooted heavily in the cultural experience of Somalia, but except for the earliest novels, they were produced elsewhere, in exile. As a political and existential condition, exile is the signature of Farah's works and, also profoundly, of his life.

Farah was born in Baidoa, in the Italian section of colonial Somalia, to a mother who was an accomplished storyteller and a father who was a merchant and later an interpreter for the British colonial government in another sector of Somaliland. He spent most of his childhood and youth in the Ogaden, a Somali-speaking region under Ethiopian control, where his family had been exiled by the Italian colonial authorities. After attending Koranic and local schools, Farah studied at the University of Chandigarth in India, graduating with a degree in literature and philosophy. After returning to Somalia in early 1969, Farah worked at a high school and also began writing fiction, publishing his first novel in English, *From a Crooked Rib*, in 1970. His only novel in Somali, *Tallow Waa Telee Ma*, was initially serialized in a magazine, but it was censored by the government and then cancelled. In 1974, Farah was awarded a fellowship by UNESCO to study drama in London, where he stayed for two years.

Perhaps the seminal event in his life and later his writings was the coming to power of General Mohammed Siad Barre in a political coup in 1969, a process that initiated a long dictatorship that was to see Somalia become a major pawn in the cold war, as it aligned alternately with the United States and the Soviet Union. It was at this time that Farah, concerned with questions of power and its effects on social and private relationships, started writing what has come to be known as his "dictatorship trilogy." While he was traveling abroad in 1976, Farah was informed that his second English novel, *A Naked Needle*, was considered treasonable, and that he was under threat of imprisonment or execution. Farah did not return to Somalia until 1996. Although he had been forced to live and write out of his country for twenty years, Farah rejected the notion that to be an exile was to be homeless, choosing, in his own words, to keep Somalia—and his connection to it—alive through writing, and to "systematically make the rest of Africa my country." Unlike many exiled African writers, who preferred to live in Europe and America, Farah spent his twenty years of exile in different African countries—Sudan, Uganda, the Gambia, Nigeria, and post-apartheid South Africa.

Although he had decided to make the whole of Africa his home, all of Farah's novels are set in Somalia and reflect the county's unique culture and history. This uniqueness is itself apparent in the novelist's life and education. For example, he was connected through his mother to the most dominant Somali literary tradition—oral storytelling. Through his father's experience as a merchant and colonial civil servant, Farah grew up conscious of Somalia's unique location at the Horn of Africa, its connection to the Red Sea and Indian Ocean, to the Arabian Sea and India. Moreover, Farah's childhood and youth reflected the bizarre cartography of colonialism. He was the subject of a Somalia that had been divided between four imperial powers: France, Italy, Britain, and Ethiopia. His early years were spent crossing boundaries that were at once artificial and arbitrary, yet also the source of painful divisions and experience. His mature novels, including *Maps*, are at their most powerful when they question the authority of boundaries.

At the same time, however, the unstable boundaries of the colonial world had their uncanny rewards. One of the most outstanding aspects of Farah's fiction is its grounding in the local details of Somali life and history and, simultaneously, its larger sense of the cosmopolitanism of Somalia. Like many of the educated subjects who populate his novels, Farah grew up multilingual, speaking, in addition to his native Somali, English, Arabic, French, and Italian. The characters of his novels are obsessed with the meaning of their Somaliness, and the tragedies in their lives are tied up with the country's tortured colonial and postcolonial history, but their range of reference reaches out to the whole East African region, to the rest of Africa, and to global culture.

Farah's literary output to date can be divided into four phases, which are connected thematically but have important variations in style and language. The first phase, represented by *From a Crooked Rib*, marked Farah's relation to, and difference from, the African tradition of letters as it had emerged in the 1950s and 1960s. In this story of a young woman struggling with the power of patriarchy and tradition, Farah took up what were then familiar themes in African literature: the struggle between a past rooted in an oral tradition and the literate culture ushered in by colonial modernity, women's location between the demands of culture and their desire for freedom, and the movement from rural to urban space.

Farah's first novel was written in a simple and straightforward narrative style and did not display the kind of experimentation with language that was to characterize his mature works, but it was still notable for two reasons. First, it displayed an almost sacrilegious rejection of tradition as a place of identity and the recovery of self. Where other African writers had tended to perceive tradition as the counter to colonialism and its destructive energies, Farah produced a narrative in which the forces of traditionalism were associated with cultural regression and authoritarianism, an association that was to be elaborated in his dictatorship trilogy of the mid- and late 1970s. Second, Farah's novel was informed by what some critics and readers considered a feminist sensibility unusual among the writings of male African writers. For running through the tragic story of Elba, especially her entrapment between the clan and the city, was the then unusual claim that women were not the symbolic representations of nation but the primary victims of the nationalist tradition.

The second phase of Farah's career is represented by the four novels *A Naked Needle*, *Sweet and Sour Milk*, *Sardines*, and *Close Sesame*, the last three written as a trilogy collectively known as *Variations on a Theme of African Dictatorship*. All four novels were specific responses to the Siad Barre regime in Somalia that Farah allegorized as both a representation of regimes of power in Africa in a period (the 1970s) dominated by military governments and as the logical embodiment of the authoritarianism of tradition. While these novels are concerned overtly with questions of power, especially of the ways in which courageous individuals struggle to create a space of freedom and to deny the military dictatorship its legitimacy, even to undermine its rhetoric of revolution, they are also memorable for their valorization or even celebration of the language of modernism and indeed the international avant-garde. Farah's goal in these novels was to narrate the subjective lives of characters who had retreated into their own worlds to secure their identity and sanity (characters such as Koschin in *A Naked Needle* or Medina in *Sardines*) while at the same time mapping out the exterior landscape controlled by the dictatorship. In order to narrate the geography of dictatorship and the psychology of his subjects, he needed a form that would represent both the inner and outer worlds of Somalia. In this sense, Farah did not entirely break with the realism of his peers (he still needed to represent the Somali world he had left behind), but the use of scatology, fragmented language, and allusion placed him squarely within the aesthetic ideology of international modernism.

The third phase of Farah's career produced *Maps*, the novel that brought him international acclaim. This phase can be described as Farah's postnationalist phase and, indeed, the success of *Maps* can be attributed to the fact that the central theme in this novel captured a generalized African fatigue with the claim that the liberated nation would embody freedom. For in telling the story of Askar, orphaned by nature and war, born both Ethiopian and Somali, bereft of family and nation, Farah complicated the ideologies of boundaries and localities that had been invoked by African dictatorships as sources of legitimacy. Where other radical African writers produced novels aimed at recovering the ideals of nationalism from the rhetoric of dictatorship, Askar's story was about redefining boundary or nation as a prelude to transcending it. This desire for a postnationalist future is evident in the other two novels from this phase, *Gifts* and *Secrets*, both of which are concerned with the aftermath of the collapse of both the dictatorship and the state in Somalia and the destruction left in their wake.

In 1996, after twenty years in exile, Farah was able to return to Somalia, and the fourth phase of his career has been characterized by the anxiety of home and exile and the search for a possible space between those two extremes. One of the consequences of the crisis in Somalia was the displacement of large sections of the population, which led to the emergence of a Somali diaspora in Europe, America, the rest of Africa, and the Persian Gulf region. In *Voices of Yesterday*, Farah documented the fears and desires of Somalis in the diaspora and their complex relation with both their ancestral and adopted homes, and he narrated the painful search to reconnect with the homeland in *Links* (2003). In these two works, Farah sought a language that went beyond the critique or celebration of both nation and exile and to understand how the experience of both was transformative.

PRIMARY TEXTS

Farah, Nurrudin. *From a Crooked Rib*. London: Heinemann, 1970.

——. *A Naked Needle*. London: Heinemann, 1976.

——. *Sweet and Sour Milk*. London: Heinemann, 1980.

——. *Sardines*. London: Allison & Busby, 1981.

——. *Close Sesame*. London: Allison & Busby, 1983.

——. *Maps*. New York: Pantheon Books, 1986.

——. *Gifts*. London: Serif, 1993.

——. *Secrets*. New York: Arcade, 1998.

——. *Voices of Yesterday: Voices from the Somali Diaspora*. London: Cassell, 2000.

——. *Links*. New York: Riverhead Books, 2004.

REFERENCES

Ahmed, Ali Jimale. *Tradition, Anomaly, and the Wave for the Future: Somali Oral Literature, Nuruddin Farah, and Written Somali Prose Fiction*. 1989.

Alden, Patricia, and Louis Tremaine. *Nuruddin Farah*. New York: Twayne, 1999.

Cobham, Rhonda. "Boundaries of the Nation, Boundaries of the Self: African Nationalist Fictions and Nuruddin Farah's *Maps*." *Research in African Literatures* 22, no. 2 (Summer 1991): 83–98.

Gikandi, Simon. "Nuruddin Farah and Postcolonial Textuality." *World Literature Today* (1998): 753–759.

Ngaboh-Smart, Francis. "Dimensions of Gift Giving in Nuruddin Farah's *Gifts*." *Research in African Literatures* 27, no. 4 (Winter 1996): 144–156.

——. "Nationalism and the Aporia of National Identity in Farah's *Maps*." *Research in African Literatures* 32, no. 3 (Fall 2001): 86–102.

Wright, Derek. *Emerging Perspectives on Nuruddin Farah*. Trenton, N.J.: Africa World Press: 2003.

——. *The Novels of Nuruddin Farah*. Rev. ed. Oxford: James Currey, 2003.

[Gikandi]

Fikré, Tolossa (b. 1947)   Ethiopian playwright and essayist. He is best known for his play *The Coffin-Dealer and the Gravedigger* and his numerous essays on Ethiopian philosophy, culture, and politics published in the North America–based *Ethiopia Review*. Fikré came to prominence in the late 1970s, when his scripts and poems were first performed on Ethiopian Radio and Television in Addis Ababa. On the basis of his first collection of short stories, he won a scholarship to the Soviet Union, where he studied creative writing at the famous Gorky Institute for Literature. His work at the institute was considered outstanding, and he even sold a play to the Ministry of Culture. He later undertook graduate work at the University of Bremen in Germany, from where he graduated with a PhD in comparative literature in 1982. Fikré later moved to the United States, where he has been a professor of literature and college administrator.

Although he has written over eighteen stage plays and at least two film scripts, Fikré's reputation as a writer rests primarily on his satirical play *The Coffin-Dealer and the Gravedigger*. Written in the fashion of Gogol, the play is a mixture of absurd comedy and serious social commentary. In the play, Fikré presents two characters who are forced by their professions to live on the results of the failure of modern Ethiopian society. The central paradox in the life of the Coffin Dealer and the Gravedigger is that their lives depend on the death of their neighbors and the absence of death leads to impoverishment and a sense of failure. In the play, Fikré presented his audience with a medium for observing the failure of Ethiopian society without giving in to despair or cynicism, and his deft use of social satire perhaps explains the popularity of the play, which has been performed in Ethiopia regularly since the 1970s and has recently proven equally popular with members of the Ethiopian diaspora in North America.

PRIMARY WORKS (IN ENGLISH)

Fikré, Tolossa. *The Coffin-Dealer and the Gravedigger; A Foot of Land: Two Plays*. Bremen: Übersee-Museum, 1982.

CRITICISM

Fikré, Tolossa. "Realism in Haddis Alemayehu." In *Silence Is Not Golden: A Critical Anthology of Ethiopian Literature*, edited by Taddesse Adera and Ali Jimale Ahmed, 123–134. Lawrenceville, N.J.: Red Sea Press, 1995.

[*Gikandi*]

Gabre-Medhin, Tsegaye (b. 1936) Ethiopian playwright and poet. Gabre-Medhin's long writing career spans the key periods of late twentieth-century Ethiopian history, and he is considered to be one of the most distinguished modern writers working both in Amharic and English. He has been a witness to the restoration of the empire after the Italian occupation, the military coup that ushered in the rule of the *Durgue*, and the postrevolutionary period. Under each of these regimes, Gabre-Medhin was often honored as an icon of modern Ethiopian culture, but he was also ruthlessly censored, especially for his use of drama as a tool for criticizing abuses of power by officials.

Gabre-Medhin was born in the Shewa region during the Italian occupation of Ethiopia, and like most members of his generation, his life was marked by the trauma of fascist rule and, most particularly, his country's loss of its independence for the first time since the early Christian period. Born into a family that was an unusual amalgam of the Amharic and Oromo cultures, the two most dominant groups in Ethiopia, Gabre-Medhin was educated by both the religious institutions run by the local Ethiopian Coptic Church and the modern European-style school. From the church school, he acquired an intimate knowledge of traditional poetic forms, especially those associated with the liturgy; at the European schools, he was introduced to modern poetry and drama. Consequently, his works are marked by attempts to fuse the two traditions while exploring the tension between Ethiopian and European systems of values, especially the conflict between religious and secular systems.

After his secondary and higher education at the Wingate School and Commercial College in Addis Ababa, where he was heavily involved in drama, Gabre-Medhin studied in the United States and qualified as a lawyer at the Blackstone School of Law in Chicago. But his major interest continued to be the theater. In the 1950s, he studied drama in Britain, France, and Italy, and it was during this period that he produced his major works in Amharic. In the 1960s, Gabre-Medhin became interested in experimental theater, and he began to adapt the works of major European playwrights—Shakespeare and Moliere, for example—for the Ethiopian stage. Most of his plays in Amharic were banned during the 1960s, although, paradoxically, he was considered important enough to be awarded the prestigious Haile Sellassie I Prize for Amharic Literature. He was the director of the Ethiopian National Theater from 1961 to 1971.

During the late 1960s and for most of the 1970s, Gabre-Medhin was a major figure in pan-Africanist theater, presenting influential papers at congresses such as the 1966 Festival of African and Black Arts. For a brief period in the late 1970s, a period of turmoil and revolution during which radical students and intellectuals launched their final assault on the imperial system, Gabre-Medhin served as the vice minister for culture and as a professor of drama at the University of Addis Ababa. Most of his work from this period, which included Amharic adaptations of the works of the radical German playwright Bertolt Brecht, were banned by the government. In the 1980s, when Ethiopia was governed by a military dictatorship, Gabre-Medhin turned to historical subjects, writing and producing plays on important Ethiopian figures such as the emperors Menelik and Tewodros. These historical plays, including two works on the Ethiopian Revolution, were immediately banned. In the 1990s, Gabre-Medhin turned his attention to the larger problem of Africa's identity, lecturing on and writing about the ancient cultures of the continent.

While Gabre-Medhin has won the greatest acclaim for his work in Amharic, his two works of drama in English, *Oda-Oak Oracle* (1966) and *Collision of Atlas* (1977), have been considered central to the canon of Af-

rican drama, especially with regard to the question of tragedy and form. Indeed, B. Jeyifo has described Gabre-Medhin as "one of the most self-conscious aesthetes working in the contemporary African theatre" (*Modern African Drama*, 577). *Oda-Oak Oracle* is a ritualistic verse drama revolving around the story of a man, Shanka, who discovers that his first-born is cursed and must be sacrificed to ancestral spirits. In trying to deal with this fate, he becomes caught between the claims of powerful religious traditions and simple questions of existence. For Gabre-Medhin, the tragic form is central to understanding the Ethiopian condition; tragedy emerges out of the Ethiopians' desire to rise beyond the visitation of wars and violence to assert their freedom. "The Ethiopian continues to sustain war and suffering in order to preserve his freedom" (quoted in Ayele, "Poet Laureate Tsegaye Gabre-Medhin of Ethiopia," 6).

The relationship between suffering and freedom is also a major theme in *Collision of Atlas*, a play set in the ancient empire of Axum in the sixteenth century. The play dramatizes the rise and tragic fall of King Kaleb, the struggle to succeed him, and the political conflicts that ensue. In the preface to the play, Gabre-Medhin asserts that his turn to historical subjects is part of the desire to encourage a new generation of Africans to come to terms with their historic past, "even that historic past often torn and denied against [them]" (quoted in Jeyifo, *Modern African Drama*, 570). It is perhaps a major sign of the play's success in making the past a mirror of the political and social problems of the present that all three Ethiopian governments since the 1950s have rarely hesitated in banning Gabre-Medhin's historical plays. At the same time, these governments have not been oblivious to Gabre-Medhin's national and international significance to Ethiopian culture in general and theater in particular. It has not been unusual for the playwright to be appointed a vice minister of culture in one year and be imprisoned the next, or to have his works banned even as he is celebrated as his country's poet laureate.

PRIMARY TEXTS (IN ENGLISH)

Gabre-Medhin, Tsegaye. *Oda-Oak Oracle.* London: Oxford University Press, 1965.

——. *Collision of Atlas.* London: Rex Collings, 1977.

REFERENCES

Ayele, Negussay. "Poet Laureate Tsegaye Gabre-Medhin of Ethiopia: A Profile of the Man and His Writings." Available at http://www.ethiopians.com/tsegaye/.

Jeyifo, Biodun. *Modern African Drama: Backgrounds and Criticism.* 1st ed. New York: W.W. Norton, 2002.

Sumner, Claude, et al. *La Couleur De Mon Chant: Quatre Drames Éthiopiens, Petros, Le Rêve Du Roi, Le Silence Des Cordes, Oda, Adaptés De Quatre Pièces, Petros at the Hour, Tewodros, Azmari, Oda-Oak Oracle De Tsegaye Gabre-Medhin.* Yaoundé, Cameroon: Éditions Clé, 1977.

[Gikandi]

Gakwandi, Arthur Shatto (b. 1943) Ugandan novelist, short-story writer, and diplomat. Born in Kajara, Gakwandi was educated at Makerere University College, where he earned his BA, later receiving his MLitt degree at the University of Edinburgh. After years of teaching literature at Makerere, he joined the Ugandan diplomatic service in 1989 and served in various capacities as an ambassador. Proficient in English, French, Swahili, and Luganda, Gakwandi's writings represent an important interface between languages. His first novel, *Kosiya Kifefe* (1998) is a story of growing up in postindependence Uganda. It follows Kosiya's life from his humble rural background to his high status as part of the ruling elites in Africa, who despite their façade of sophistication are as rustic as the society they patronize. "Seasons," a short story, was published in *Short Story International* in 1995. However, Gakwandi is best known for *The Novel and Contemporary Experience in Africa* (1977), a work of African literary criticism, in which he discusses the writings of Ngugi wa Thiong'o, Chinua Achebe, and Ayi Kwei Armah, among others.

PRIMARY TEXTS

Gakwandi, Arthur Shatto. *The Novel and Contemporary Experience in Africa.* London: Heinemann; New York: Africana Publishing House, 1977.

——. "Seasons." *Short Story International,* no. 26 (October 1995).

——. *Kosiya Kifefe.* Nairobi: East African Educational Publishers, 1998.

[Mwangi]

Gatheru, Mugo (b. 1925) Kenyan autobiographer, lawyer, and journalist. Born in the Fort Hall (now Murang'a) district in the Central Province of Kenya, Gatheru grew up in Kenya's "white highlands," where his parents worked as squatters. He was educated at Weithaga and Kambui Primary School in the early 1940s and later worked as an assistant in the government's Medical Research Laboratory in Nairobi. Like most children of African squatters in Kenya, Gatheru became involved in nationalist politics at an early age, and in 1946 he became the associate editor of the *African Voice*, a newspaper committed to airing the grievances of Africans against the injustice of the colonial system. It was during his period as a newspaper editor that Gatheru became determined to seek an education in the United States. Unable to secure a certificate of good conduct, which was needed for a visa, Gatheru left Kenya for India in 1949, to study at Allahabad University, and a year later he was allowed to enter the United States, where he studied at Roosevelt University in Chicago. He later studied law at Lincolns Inn in London. From 1969 to 2002, Gatheru was a professor of history at California State University, Sacramento.

Although he wrote many commentaries for American publications, Gatheru gained international attention with the publication of his autobiography, *A Child of Two Worlds*, in 1964, a year after Kenya became independent. In this work, as its title suggests, Gatheru narrated his experiences as a child growing up between two cultural systems, the Gikuyu world of his parents, organized around rites of passage and traditional wisdom, and the world of colonial modernity, represented by a new system of formal education and the exploitation of African labor. He also focused on the grievances that led to the development of radical politics among members of his generation in the 1940s, the development of a nationalist consciousness, and the discovery of the African diaspora in the United States.

While this work followed a common pattern in African autobiography, one in which the experiences of an individual's life are seen as representative of an awakening into political consciousness, *A Child of Two Worlds* crystallized a set of themes that were germane to the rise of radical nationalism in Kenya during the crucial period between 1945 and 1955: the centrality of education in the development of political consciousness, the tension between the claims of modernity and tradition, and the role of culture in the process of decolonization. Mugo opened his autobiography with a chapter on Gikuyu origin myths; he ended it with a rallying call for what he called a "bond of mutual sympathy" among people of African descent and a celebration of Kenyan independence as the event that made it possible to make "sense of my life and those of others." *From Beneath the Tree of Life: A Story of the Kenyan People of Ngai* is a retelling of the Gikuyu myth of creation directed at a young-adult readership. Mugo is also the author of *Kenya: From Colonisation to Independence, 1888–1970*, a general history of Kenya.

PRIMARY TEXTS

Gatheru, Mugo. *A Child of Two Worlds*. London: Kegan and Paul, 1964.
——. *From Beneath the Tree of Life: A Story of the Kenyan People of Ngai*. Mansfield, Ohio: Bookmasters, 2002.
——. *Kenya: From Colonisation to Independence, 1888–1970*. Jefferson, N.C.: McFarland & Company, 2005.

REFERENCES

Lonsdale, John. "Mau Maus of the Mind: Making Mau Mau and Remaking Kenya (in Colonial Minds)." *The Journal of African History* 31, no. 3 (1990): 393–421.
Neubauer, Carol E. "One Voice Speaking for Many: The Mau Mau Movement and Kenyan Autobiography." *The Journal of Modern African Studies* 21, no. 1 (1983): 113–131.

[Gikandi]

Gender and Feminist Criticism For a long time, the images of women found in the writings of major East African writers have been generally negative. In popular literature, women have often been cast as sex objects to be consumed by men, while politically engaged literature has historically subordinated women to the nationalist project, presenting them as symbols of the motherland but not endowing them with agency or subjectivity. Nici Nelson demonstrates that, with the exception of a few novels, women in the cities are portrayed negatively as people given to "manipulating their sexual attractiveness to men to entice, tantalize and entrap male characters. Either that or they are represented as sexual objects with nothing to offer a man but sex" (Nelson, "Representations of Men and Women," 148).

However, the emergence of a critical practice informed by gender analysis generated some important changes in the 1980s, as creative writers attempted to rethink the role of women in society, politics, and culture. Still, in the early phase of gender criticism, critics were cautious not to be mistaken for Western feminists, and energetic feminist analyses of East African literature tended to come from outside the region rather than from locally based critics. The first sustained attempt to redefine the place of women in African literature was Florence Stratton's *Contemporary African Literature and the Politics of Gender*, which exposed how African women writers had been excluded or marginalized from the male-dominated canon, using the work of Grace Ogot as one of its many examples. The book also exposed the stereotyped representation of women in even the most progressive male writers. Like Stratton, Elleke Boehmer explored the patriarchal blind spots in progressive male writers' view of women, singling out Ngugi's writing as an example of the neglect of the gendered nature of power, which "ultimately works to inhibit his rousing call for a new dispensation in Kenya" (Boehmer, "Master's Dance," 189).

Some feminist analyses of East African literature have been criticized because of what is construed to be their universalization of feminism and its trafficking in Western prejudices about Africa. A case in point is Maryse Conde's analysis of Grace Ogot's writing, in which she argues that

> Grace Ogot lacks neither style nor imagination. But her talents are totally wasted. She is so blinded by her respect for European behavior, so confused as to the place of her traditional beliefs that her female characters possess neither coherence nor credibility. . . . She may believe that she is an emancipated woman "who reads books" but what she offers her fellow country women is a dangerous picture of alienation and enslavement. (142)

In *Contemporary African Literature and the Politics of Gender*, Stratton dismisses Conde's reading of Ogot as "perverse," as it "overlooks the cultural and historical specificity of western feminism which she represents as universal" (61). Gloria Chukukere takes a similar position with regard to Conde's criticism of Grace Ogot, arguing that Conde's misjudgment of the writer stems from the fact that she is assessing African writers against the aggressive and militant forms of protest common in Western feminism at the time the essay was written (Chukukere, *Gender Voices and Choices*, 218).

Thus the challenge for feminist critics of East African literature has been to reject what is seen as a universalizing Western feminism and thus to present gender differences in African writing as historically and socially situated. It is with this project in mind that Kathleen McLuskie and Lynn Innes offer a general picture of women's writing in Africa. They note a continuum between colonial and postcolonial literature in portraying the continent as an enigmatic woman. For them, Wanja in Ngugi's *Petals of Blood* hovers between realism and symbolism in the novel's portrayal of the exploitation of Africa. They argue that "whether as wives or prostitutes, African women are rarely portrayed *except* in relation to men, or their *otherness* to men. One rarely catches a glimpse of women operating independently, although in most parts of Africa, women did not have their own bit of land, their own crops, their own market stalls" ("Women and African Literature," 4).

Critics of East African literature have also been concerned with the domination of the institutions of literary study and interpretation by male critics. In her essay "Freedom of Choice: Kenyan Women Writers," Sophie W. Macharia comments on the domination of the literary academy by male writers, noting that although East African women writers have explored the themes that male artists have analyzed, they are rarely recognized. In "Feminist Issues in the Fiction of Kenya's Women Writers," Jean F. O'Barr discusses seven female writers from Kenya and shows their marginalization by institutions of criticism. Alternatively, some critics have focused on how writings that center on women's experiences tend to be excluded from the canon. In "Problems of Nationhood in Grace Ogot's Fiction," Grace Ify Achufusi notes that "because most of Ogot's themes centre on women, women's issues have also formed the matrix within which socio-historical or socio-political phenomena are discussed" (187). Achufusi compares Ogot to male writers such as Ngugi, Chinua Achebe, and Wole Soyinka and shows that while they are preoccupied with issues such as corruption, which are seen as threats to nationhood, these issues are mentioned mostly in passing in Grace Ogot's work, as her texts concentrate on relationships and moral issues.

Some feminist critics like Mineke Schipper have argued that the solution to the problem of negative images of women in male fiction is the one provided in the works of women writers themselves: "They pick up their pens and express their own ideas about women and African society, and thus correct or complement the one-sidedness of certain perspectives" ("Mother Africa on a Pedestal," 49). This view is supported by Chiarunji Chesaina, who argues that "the best writers to use literature as a tool for liberation of women are women themselves. Having experienced gender discrimination or having witnessed the oppression of their fellow-women, they are in a better position

to discuss and get involved in women's issues than their male counterparts" (*Perspectives on Women in African Literature*, 5). Elsewhere, Chesaina qualifies this point by asserting that "it would be a misconception of the situation to claim that male writers cannot contribute to women's liberation," but still insists that "women writers can articulate the cries of their fellow women better than their male counterparts" ("Grace Ogot: A Creative Writer," 73, 74).

Finally, it is important to note that women writers have formed groups to champion women's issues in writing. Ugandan women artists formed Femrite in 1997 to "promote women's writings as a means of breaking through the literary recess and be able to include the literature generated from communities as a basis for functional literacy program" (Women of Uganda Network Web site, http://www.wougnet.org/profiles/femrite.html). The group has published some of the finest literary works to come out of East Africa. These include Goretti Kyomuhendo's *Secrets No More*, a feminist presentation of the genocide in Rwanda, and Ayeta Anne Wangusa's *Memoirs of a Mother*, a first-person narrative by a Ugandan woman forced to trade the romantic idealism of her youth for a mundane marriage based on outmoded rules and obligations.

REFERENCES

Achufusi, Ify. "Problems of Nationhood in Grace Ogot's Fiction." *Journal of Commonwealth Literature* 26, no. 1 (1991): 179–188.

Adagala, Kavetsa. "Wanja of *Petals of Blood*: A Study of the Women Question and Imperialism in Kenya." Seminar presentation, University of Nairobi, April 30, 1981.

Bardolph, Jacqueline. "The Literature of Kenya." In *The Writing of East and Central Africa*, edited by G. D. Killam, 36–53. Nairobi: Heinemann, 1984.

Bjorkman, Ingrid. "Oppression and Liberation of Kenyan Women: On Orature and Modern Women's Literature." In *Culture in Africa: An Appeal for Pluralism*, edited by Raoul Granqvist, 109–122. Uddevella: Nordiska Afrikainstitutet.

Boehmer, Elleke. "The Master's Dance to the Master's Voice: Revolutionary Nationalism and the Representation of Women in the Writing of Ngugi wa Thiong'o." *Journal of Commonwealth Literature* 26, no. 1 (1991): 188–197.

——. "Motherland, Mothers, and Nationalist Sons: Representations of Nationalism and Women in African Literature." In *From Commonwealth to Post-Colonial*, edited by Anna Rutherford, 229–258. Sydney: Dangaroo, 1992.

——. "Transfiguring: Colonial Body into Postcolonial Fiction." *Novel* (Winter 1993): 268–277.

Brinkmann, Inge. *Kikuyu Gender Norms and Narratives*. Leiden: Research School CNWS, 1996.

Brown, Lloyd W. *Women Writers in Black Africa*. Westport, Conn.: Greenwood, 1981.

Chesaina, Ciarunji. "Grace Ogot: A Creative Writer's Contribution to Cultural Development and Women's Emancipation." *Writers' Forum: A Journal of Writers' Association of Kenya* 1 (1992): 73–80.

——. *Perspectives on Women in African Literature*. Nairobi: Impact, 1994.

Chukukere, Gloria. *Gender Voices and Choices: Redefining Women in Contemporary African Fiction*. Enugu, Nigeria: Fourth Dimension, 1995.

Conde, Maryse. "Three Female Modern Africa Writers: Flora Nwapa, Ama Ata Aidoo, and Grace Ogot." *Presence Africaine* 82, no. 2 (1972): 132–143.

Frank, Katherine. "Women Without Men: The Feminist Novel in Africa." *African Literature Today* 15 (1987): 14–34.

Mabala, Richard S. "Gender in Tanzanian Kiswahili Fiction." In *Gender Relations and Women's Images in the Media*, edited by D. A. S. Mbilinyi and C. K. Omari, 159–206. Dar es Salaam: Dar es Salaam University Press, 1996.

McLuskie, Kathleen, and Lynn Innes. "Women and African Literature." *Wasafiri* 8 (1988): 3–7.

Murray, Stephen O., and Will Roscoe. *Boy-Wives and Female Husbands: Studies in African Homosexualities*. New York: St. Martin's Press, 1998.

Nelson, Nici. "Representations of Men and Women, City and Town in Kenyan Novels of the 1970s and 1980s." *African Languages and Cultures* 9, no. 2 (1996): 145–168.

Nnaemeka, Obioma, ed. *The Politics of (M)othering: Womanhood, Identity, and Resistance in African Literature*. London: Routledge, 1997.

O'Barr, Jean F. "Feminist Issues in the Fiction of Kenya's Women Writers." *African Literature Today* 15 (1987): 55–70.

Schipper, Mineke. "Mother Africa on a Pedestal: The Male Heritage in African Literature and Criticism." *African Literature Today* 15 (1987): 35–54.

Stratton, Florence. *Contemporary African Literature and the Politics of Gender*. London: Routledge, 1994.

——. "The Shallow Grave: Archetypes of Female Experience in African Fiction." *Research in African Literatures* 2 (1988): 143–169.

Taiwo, Oladele. *Female Novelists of Modern Africa*. London: Macmillan, 1984.

[Mwangi]

Genga-Idowu, Florence M. (1960–1998) Kenyan novelist, schoolteacher, children's rights advocate, children's writer, editor, and critic. She is best known for her two novels *Lady in Chains* (1993) and *My Heart on Trial* (1997), which examine the role of women in contemporary African societies against the background of poverty, misogyny, and dying precolonial traditions. Full of pathos, her work examines the crises of masculinity as modernity brings in its wake more liberating possibilities for the African woman. Her male characters are depicted as threatened by a mysterious power that women seem to possess beneath their veneer of female marginality. *Lady in Chains* tells the story of Susan, who is leased out by her husband, Ochola, to another man, in order to enable the family meet its basic needs. When they move from the rural areas to the city in search of opportunities, they are met by the harsh reality of destitution in the Nairobi slums, where Ochola works as a night watchman and Susan as a distiller of an illicit beverage. They arrange for Ochola to pose as Susan's father, in order to marry her off to Polycarp, a rich suitor and the son of a politician. However, instead of returning as planned to Ochola after Polycarp has paid the lucrative dowry, Susan chooses to remain in her fictitious social role as Polycarp's wife. On the surface, Susan comes through as predatory and selfish, but the story celebrates her ability to exploit gender codes to get what her society has denied her.

Woven into the narrative of the gender war between a man and his wife is the portrayal of a postcolonial condition ordered by corruption, police brutality, unequal distribution of resources, and abject poverty. While exposing the moral decay in modern society, the novel deconstructs the traditional notion of the prostitute as morally degenerate. It shows the social reasons that compel a woman like Susan to embrace commercial sex work and signals that working as a prostitute is more empowering than living as a subservient wife. When she starts working as a prostitute at Sabina Joy, in scenes that evoke and deconstruct Meja Mwangi's *Going Down River Road*, Susan emerges as a far more powerful woman than ever before. For its part, *My Heart on Trial*, a novel about a brutal political murder, spans an array of settings to expose the moral de-

cay and political callousness in modern Kenya. It is rich in traditional idiom, but is at once critical of the marginal roles women have been assigned by African traditional cultures, especially the treatment of female children as second-class human beings, the mistreatment of widows, and the early marriages of African girls. At the same time, the novel portrays the conflict between Christianity and traditional Luo culture and investigates what modernity means for the African woman.

Born into a polygamous rural family in the Migori District and educated in a Catholic missionary girls' high school before entering the University of Nairobi in 1979 and marrying a Nigerian in 1988, Genga-Idowu's writing is laced with Christian references and the ethos of both Kenyan and Nigerian cultures. In *Memories Into Marriage* (1995), a heavily didactic novel, Genga-Idowu examines the plight of African girls by questioning the traditional socialization that subjugates them. Using prayers as epigraphs and a doctor's first-person observations to articulate its beliefs, the novel offers no room for doubt about its author's belief in the unequivocal and immediate liberation of African women from subordinating social structures. Her equally didactic children's stories have appeared in *Pied Crow*, a Nairobi-based children's magazine that she at one time edited, and in various German-language publications in Germany and Switzerland. Her work has also appeared in Nigerian and American magazines. *The Hero of the Ridges and Other Stories* (2000) is a collection of children's short stories that draw on Kenyan and Nigerian oral traditions.

PRIMARY TEXTS

Genga-Idowu, Florence M. *Lady in Chains*. Nairobi: East African Educational Publishers, 1993.

——. *Memories Into Marriage*. Nairobi: Paulines, 1995.

———. *My Heart on Trial.* Nairobi: East African Educational Publishers, 1997.

———. *The Hero of the Ridges and Other Stories.* Nairobi: Paulines, 2000.

REFERENCES

Kruger, Marie. "Just a Brilliant Disguise: Postcolonial Identities and the Performance of Gender." *The Nairobi Journal of Literature* 1 (2003): 23–33.

Muriungi, Colomba. "The 'Sweet Pepper': Prostitution Declosetted in Kenyan Women's Writing." *EnterText* 4, no. 2 (Winter 2004–2005): 288–312.

Ng'ang'a, Elias. "The Social Vision of Genga-Idowu's Fiction." MA thesis, University of Nairobi, 2003.

[Mwangi]

Geteria, Wamungunda (b. 1945) Kenyan writer born in Embu District. Geteria's works belong to the tradition of popular fiction in East Africa and often deal with topical issues such as corruption and disease with a light and entertaining tone. His first novel, *Black Gold of Chepkube*, thematizes the black market in coffee across the Uganda-Kenya border, which in the 1970s led to the emergence of a new culture of corruption and illicit trade. He later wrote *Nice People*, which deals with the HIV/AIDS menace and the high prices of drugs needed to control it. Geteria is also an avid collector of folklore from the Embu and Mbeere people of eastern Kenya.

PRIMARY TEXTS

Geteria, Wamungunda. *Black Gold of Chepkube.* Nairobi: Longman, 1985.

———. *Nice People.* Nairobi: East African Educational Publishers, 1992.

[Mwangi]

Gicheru, Mwangi (b. 1947) Kenyan popular novelist and hotelier. He was born in Ki-amwangi, Karatina, in rural Nyeri, in central Kenya. His novel *The Mixers* (1991) focuses on miscegenation during a time of colonial racial stress. Set in the Kenyan white highlands during the three decades preceding Kenya's independence and using animals to mock racial boundaries, the novel exposes the fears, anxieties, and superstitions among both settler and native communities. *Across the Bridge* (1979) revolves around a love affair between a rich girl and a poor boy and lays bare the tensions between the rich and the poor in postindependence Africa. It is the typical story of a powerful rich man (Kahuthu) employing a poor houseboy (Chuma), who falls in love with the rich man's daughter (Caroline) and impregnates her before running away and getting involved in crime. The novel ends with Chuma's repentance and reunion with Caroline. Gicheru's other novels include *The Ivory Merchant* (1976), a crime novel about smuggling, and *The Double Cross* (1981), also set in the mysterious world of smugglers, which captured the East African imagination in the later 1970s, especially during the period of illicit cross-border trade in coffee between Kenya and Uganda. *Two in One*, one of the most popular of Gicheru's novels, is based on a real-life incident, in which the author's daughter was abducted by thugs.

PRIMARY TEXTS

Gicheru, Mwangi. *The Ivory Merchant.* Nairobi: EAEP, 1976.

———. *Across the Bridge.* Nairobi: Longhorn, 1979.

———. *The Double Cross.* Nairobi: Longhorn, 1981.

———. *Two in One.* Nairobi: Longhorn, 1981.

———. *The Mixers.* Nairobi: Longhorn, 1991.

[Mwangi]

Gurnah, Abdulrazak (b. 1948) Tanzanian (Zanzibari) novelist and university lecturer.

Born on the island of Zanzibar during the late colonial period, Gurnah was educated in local schools in East Africa before he left for higher education in Britain in 1968. He has lived and worked in Britain since then, mostly at the University of Kent at Canterbury, where he has taught postcolonial literatures. Although they range from the autobiographical to the historical in their themes and interests, Gurnah's fictional works can be read as attempts to bridge his early life in East Africa in the 1950s and 1960s, where he was part of a thriving Afro-Arab and Muslim tradition, and his experience as a migrant and thus minority in Britain. These works are concerned with both questions of memory (the act of recalling the past in narrative) and the process of departure, the movement from home to exile in both a real and metaphorical sense. In all cases, there is a strong autobiographical element in Gurnah's novels. Indeed, his first work, *Memory of Departure* (1987), the story of a boy who leaves his traditional Islamic home on the East African coast to be educated in the capital, Nairobi, and subsequently to prepare for an European sojourn, is based on Gurnah's own experiences and reflects his keen sense of the tension between one's desire to be rooted in a landscape and the inevitability of exile.

The same movement—from home on the East African coast to a cold British landscape—is reappraised in *Admiring Silence* (1996), published over ten years later. Other novels, including *Pilgrim's Way* (1988) and *Dottie* (1990), continue to narrate the memories and experiences of East Africans trying to come to terms with postimperial Britain and its ambivalent attitude toward its former subjects. In *By the Sea* (2001), Gurnah uses the story of Saleh Omar, an asylum seeker in Britain, to represent the strange juxtaposition of departure with the memories of the places left behind, foregrounding the ironic apprehension of home as a place that has to be abandoned and of exile as an alien space that is also a place of belonging.

Paradise (1994), which was nominated for the prestigious Booker Prize, is an exception to these narratives of home and departure. It is a historical portrait of East Africa during World War I, in which Gurnah tries to bring together the unique cultural geography of the East African coast, which is connected to Arabia through Islam, to India and the Indian Ocean coast through trade, and to Europe through colonialism. Revolving around several doomed cross-cultural love affairs, *Desertion* (2005) deals with the themes of exile, colonial takeover of East Africa, and ideological construction of race. It is the story of Martin Pearce, an Arabic-speaking English Orientalist, historian, writer, and traveler, who in 1899 is found stranded in the desert by Hassanali, a Kenyan coastal Muslim man of mixed Indian and African descent. He has been abandoned to die by his guide, but Hassanali takes care of him until a colonial officer, Fredrick Turner, relocates him to his house to save him from being harmed by the natives. When Martin Pearce returns to thank the good Samaritan who saved him, he falls rapturously in love with his sister, Rehana, whom he nevertheless deserts after the end of colonial rule.

Although Gurnah's novels are located in the cultural space between East Africa and Britain and constitute powerful meditations on the historical movements and personal journeys that connect the regions, his style eschews the magical realism of some of his more famous contemporaries like Salman Rushdie and Ben Okri. His style is reminiscent of a previous generation of postcolonial writers (Narayan and Ngugi), who were concerned with developing narratives of individuals whose inner life reflected the transformations of their communities.

PRIMARY TEXTS

Gurnah, Abdulrazak. *Memory of Departure.*
London: Jonathan Cape, 1987.
——. *Pilgrim's Way.* London: Jonathan
Cape, 1988.
——. *Dottie.* London: Jonathan Cape, 1990.
——. *Paradise.* London: Hamish Hamilton,
1994.
——. *Admiring Silence.* London: Hamish
Hamilton, 1996.
——. *By the Sea.* London: Bloomsbury,
2001.
——. *Desertion.* New York: Pantheon, 2005.

EDITED WORKS

Gurnah, Abdulrazak, ed. *Essays in African
Literature: A Re-evaluation.* Oxford: Heinemann, 1993.
——, ed. *Essays on African Writing 2: Contemporary Literature.* Oxford: Heinemann, 1993.

REFERENCES

Bardolph, Jacqueline. "Abdulrazak Gurnah's
Paradise and *Admiring Silence*: History,
Stories, and the Figure of the Uncle." In
Contemporary African Fiction, edited by
Derek Wright, 77–89. Bayreuth: Bayreuth
University Press, 1997.
Schwerdt, Dianne. "Looking in on Paradise:
Race, Gender, and Power in Abdulrazak
Gurnah's *Paradise*." In *Contemporary Af-
rican Fiction*, edited by Derek Wright,
91–101. Bayreuth: Bayreuth University
Press, 1997.

[Gikandi]

Hokororo, Anthony M. (b. 1934?) Tanzanian novelist and information officer.
Hokororo was among the first group of literature students at Makerere University
College, from where he graduated in 1959.
His first short story, "A Day Off," was published in *Origin East Africa*, the pioneering
anthology of creative writing from East
Africa. It is considered to be one of the first
East African stories to narrate the possibilities of a liberated woman in postcolonial society. It tells the story of Zale, who is taken
for granted by her husband, Abdu, who demands subservience. The story depicts how
Zale learns that she can indeed live a life free
from her husband and his needs.

After his debut story, Hokororo spent
many years working as an information officer in Tanzania, and it was not until the
1990s that he returned to writing serious fiction. *Salma's Spirit* (1997) uses postmodern
techniques, mixing myth, fable, and realism
to represent the postindependence condition of Tanzania. The novel tells the story of
Sam Mbogo, the director of personnel at the
Ministry of National Tribulations and Anxieties, who finds himself tormented by his at-
traction to the beautiful Selma. His boss,
Mr. Kondo, has also been plagued by strange
events linked to the death of his wife and
daughter in a road accident. Physical evidence disappears from sight as the police
look for Selma and Sam. Beneath the novel's
postmodern playfulness, it uses symbols
and images to situate its action within a specific historical time and place.

PRIMARY TEXTS

Hokororo, Anthony M. "A Day Off." In
Origin East Africa, edited by David Cook
and David Rubadiri, 29–35. London:
Heinemann, 1965.
——. *Salma's Spirit.* Dar es Salaam: Mkuki
na Nyota, 1997.

[Mwangi]

Hussein, Ebrahim (b. 1943) Tanzanian
playwright, academic, and drama critic.

Hussein is considered to be one of the best playwrights in the Swahili language but because all his plays have been written in that language, he has perhaps not garnered the international acclaim of some of his contemporaries. Hussein's plays are, nevertheless, central to discussions about the nature of drama in Africa and exemplify, in particular, the ongoing debate over the relation between theater and politics. His Swahili plays have been a staple of the high school and college curriculum, and *Kinjekitile*, which was translated by the author into English, has been anthologized and discussed in some of the leading works on African drama.

Born in southeastern Tanzania, Hussein was educated at University College, Dar es Salaam, and later did graduate work at Humboldt University, in the former East Germany, where he wrote his PhD thesis on the development of theater in East Africa and came under the influence of Bertolt Brecht. His early drama, including *Kinjekitile* and *Mashetani*, reflected the political and aesthetic influence of Brecht, taking on major historical themes and privileging the pedagogical function of drama. *Kinjekitile*, which discusses the events surrounding the Maji Maji uprising against German rule in Tanganyika between 1905 and 1907, is considered by many critics to be one of the most innovative works of political theater in Africa.

But Hussein's reputation in the 1970s did not rest solely on his mastery of the Brechtian theater of alienation. He was also a master of the Swahili language and its idiom, and his free verse in that language has been cited as exceptional. In later years, Hussein seems to have become disillusioned with political theater, and his later Swahili plays (*Jogoo Kijijini* and *Arusi*) tend to be more subjective and introspective, focusing on the alienation of individuals in the modern landscape rather than the drama of history.

PRIMARY TEXTS (IN ENGLISH)

Hussein, Ebrahim. *Kinjeketile.* Dar es Salaam: Oxford University Press, 1970. Translated from Kiswahili into English by the author.

——. *Mashetani.* Dar es Salaam: Oxford University Press, 1971. Translated from Kiswahili into English by the author.

REFERENCES

Jeyifo, B. *The Truthful Lie: Essays in the Sociology of an African Drama.* London: New Beacon Books, 1985.

Ricard, Alain. *Ebrahim Hussein: Swahili Theatre and Individualism.* Dar es Salaam: Mkuki na Nyota Publishers, 2000.

[Gikandi]

Huxley, Elspeth (1907–1997) Kenyan novelist and essayist. Huxley was part of a small group of writers of British origin who dominated the representation of Kenyan images and experiences before the period of decolonization. Although born in Britain, she spent most of her childhood in Kenya, among the southern Kikuyu, and her family was part of the early history of what was to become the Kenyan colony. Educated in the European school in Nairobi, Huxley was sent to Britain and studied agriculture at the University of Reading and, later, at Cornell University in the United States. In 1929, she joined the Empire Marketing Board as a press officer and traveled widely in the United States and Africa. From 1952 to 1959, she was a member of the General Advisory Council for the BBC and the Monckton Advisory Commission on Central Africa. During the Mau Mau conflict in Kenya, she was deployed by the colonial government as one of its so-called Kikuyu experts, a group of white Kenyans (the most prominent being Louis Leakey) who were often called upon to provide ethnographic explanations of the sources of the nationalist conflict. Like Leakey, Huxley had grown up among the Kikuyu, speaking their language and mastering their customs, and her most important book is perhaps her childhood memoir *The Flame Trees of Thika* (1959), which was popularized in a television series in the early 1980s. In this memoir, Huxley provided a compelling portrait of the settlement of Kenya at the beginning of the twentieth century and of the intricate encounters between Africans and Europeans as they negotiated their relationships.

Twenty years earlier, Huxley had tried to provide an ethnographic portrait of Kikuyu life in the novel *Red Strangers*, drawing on her extensive conversations with community elders and the ethnographic works of S. Routledge and Leakey. The novel was intended to be a documentary on the colonial encounter seen from the perspective of the Kikuyu themselves, but Huxley operated under the premise that her Africans could not represent themselves and thus needed a European interlocutor familiar with their language and traditions. This is the assertion she made in the foreword to *Red Strangers*, where she disclaimed any intention of speaking for the Kikuyu but insisted that it was only through her works that their voices could be represented.

Huxley's literary output was extensive and included biographical essays on colonial explorers such as David Livingstone and Mary Kingsley, works of travel, memoirs, and novels. Her reputation, however, rests on *The Flame Trees if Thika*, the memoir of her African childhood.

PRIMARY TEXTS

Huxley, Elspeth. *Red Strangers*. London: Chatto & Windus, 1939.

——. *Four Guineas: A Journey Through West Africa*. London: Chatto & Windus, 1954.

——. *The Flame Trees of Thika: Memories of an African Childhood*. London: Chatto & Windus, 1959.

——. *The Mottled Lizard*. London: Chatto & Windus, 1962.

[Gikandi]

Imbuga, Francis Davis (b. 1947)   Poet, novelist, and Kenya's leading playwright and theater personality. Imbuga's success as a dramatist stems from his choice of topical social and political themes and his fusion of English and elements of modern drama with African idioms such as proverbs, sayings, and dance, which appeal to the tastes and sensibilities of local communities. A versatile artist, he has written cartoon strips and humor columns in Kenyan media. He has served as an adjudicator in the Kenya National School's Drama Festival for many years, and his plays have been studied as compulsory texts in Kenyan high schools, making him the most influential dramatist in the country.

Imbuga was born in Wenyange Village, West Maragoli. His rural clan, Vamembe, appears in the play *Aminata* as Wembe. Imbuga started showing interest in theater while attending the prestigious Alliance High School, where his play *Omolo* (1969) was selected for the finals in the Kenyan National Schools Drama Festival. He played the lead role in the play and won the Best Actor's Award. Between 1970 and 1973, he wrote the "Omolo" series for Voice of Kenya television. During the same period, he acted in over fifty plays in the Voice of Kenya African theater series, combining his studies at the University of Nairobi with work in dramatic productions. He received his BA in education in 1973 and an MA in drama in 1975. He studied for a PhD at the University of Iowa between 1988 and 1992, where he wrote his first novel, *Shrine of Tears*.

As a visiting student at the University of Ghana, Legion, and the University of Ibadan, Nigeria, Imbuga focused on works with nationalistic themes, such as the writings of Okot p'Bitek, Ngugi wa Thiong'o, Peter Nazareth, and Jonathan Kariara. The influence of these writers was evident in his own writing. For example, tensions between rural and urban Kenya form a recurrent motif, as does his critique of the chaos wrought by modernity. His first play, *The Married Bachelor* (1971), portrays the escapades of Denis, a university lecturer of culture, who is caught between the conflicting claims of his father's traditional culture and the demands of urban life. In *The Kisses of Fate* (1971), Imbuga dramatizes the stereotypical story of two youths who unwittingly fall in incestuous love, while *The Fourth Trial* (1971) is a humorous play centered on the story of a childless couple, Musa and Hellen, who blame each other for their inability to have a child. Imbuga's earlier plays are melodramatic and do not resolve conflicts without resorting to coincidence.

As a graduate student, Imbuga met and became friends with Joe de Graft, the Ghanaian poet and playwright then teaching at the University of Nairobi. He also toured Britain, Ghana, and Nigeria, widening his experience in dramaturgy and sharpening his theatrical skills. The result of these experiences was *Betrayal in the City* (1978), the play that put Imbuga on the national and regional literary map. It was chosen as one of the two plays to represent Kenya in the Second World Black and African Festival of Arts and Culture (FESTAC). The play revolves around the murder of a student activist, Jasper Wendo, by a dictatorial postcolonial regime, and this murder is used to dramatize the abuse of power, nepotism, corruption, and repression in the fictional postindependence state Kafira, an anagram of "Africa." The play begins at Jasper Wendo's grave and ends at the same spot, with almost the same dialogue. The cyclic plot suggests cynicism, and some of the lines, especially those coming from intellectuals, express a bleak future for Africa. For example, a former university professor now in jail because the regime considers him subversive suggests that colonialism would be better than the current situation, which offers little hope for change:

> It was better while we waited. Now we have nothing to look forward to. We have killed our past and are busy killing the future. Sometimes I sit here and look far into the past. There I see my mother slaughtering the biggest family cock. Once every year she slaughtered a senior cock to mark the birth of Christ. Our children will never have such memories. Now there is blood everywhere. Cocks are slaughtered any day, many times a week.   (33)

The dictator is eventually overthrown in a dramatic rehearsal of a play of the same title.

The sequel, *Man of Kafira* (1982), also exploits play-within-a-play techniques as it follows the fortunes of Boss, the dictator, in exile in Abiara (an anagram of "Arabia"), where he is haunted by his past but still dreaming of recapturing power. The figure of Boss in the two plays is a thinly veiled portrait of Idi Amin, the Ugandan dictator who ruled that country between 1972 and 1979 before he was forced into exile in Saudi Arabia.

In his later plays, Imbuga presents a candid picture of the suffering that ordinary people endure at the hands of autocratic African dictators. This is the theme of *Game of Silence* (1977), which premiered at the Kenya National Theatre. His other plays include *The Successor* (1979), a satire about the greed for power that informs African succession politics; and *Aminata* (1988), specifically written for the Second World Women's

Conference held in Nairobi in 1985, about a young woman lawyer with a bright legal career before her who has to bear the burden of womanhood. Aminata's father leaves her a piece of land in his will, but this creates a conflict between her and her brothers because according to tradition, a woman should not inherit land. While the topical issue makes it a popular piece of art, it is the technique that makes the play compelling, especially Imbuga's use of local expressions, dance, and proverbs to capture the link between rural and urban Kenya.

Imbuga's first novel, *Shrine of Tears* (1993), examines the politics of theater in East Africa. It is a thinly veiled thematization of the controversy surrounding the Kenya National Theatre in the 1970s and 1980s, when it was contested by forces aligned with the British government and radical intellectuals. The novel explores the dilemma of an evolving African theater caught between the struggle against intolerant regimes and Western cultural hegemony. His second novel, *Miracle of Remera* (2004), deploys a nonrealistic mode of narration to present the myths surrounding HIV/AIDS in Africa and to explore the possibilities of using theater and other artistic forms to combat the scourge. The miracle of the title refers to the discovery of a home-grown cure for HIV by a locally trained scientist, who uses a commonplace traditional concoction to reverse the spread of the virus. Imbuga has also written children's books, the most famous of which is *Kagai and Her Brothers*. During his long and distinguished career, Imbuga has been a professor of literature at Kenyatta University, Kenya, and in Rwanda, and in this role he has combined theater and pedagogy to respond to developmental issues. Imbuga has written scripts commissioned by various government ministries and nongovernmental organizations: *The Day of the Tree* was commissioned by the Forestry Department for the government's efforts to conserve the environment. In the early 1980s, he wrote educational radio dramas entitled *You and Your Health* and *Food and Nutrition*.

PRIMARY TEXTS

Imbuga, Francis Davis. *Betrayal in the City: A Play*. Nairobi: East African Publishing House, 1976.
——. *Game of Silence*. Nairobi: Heinemann Educational Books, 1977.
——. *The Successor*. Nairobi: Heinemann Educational Books, 1979.
——. *Man of Kafira*. Nairobi: Heinemann Educational Books, 1984.
——. *Aminata: A Play*. Nairobi: Heinemann Kenya, 1988.
——. *The Burning of Rags: A Play*. Nairobi: Heinemann Kenya, 1989.
——. *Shrine of Tears*. Nairobi: Longman Kenya, 1993.
——. *Miracle of Remera*. Nairobi: Africa-wide Network, 2004.

REFERENCES

Harbnel, Ahmad. "The Aesthetics of Francis Imbuga: A Contemporary Kenyan Playwright." *Literary Review* 34, no. 4 (1991): 571–583.
Makini, Gacugu. "The Drama of Francis Imbuga." MA thesis, University of Nairobi, 1979.
Obyerodhyambo, Oby. "Of Betrayal in *Betrayal in the City*." *Literary Review* 34, no. 4 (1991): 583–589.
Olagun, Modipe. "Dramatizing Atrocities: Plays by Wole Soyinka, Francis Imbuga, and George Seremba Recalling the Idi Amin Era." *Modern Drama* 45, no. 3 (2002): 430–449.
Ruganda, John. *Telling the Truth Laughingly. The Politics of Francis Imbuga's Drama*. Nairobi: East African Educational Publishers, 1992.

[Mwangi]

Isegawa, Moses (b. 1963) Ugandan novelist. Isegawa was educated in a Catholic seminary in Uganda and taught history in Kampala before he emigrated to the Netherlands in 1990. *Abyssinian Chronicles* (2000), first published in Dutch as *Abessijne kronieken* in 1998, is an ambitious novel that uses the experiences of the growing up of its precocious main character, Mugezi Muwaabi, to portray the corruption, chaos, and carnage of postindependence Uganda. Although it primarily focuses on the Idi Amin years of the 1970s, it suggests that preceding and later regimes appear democratic only in comparison to Amin's monstrosity. Like the narrator Saleem in Salman Rushdie's *Midnight's Children*, the restless and self-conscious narrator in *Abyssinian Chronicles* shares his birthday with his country, Uganda. Though the story is told in an autobiographical mode, the narrator seems to enjoy omniscience and is even able to narrate in the third-person voice the intimate particulars of the night he was conceived by his easily agitated and ironically named father, Serenity, and his prudish mother, Padlock. Mugezi's uncanny omniscience enables the novel to present a national history beyond the limits of personal experience. The tyranny of his parents seems to parallel that of the nation's leaders, and the novel examines in gritty detail the Muwaabi family's endangered genealogy and the way it intersects with the politics of postcolonial nations. The novel presents the expulsion of Indians from Uganda in the 1970s and the experiences of African exiles in Western ghettos. Detailing the corrupt regimes that precede and succeed Amin's and depicting the onset of the AIDS scourge on a war-ravaged Uganda, the novel puns in its title on the word "abyss," to indicate the depth of the malaise and the failure of postcolonial nation states. Uganda is described as a "land of false bottoms where under every abyss there was another one waiting to ensnare people" (469).

Composed earlier than *Abyssinian Chronicles*, Isegawa's other novel, *Snakepit* (2004), was first published in Dutch in 1999, as *Slangenkuil*. It examines in detail corruption and violence in Uganda in the 1970s through the story of Bat Katanga, who returns to his homeland in the 1970s after graduating with an advanced mathematics degree from Cambridge University. Like Obi Okonkwo in Achebe's *No Longer at Ease*, Bat falls into the sleaze and corruption that defines civil service in Idi Amin's Uganda. He immediately lands a job as the head of the Ministry of Power and Communications, thanks to some help from the ambitious Samson Bazooka Ondogar, who directs Amin's murderous Anti-Smuggling Unit. As paranoid as the regime he serves, General Bazooka plants a beautiful female spy and his former lover, Victoria, on his protégé. Victoria, however, falls in love with Bat, but when they become estranged following his interest in his village sweetheart, Victoria brutally takes her revenge. While on a trip abroad, Bat is forced to take a bribe from a Saudi prince, and he is later hounded into prison, where he is terrorized by his seniors into a near nervous breakdown. Bat's release from prison coincides with the downward spiral of the nation, in a trajectory that signals the impossibility of individual regeneration in a perverse nation. The novel uses details of massacres, rapes, and pillaging as examples of the despair and degeneration of the postcolonial nation in its first decade of independence. It is also a study of the paranoia, power struggles, rivalries, revenge, and enmity of Amin's regime.

The short story "The Astrologer" is a slightly reworked version of a section of *Snakepit*, in which Isegawa satirizes the squandering of national resources on superstitions and draws connections between Idi Amin and other African megalomaniacs. Told from the perspective of a teacher,

Beeda, whose mother's school is on the verge of an attack by children militia, the short story "The War of the Ears" (2005) portrays Uganda gripped by the terror of civil war, in which the government is fighting a quasi-religious guerrilla movement. In the story, children soldiers who question the wishes of their seniors get their ears chopped off while the government uses loudspeakers to hammer home its propaganda.

PRIMARY TEXTS

Isegawa, Moses. *Abyssinian Chronicles*. New York: Random House, 2001.

——. "The Astrologer." *Transition* 10, no. 2 (2001): 84–90.

——. *Snakepit*. New York: Random House, 2001.

——. "The War of the Ears." *Granta* 92 (Winter 2005): 43–60.

REFERENCES

Filbin, Thomas. "Up Close and Personal." *Hudson Review* 57, no. 3 (2004): 509–514.

Jones, Jacqui. "Traversing the Abyss: Moses Isegawa—An Interview and Commentary." *English in Africa* 27, no. 2 (2000): 85–102.

[Mwangi]

Journals Although they have been sporadic and precarious, East African literary journals and magazines have been critical in the propagation of a literary culture and in exposing new artists to a wide readership, especially in the shorter-form genres. From the 1960s onward, journals from the region gave international exposure to narrative prose and drama, in the form of reviews and extracts. Associated with university departments, the journals were vital in establishing and debating interpretive strategies in East African literature. As Bernth Lindfors has noted, almost all the major literary names in East Africa originally either contributed to journals or edited them before launching themselves internationally: "Little magazines have played a big role in the development of Anglophone African Writing. Indeed, virtually all the major authors in English-speaking Africa today got their start in local periodicals of very limited circulation. They wrote for their peers rather than for international consumption" (*Loaded Vehicles*, 43). Ngugi wa Thiong'o, Peter Nazareth, Richard Ntiru, and John Nagenda all served as editors of *Penpoint*, the journal of the English department at Makerere University College. Some of the most important East African writers, including Grace Ogot, Jared Angira, Timothy Wangusa, Jagjit Singh, and Stephen Lubega, cut their literary teeth in the pages of *Penpoint* and the *Makerere Beat*.

The late 1960s and 1970s witnessed a remarkable growth of journals dealing with East African literature and art from other parts of the continent. Student journals provided a forum for budding writers. From Dar es Salaam University College in Tanzania came the *Darlite* (1966), which was followed by *Umma* (1970); from Nairobi came *Nexus* (1967), followed by *Busara* (1968); Makerere's *Penpoint* (1958) was superseded by *Dhana* (1971). Other journals included *Ghala* (published by the East African Cultural Trust) and *Joliso* (published at the University of Nairobi). Magazines based elsewhere in Africa that also published East African authors included *Okike*, based in Enugu, Nigeria, and *Black Orpheus* from Lagos, Nigeria.

However, the most important literary magazine to come out of East Africa was *Transition*, started in Kampala, Uganda, by Rajat Neogy (1938–1995) in 1961. *Transition*'s aim, as defined by Neogy in his introduction to the premier issue, was to offer "a monthly reflection of the cultural and social scene in East Africa: and its constant aim is to search and encourage writers and poets from East Africa." *Transition* aimed to be different from other news magazines by providing "an intelligent and creative backdrop to the East African scene, to give perspective and dimension to affairs that a weekly or daily press would ether sectionalize or ignore." The journal was an important outlet for creative writing and critical thought in East Africa, and it published almost every major writer and intellectual from the region as well as others from outside.

In the late 1960s, the University of East Africa was broken up into individual public universities, and the departments of English went separate ways. Each university had its own literary publications, but writers continued to contribute to journals across territorial boundaries and continued to be featured in anthologies and journals published outside the region. The *Literary Half-Yearly* (published in Mysore, India) carried articles on East Africa, as did *English in Africa* (Witwatersrand, South Africa) and *Research in African Literatures* (originally based at the University of Texas).

Political crackdowns by intolerant regimes, lack of adequate funding, and low morale among academics adversely affected literary journals in East Africa. In Kenya, for example, the government passed a new law in 2002 requiring publishers to sign a bond of Sh1 million (US$12,990) in order to run publications. Although the law was intended to control oppositional and pornographic tabloids, it also threatened the existence of various academic publications including *Wajibu*, a quarterly journal founded in Nairobi in 1985. Even before the passage of the media bill, the Kenyan government often used its power to control student journals and newspapers. *Mzalendo*, a journal published by University of Nairobi students, was banned by the Kenyan government in the 1980s because of its heavy political content.

REFERENCES

Elder, Arlene A. "English-Language Fiction from East Africa." In *A History of Twentieth Century African Literatures*, edited by Oyekan Owomoyela, 49–84. Lincoln: University of Nebraska Press, 1993.

Lindfors, Bernth. *Loaded Vehicles: Studies in African Literary Media.* Trenton, N.J.: Africa World Press, 1996.

Zell, Hans M. "Publishing in Africa: The Crisis and Challenge." In *A History of Twentieth Century African Literatures*, edited by Oyekan Owomoyela, 369–387. Lincoln: University of Nebraska Press, 1993.

[Mwangi]

K

Kaggia, Bildad (1922–2005) Kenyan freedom fighter, nationalist radical, trade unionist, publisher, oppositionist, and staunch advocate of multiparty democracy in colonial and postcolonial Kenya. One of the founding fathers of the Kenyan nation, Kaggia and Jomo Kenyatta were jailed in the 1950s by the colonial government for their opposition to British rule. Kaggia was appointed an assistant minister of education upon independence in 1963. He strongly believed in principles of equity and opposed the corruption, elitism, and materialism of successive Kenyan regimes, a fact that led to his marginalization in the capitalist postindependence order. He fell out with the Kenyatta government in the late 1960s for aligning himself with Kenya Peoples Union, a leftist party led by Oginga Odinga, and consequently lost his parliamentary seat in

1969, in polls that were widely thought to have been rigged in favor of the Kenyatta-led Kenya African National Union candidates. Before the polls, which Kenyatta had openly vowed to rig in favor of Kaggia's opponent, Kaggia was arrested for holding an unlicensed meeting and imprisoned for six months. During his jail term, he was made a public spectacle, forced to sweep the streets of his home town as his constituents watched. He retired from politics in the 1970s and died in humiliation and poverty. His experiences in postindependence Kenya exemplify the excesses of the postcolonial nation in silencing to near submission dissenting voices. In popular discourse, he instantly became the quintessential figure of the unrewarded anticolonial nationalist.

His memoir *Roots of Freedom* (1975) chronicles his development from a poor child in colonial Kenya to an urban Mau Mau organizer. The book details his recruitment into the Kenya African Rifles (a multi-battalion British colonial regiment raised from the various British possessions in East Africa from 1902 until independence in the 1960s), the part he played in World War II campaigns, and the influence his experiences in Britain and the Middle East had on his anticolonial and antimissionary beliefs. He describes how, like other young people from the colonies, he learned from his involvement in World War II that the British, whom he had previously considered all too powerful, could also be defeated in battle. Prefiguring his oppositionist positions, Kaggia underscores moments when he led the Kenya African Rifles soldiers in demanding their rights from their colonial seniors. The memoir shows how African participation in the war and their stints in Europe prodded the colonized peoples to demand the freedom of their nations when they returned home. His newspaper, *Inoro ria Gikuyu* (*The Sharpener*), counteracted the imperialist press with vernacular opin-ions. While much of the literature on the controversies surrounding the freedom struggle focuses mainly on guerrilla warfare in ethnically defined rural areas, Kaggia's memoir shows the urban, interracial, and more cosmopolitan efforts to dislodge colonialism. It describes the escalation of the urban anticolonial struggle and the "coups" staged within the nationalist movement by the more militant leftist wings of the political organizations and trade unions.

It is highly likely that the memoir, which was published more than a decade after independence—when Kaggia had already fallen out of favor with the Kenyan government and had become one of Kenyatta's most vocal critics—was censored to leave out details of his disillusionment with the postcolonial dispensation. The memoir also discusses his break with the mainstream versions of Christianity, which he claims not only mistranslated certain Gikuyu language terms in order to demonize local practices, but also deliberately misinterpreted the Bible to justify exploitation of Africans. A charismatic leader, Kaggia describes in his memoir the religious movement he founded to counter conventional Christianity and his break with traditional practices such as paying a bride price.

PRIMARY TEXTS

Kaggia, Bildad. *Roots of Freedom, 1921–1963: The Autobiography of Bildad Kaggia.* Nairobi: East African Publishing House, 1975.

REFERENCES

Gertzel, C. J., et al., eds. *Government and Politics in Kenya: A Nation Building Text.* Nairobi: East African Publishing House, 1969.

Kyle, Keith. *The Politics of the Independence of Kenya.* New York: St. Martin's Press, 1999.

Maloba, Wunyabari O. *Mau Mau and Kenya: An Analysis of a Peasant Revolt.*

Bloomington: Indiana University Press, 1993.

Shiroya, O. J. E. *Kenya and World War II: African Soldiers in the European War.* Nairobi: Kenya Literature Bureau, 1985.

Spencer, John. *The Kenya African Union.* Boston: KPI, 1985.

[Mwangi]

Kahiga, Samuel (b. 1946) Kenyan novelist and short-story writer. Born in Kabete, outside Nairobi, Kahiga's early childhood was marked by the state of emergency in Kenya in the 1950s and the Mau Mau revolt against British colonialism. He was educated in local schools, studied design at the University of Nairobi, and later worked as an illustrator for magazines and books. It was while he was at the University of Nairobi that Kahiga started writing fiction, coming into prominence as a writer during the great creative and cultural revival in East Africa during the first decade of independence (the 1960s). Most of his early works were short stories, submitted to prominent journals, magazines, and newspapers in East Africa. While later in his career he devoted himself to writing novels, Kahiga's reputation as a writer rests on his early stories collected in *Potent Ash*, jointly published with his older brother, Leonard Kibera.

On their publication in 1968, these stories stood out as the first vivid expressions of what it might have meant to live and come of age under a state of colonial terror. Like his brother Kibera, his focus in these stories was on Mau Mau as an immediate and lived experience, one not mediated by the political concerns or historiographic debates that were to shadow the representation of the movement in the 1970s. One of Kahiga's stories in this collection, "Departure at Dawn," is equaled only by Ngugi's *Weep Not, Child* in its ability to capture both the fears and hopes surrounding the anticolonial struggle in Kenya and, more particularly, a child's perspective on the overwhelming and often invisible forces moving the world around him. But Kahiga's stories in *Potent Ash* are not all about Mau Mau; less concerned with the larger drama of politics than his brother Kibera, Kahiga's stories are structured by the struggle between larger natural events (such as floods) and individual subjects who find themselves trapped in them. As in "God's Waters," these stories are driven by the transformations that take place when people struggle to contain larger natural events.

After an absence of almost nine years, Kahiga returned to writing fiction with a series of novels published in the 1970s: *Lover in the Sky, The Girl from Abroad, Flight to Juba,* and *When the Stars Are Scattered.* In thematic terms, these novels are aimed at a popular readership and thus tend to focus on romantic relationships, adventure, and entertainment, and are presented in a tone that contrasts sharply with the sober note of the stories in *Potent Ash*. But while these novels have not made it into the canon of East African literature, they represent some of the best qualities in Kahiga's prose: namely, his ability to capture the tense relation between individuals and their social environment, his vivid and dramatic presentation of scenes, and his use of an accessible style to mediate complex social relationships. The qualities are evident in *Dedan Kimathi*, Kahiga's most significant work to date, a novel in which he seeks to unravel the mysterious life of a famous Mau Mau hero while at the same time both producing a thriller about the war between nationalist and colonial forces in the forests of central Kenya and capturing the psychological conflicts that arise when personal desire and public duty come into conflict.

PRIMARY TEXTS

Kahiga, Samuel. *Potent Ash*. Nairobi: East African Publishing House, 1968.

——. *The Girl from Abroad*. London: Heinemann, 1974.

——. *Dedan Kimathi*. Nairobi: Longman Kenya, 1990.

——. *Flight to Juba*. Nairobi: Longman Kenya, 1979.

——. *Lover in the Sky*. Nairobi: Spear, 1975.

——. *Paradise Farm*. Nairobi: Longman Kenya, 1993.

——. *When the Stars Are Scattered*. Nairobi: Longman Kenya, 1979.

REFERENCES

Nazareth, Peter. "The Social Responsibility of the East African Writer (in African Literature)." *Callaloo* 8, no. 10 (1980): 87–105.

Simatei, Peter. "Versions and Inversions: Mau Mau in Kahiga's Dedan Kimathi: The Real Story." *Research in African Literatures* 30, no. 1 (Spring 1999): 154–161.

[Gikandi]

Kalimugogo, Godfrey (b. 1943) Ugandan novelist and short-story writer. Educated at Makerere University, where he graduated with an honors degree in English, and the University of Dar es Salaam, where he studied African and Caribbean literature, Kalimugogo has worked as a civil servant since the 1970s, and his works, which draw on his experiences in the government, represent the anxieties facing the civil service in Africa. His first novel, *Pilgrimage to Nowhere* (1974), is based on the conflict between a tranquil village experience and the debased life of the city. Bwengye, a widower from the peaceful M'kyogo villages, sets out for the city to look for his son Kwita. Bwenye discovers that Kwita is no longer the beloved son, but a drunkard, thief, and pimp.

Perhaps Kalimugogo's most successful work is *The Department* (1976), a satirical novel that lampoons the absurdities of bureaucratic practices in an emergent postcolony. Mutana, a new employee in the Department, finds himself at a crossroads: he is supposed to respect his culture while at the same time serve in a heartless bureaucracy, one that declares mere superstition his attendance at his mother's burial, as mandated by tradition. But Mutana is not alone in this split. Even his bosses cannot make a quick decision about anything because of the stifling nature of the bureaucracy, resulting in total dehumanization. Kalimugogo describes the Department as "a super machine carefully divorced from the known ethics of men, moving along the belt of its own invention, leading to a carefully selected end: produce more money and forget yourselves as people." Kalimugogo's other works include the short-story collection *Dare to Die* (1972) and four novels: *Trials and Tribulations in Sandu's Home* (1976), *The Pulse of the Woods* (1974), *The Prodigal Chairman* (1979), and *Sandu, the Prince* (1982). The narratives deal with the themes of the collapse of traditional family values and the encroachment of corruption throughout the nation.

PRIMARY TEXTS

Kalimugogo, Godfrey. *Dare to Die*. Nairobi: East African Literature Bureau, 1972.

——. *Pilgrimage to Nowhere*. Kampala: East African Literature Bureau, 1974.

——. *The Pulse of the Woods*. Kampala: East African Literature Bureau, 1974.

——. *The Department*. Kampala: East African Literature Bureau, 1976.

——. *Trials and Tribulations in Sandu's Home*. Kampala: East African Literature Bureau, 1976.

——. *The Prodigal Chairman*. Nairobi: Uzima, 1979.

——. *Sandu, the Prince*. Nairobi: Kenya Literature Bureau, 1982.

REFERENCES

Gakwandi, Shatto Arthur. *The Novel and Contemporary Experience in Africa*. New

York: Africana Publishing Company, 1977.

Wanjala, Chris (Lukorito). *For Home and Freedom*. Nairobi: East African Publishing House, 1980.

———. *Season of Harvest: Some Notes on East African Literature*. Nairobi: Kenya Literature Bureau, 1978.

[Mwangi]

Karanja, David (b. 1971) Kenyan novelist. He attended Arap Moi Primary School and Oloolaiser Secondary School before matriculating at the University of Nairobi in the early 1990s to study anthropology. As a university student, he pursued his interests in journalism and writing fiction. His first novel, *The Girl Was Mine* (1996), the story of a budding novelist, is a playful examination of the marginalization of the poor in postcolonial Kenya. When author Douglas Kamau falls in love with Nancy Wanja, the daughter of the rich governor of the Central Bank, her father is not amused, because he would like to use her possible friendship with an American tycoon to curry favors with the West and win himself a job with the World Bank. The lovers' lives are placed in danger, prompting them to flee to Namibia, where Douglas writes an autobiographical short story entitled "Lovers on the Run." In Namibia, Douglas is arrested at the instigation of Wanja's father, but he is released when the authorities fail to find enough evidence to convict him. However, things are different in Kenya. On his arrival home, he is charged with two counts—one of which is "damaging Kenya's good image in Namibia by going around Windhoek raping women." He is sent to jail, where he writes the novel *The Girl Was Mine*. Nancy leaves Douglas for the American tycoon, but the novel Douglas writes in prison becomes an instant bestseller. Karanja integrates romance with commentaries on social injus-

tices and the gap between the rich and the poor, using Nancy Wanja as the metaphor for her nation, prostituted by her father to perpetuate the exploitation of the Third World.

A Dreamer's Paradise (2001) is a more sophisticated story. Its account of Kenyan politics led to its rejection by Kenyan publishers and it had to be published in South Africa. It uses folkloric materials and techniques to thematize ideological ignorance in a society battered by years of dictatorship. A novel of growing up, *A Dreamer's Paradise* presents Mathina (a Gikuyu word for "problems" or "poverty") as he tries to comprehend his position in a stifling environment where the immoral power elites can end human life without batting an eyelid. The boy attends Mariga (Gikuyu for "incomprehensible") Primary School but remains puzzled all his life, overwhelmed by the activities of Gitonga (Gikuyu for "the rich one"), who unfairly sacks his father and ends up winning the elections against the morally upright teacher Mbogo. Lives are destroyed by the cynicism of the rich and the attitude of the government toward the poor, while the school system serves to maintain the status quo. So confounding is the world he dwells in that Mathina eventually loses his mind and chooses to spend his life in a tree. Told from Mathina's hazy perspective, the novel opens as an oral narrative, emphasizing that the events presented are as incomprehensible to the character as they are to the people observing him. At the time the story begins, the character is already dead. Its cyclic structure indicates not despair, but a call for the rejection of power structures that silence the ruled or drive them mad. Although the novel presents historical facts about the Moi regime of the Kenya of the 1980s, it disguises itself as a dystopian narrative set in no particular country. It manages to probe the effects of dictatorship in postindependence Africa, especially on poor families and on innocent children.

Since graduating from the University of Nairobi in 1995, Karanja has worked as a journalist, writing and editing for publications in Kenya, Zimbabawe, the United Kingdom, and the United States. While refreshing in its own right, Karanja's fiction serves to demonstrate the hold Ngugi wa Thiong'o, whose ideas and characterizations are echoed in Karanja's work, has on a younger generation of writers.

PRIMARY TEXTS

Karanja, David. *The Girl Was Mine.* Nairobi: Spear Books, 1996.

———. *Dreamer's Paradise.* Cape Town: Kwela, 2001.

REFERENCES

Muhoma, Catherine. "A Failed Romance: Reading Masculinity and Love in David Karanja's *The Girl Was Mine.*" *Africa Insight* 35, no. 2 (2005): 26–32.

[Mwangi]

Kariara, Jonathan (1935–1993) Kenyan publisher, poet, and short-story writer. Kariara was born into a pioneering Christian family at the Church of Scotland Mission, Tumutumu, where he received his early education. He attended Kagumo and Kangaru Government Schools before studying at Makerere University College in Uganda, where he was one of the first honors students in English. At Makerere, Kariara was editor of *Penpoint*, the college's literary magazine, and it was during his editorship that some of the most prominent writers in East Africa, including the novelist Ngugi wa Thiong'o, published their first works. After graduating from Makerere, Kariara worked as a book editor for the East African Literature Bureau and later for Oxford University Press. From the late 1960s and 1970s, he edited *Zuka*, a literary magazine sponsored by the literature department of the University of Nairobi.

Kariara's creative writing belongs solidly to what has come to be known as the Makerere School of English, a tradition characterized by attempts to use local materials and backgrounds while maintaining the formal conventions of English writing in both verse and prose. In his earliest short stories and poems published in *Origin East Africa*, an anthology of writing by Makerere students edited by David Cook and David Rubadiri, Kariara's work is characterized both by a keen sense of the Gikuyu landscape and patterns of life and his mastery of the inner psychology of characters and their struggle for the moral high ground associated with F. R. Leavis's notion of the best of English writing. Kariara never overtly engaged with the politics of nationalism that constituted the defining moment of his generation, nor did he seem to have a specific interest in cultural nationalism, but in the two short stories published in *Origin East Africa* and others later collected in *The Coming of Power*, he seemed to conceive of the condition of the new African as a struggle between the subtle yet malevolent forces of nature and the claims of the new Christian culture.

Born into a family that was very much part of this new order, Kariara nevertheless sought to use his prose to capture what he saw as the disappearing world of Gikuyu life, one he closely associated with the landscape and the rhythms of everyday life. Avoiding elevated subjects and often focusing on the most common aspects of social life, Kariara's short stories exhibited keen psychological insight into how personal struggles emerging out of the most ordinary circumstances (disputes over land in "Bringing in the Sheaves," for example) could turn into larger generational and class conflicts. But it was perhaps in verse, including his often anthologized poems

"Grass Will Grow" and "A Leopard Lives on the Muu Tree," that Kariara was most experimental and yet conventional, carefully balancing the technical aspects of English verse, especially meter, with themes drawn from his native Kenyan landscape.

PRIMARY TEXTS

Kariara, Jonathan. Various poems and short stories collected in *Origin East Africa: A Makerere Anthology*, edited by David Cook and David Rubadiri. London: Heinemann, 1965.

——. Various poems collected in *Poems from East Africa*, edited by David Cook and David Rubadiri. London: Heinemann, 1971.

——. *The Coming of Power and Other Stories*. Nairobi: Oxford University Press, 1986.

SECONDARY TEXTS

Kariara, Jonathan, and Ellen Kitonga. *An Introduction to East African Poetry*. Nairobi: Oxford University Press, 1976.

[Gikandi]

Kariuki, Josiah Mwangi (1925–1975) Kenyan nationalist politician and autobiographer. Kariuki was born in Kabati in the Rift Valley, where his parents had migrated to work as squatters on a white settler's farm. His early education was at a Kikuyu Independent School Association (KISA) institution founded by a group of African Christians who in the 1920s had broken away from the mainstream Protestant churches over the issue of female circumcision. In the 1940s, Kariuki attended the Nakuru African School and later the Kerugoya Intermediate School. In 1950, he went to Uganda to study at the famous King's College, Budo, a school established by Anglican missionaries to educate the children of the Baganda elite. A member since the late 1940s of the Kenya African Union, the leading nationalist movement, Kariuki was closely associated with the radical wing of nationalist politics, and he was arrested and detained in numerous prisons and camps from 1953 to 1960 for being a member of Mau Mau. After independence, he served as private secretary to Prime Minister Jomo Kenyatta. Later, he was elected to the Kenyan Parliament as the member for Nyandarua North and served as an assistant minister for agriculture.

Although a member of the Kenyatta government, Kariuki was a relentless advocate for the landless and poor in Kenya and was perhaps the most vocal advocate for the grievances of former Mau Mau fighters who had been sidelined in the postcolonial polity. He was murdered under brutal and mysterious circumstances in 1975, by what many believe were agents of the state. While Kariuki remains a symbol of radical protest in Kenya, his most important contribution to the literary culture was his autobiography, *Mau Mau Detainee*, perhaps both the first inside account of Kenyan radical nationalism and its tactics and rituals as well as being a gripping narrative of the "pipeline" of political detention that remains a controversial subject in Kenya and Britain. Kariuki was able to give his readers an insider's glimpse at the inner workings of Mau Mau among the civilian population, its genesis and transformation in the settled areas, and its ability to sustain its structures even in the massive prison system set up to contain it. As the novelist Ngugi wa Thiong'o wrote in a moving tribute to Kariuki in 1975, *Mau Mau Detainee* was the record of the kind of experiences both the colonial government and its postcolonial successor sought to repress: "Kariuki's education in the settled area, in the streets of political struggle with the masses, in the universities of Manyani and other concentration camps, had opened him to see the link which bound the peasants and workers of Kenya to all others struggling against oppression and exploitation" ("J. M.—A Writer's Tribute," 83).

PRIMARY TEXTS

Kariuki, Josiah Mwangi. *Mau Mau Detainee: The Account by a Kenyan African of His Experiences in Detention Camps, 1953–1960*. London and Nairobi: Oxford University Press, 1963.

REFERENCES

Berman, Bruce J. "Nationalism, Ethnicity, and Modernity: The Paradox of Mau Mau." *Canadian Journal of African Studies* 25, no. 2 (1991): 81–206.

Ngugi wa Thiong'o. "J. M.—A Writer's Tribute." In *Writers in Politics*, 82–85. London: Heinemann, 1981.

[Gikandi]

Kenyatta, Jomo (1893?–1978) Kenyan statesman and anthropologist. Kenyatta was born in the southern region of central Kenya at the beginning of colonial rule in East Africa, and his life closely paralleled the history of the region as a whole and the country that he was to lead to independence. In fact, there is no significant period in the modern history of Kenya that does not bear Kenyatta's mark. He was one of the first Africans to be educated at the colonial mission and school, he was among the first to take up employment in the new urban center of Nairobi and cultivate a so-called modern identity, and he was the most prominent of the first generation of young nationalists who challenged the authority of colonial rule in the 1920s.

Born Kamau wa Ngengi, Kenyatta left his traditional home at a young age to join the Church of Scotland Mission at Kikuyu, where he was taught to read and write and was also trained as a carpenter. He was baptized Johnstone by Scottish missionaries, but his relationship to the church was always troubled, and he was often brought before its council for violating church doctrines or practices such as drinking alcohol. During World War I, the Scottish mission spearheaded an effort to recruit its members to fight the Germans in Tanganyika, but Kenyatta managed to get away, and he spent the duration of the war hiding among his Maasai relatives and trading in meat.

It was while he was working as a meter reader for the Nairobi City Council in the early 1920s that Kenyatta became interested in nationalist politics, and for most of that decade he was active as a member of the Kikuyu Central Association (KCA), the major nationalist movement in colonial Kenya at the time, serving as the secretary of the association and editor of its newspaper, *Muigwithania* (*The Reconciler*). In 1929, Kenyatta was sent by the KCA to London to represent to the British government nationalist grievances, especially regarding issues of labor and land. During this period, he toured several European countries, including the Soviet Union. He briefly returned to Kenya in 1930, but went back to England the following year, staying until 1946. During his relatively long stay in Britain, Kenyatta taught Gikuyu at the University of London, collaborated with scholars working on aspects of Gikuyu phonology and lexicography, and, most important, he studied anthropology under Bronislaw Malinowski at the London School of Economics.

It was for Malinowski's seminar on the anthropology of colonialism and social change that Kenyatta wrote his most influential book, *Facing Mount Kenya*. Kenyatta intended *Facing Mount Kenya* to provide a narrative of Gikuyu social life as it was being transformed by colonialism, and to use the book as a testimony to the "tribal" culture he had known as a child, while at the same time calling attention to the deracinating nature of the colonizing process. While the book closely followed the grid established by the school of functional anthropology associated with Malinowski, focusing on the "system of tribal organization" in the first part and then on its dislocation by colonialism in the second half, Kenyatta considered his work unique because it was drawn from his own personal experience of Gikuyu life and was an intimate representation of his people's political grievances. After outlining his personal and political credentials, Kenyatta concluded his preface to *Facing Mount Kenya* by conjoining the authority of the private with that of the public:

> I can therefore speak as a representative of my people, with personal experience of many different aspects of their life. Finally, on the vitally important question of land tenure, I can claim to speak with more than ordinary knowledge, as I have explained in a note at the beginning of Chapter 2. The Gikuyu have chosen me as their spokesman before more than one Royal Commission on land matters. One was the Hilton Young Commission of 1928–29, and a second was the Joint Committee on the Closer Union of East Africa, in 1931–32. Before this Committee I was delegated to present a memorandum on behalf of the Gikuyu Central Association. In 1932 I gave evidence in London before the Morris Carter Kenya Land Commission, which presented its Report in 1934. I have studied and taken part in various discussions of this Report, and disputes arising out of it, among others the one about the removal of the Gikuyu people from their ancestral home in Tigoni; a matter which has been widely discussed in the Press and the House of Commons.   (xx)

Kenyatta's book was unique in three other respects: First, it was driven simultaneously by the desire to recover a usable Gikuyu past and by the need to produce a nationalist counterpoint to the culture of colonialism and its ethnography. Kenyatta made the question of land tenure, the major point of contention—indeed, the battlefield—between colonizer and colonized, the key to understanding Gikuyu social organization. He made the very rituals and practices the missionaries were opposing—polygamy and clidectomy, for example—pillars of the Gikuyu polity. Kenyatta's major success here was to use anthropology, a colonial instrument, against the colonizer's ambitions and notions.

Second, Kenyatta's work appealed to nationalists and pan-Africanists not simply because he was one of them, but because he had been able to present the social organization of an African culture as a rationale and structural phenomenon. It is crucial to note that while Kenyatta's work was explicitly anticolonial, it was not advocating a return to precolonial traditions, but for an alternative path to modernity. This is the point made poignantly at the end of *Facing Mount Kenya*:

> If Africans were left in peace on their own lands, Europeans would have to offer them the benefits of white civilisation in real earnest before they could obtain the African labour which they want so much. They would have to offer the African a way of life which was really superior to the one his fathers lived before him, and a share in the prosperity given them by their command of science. They would have to let the African choose what parts of European culture could be beneficially transplanted, and how they could be adapted. He would probably not choose the gas bomb or the armed police force, but he might ask for some other things of which he does not get so much to-day. As it is, by driving him off his ancestral lands, the Europeans

have robbed him of the material foundations of his culture, and reduced him to a state of serfdom incompatible with human happiness. The African is conditioned, by the cultural and social institutions of centuries, to a freedom of which Europe has little conception, and it is not in his nature to accept serfdom for ever. He realises that he must fight unceasingly for his own complete emancipation; for without this he is doomed to remain the prey of rival imperialisms, which in every successive year will drive their fangs more deeply into his vitality and strength.   (305–306)

Third, the significance of Kenyatta's book is in the influence it has had on the politics of cultural nationalism. It presented an image of precolonial African society as stable, self-generating, and enlightened, while colonialism was posited as the agency for instability and crisis. Indeed, in postcolonial Kenya the book became the official document of Gikuyu traditional culture, used in the educational system and the courts as a primary reference. Kenyatta wrote other minor ethnographic texts, but his later life was dominated by politics. Arrested and accused of being behind the Mau Mau movement in 1952, he was imprisoned for ten years in remote parts of Kenya, only to return triumphantly in 1962 as chief minister and later prime minister and president of the country.

PRIMARY TEXTS

Kenyatta, Jomo. *Facing Mount Kenya*. New York: Vintage Books, 1965. First published in London by Secker and Warburg, 1938.

REFERENCES

Desai, Gaurav. *Subject to Colonialism: African Self-Fashioning and the Colonial Library*. Durham, N.C.: Duke University Press, 2001.
Murray-Brown, Jeremy. *Kenyatta*. London: Allen and Unwin, 1972.

[Gikandi]

Keshubi, Hope (d. 2002) Ugandan novelist and educator. Born in Kabale in southwestern Uganda, Keshubi was educated at Bweranyangi and Kyebambe Girls' Schools; then at Kyambogo National Teachers College, from where she earned a diploma in education; the Institute of Teacher Education, where she received her bachelors degree; and the University College of St. Mark and St. John in the United Kingdom, where she earned a certificate in academic English and study skills for language teaching and linguistics. She was a founding member of Femrite, a women writers' movement in Uganda, and taught English and literature in various institutions in Uganda. She served as a chief editor of the *Northern Integrated Teacher Education Project* and worked as editor-in-chief of the *Support of Uganda Primary Educational Reform Project*. Her major works include *Going Solo* (1997), *To a Young Woman* (1997), and *Lopsided Justice*, which she managed to complete shortly before her death but remains unpublished.

PRIMARY TEXTS

Keshubi, Hope. *Going Solo*. Kampala: Fountain Publishers, 1997.
——. *To a Young Woman*. Kampala: Lukash Educational Publishers, 1997.
——. *Lopsided Justice*. Unpublished.

[Mwangi]

Kibera, Leonard (1942–1983) Kenyan novelist and short-story writer. Born in Kabete, outside Nairobi, Kibera was educated in local schools, the Kangaru Government School in Embu, and later at the University of California and Stanford University. After his graduate studies in the United States, he taught literature at the University of Lusaka in Zambia and later at Kenyatta University College in Kenya. Kibera came of age during the Mau Mau conflict of the 1950s, and his early short stories, in both their theme and form, reflect a young person's acute and painful perspective on the effects of that state of emergency on individuals and families. In these stories, collected in *Potent Ash*, published jointly with his brother Samuel Kahiga, Kibera was interested in capturing the struggle for survival by ordinary villagers caught in the violent clash between nationalists and colonial forces.

Writing at a time when Mau Mau was still a raw and contradictory force in many people's memories, Kibera was not interested in the larger political claims of the movement, but rather in how the violence that defined the colonial encounter affected social and communal relationships. While later writers on Mau Mau would either romanticize the movement or present it as the highest representation of nationalist ideology, Kibera was much more interested in the alienating effects of the logic of violence and its devastation of communities. In his stories in *Potent Ash*, this alienation could manifest in numerous ways: in the mean streets of the colonial city, in the unknown lives of strangers, and, most notably, in the ominous and malevolent landscape. Indeed, his most powerful stories tend to center exclusively on the alienating effect of nature (in the form of floods or dirty city streets, for example) or on the deep angst that grips individuals when they are confronted by the immensity of the forces they seem to have initiated—only to discover, belatedly, that they are mere cogs in the malevolent machine of time.

Kibera's early stories are crafted with care, but ultimately they are powerful because of the way they capture the immediacy of Mau Mau—the fear, anticipation, and terror—as it appeared to young people in the mid-1950s. Reviewing *Potent Ash* upon its publication in 1968, the distinguished English critic Arnold Kettle, then teaching at the University of East Africa, Dar es Salaam, called attention to the ability of Kibera and his brother Kahiga to produce stories that alternated between "over-sophisticated sensibility" and the "inherent conflicts" in the represented situation. Kettle preferred the inherent conflicts to the "over-sophisticated" sensibility.

But in *Voices in the Dark*, his only novel, published two years after the stories in *Potent Ash*, Kibera showed that a sophisticated sensibility, in particular a sense of modernist style, could be blended with a profound sense of the conflicts inherent in the confused and complicated cultures of postcolonialism. At times lyrical and satirical, Kibera's novel belongs to the literature of disillusionment produced by almost all major African writers in the late 1960s, which was concerned with the failure or betrayal of the hopes and dreams that had been used to rationalize the destructiveness of the 1950s. Here, Kibera would survey the new decolonized landscape through the prism of a subject at odds with the new dispensation, struggling, with a mixture of futility and bravado, to understand where decolonization had failed and, at the same time, to capture what he called "the uncertainties and the conflict" that emerged out of the new order of things. In order to represent the failure of decolonization and to present a sense of the rhetoric of failure that gripped intellectuals and artists such as Timundu, the antihero of the novel, Kibera accentuated the themes of alienation evident in his short stories, using a disjointed narrative structure and fragmented language matched only by two canonical novels published during the same period, Wole Soyinka's *The Interpreters* and Ayi Kwei Armah's *The Beautyful Ones Are Not Yet Born*.

PRIMARY TEXTS

Kibera, Leonard. *Potent Ash*. Nairobi: East African Publishing House, 1968.

———. *Voices in the Dark*. Nairobi: East African Publishing House, 1970.

REFERENCES

Gikandi, Simon. "The Growth of the East African Novel." In *The Writing of East and Central Africa*, edited by G. D. Killam, 231–246. London: Heinemann, 1984.

Walker, James Franklin. *Fingering the Wounds of Freedom: Leonard Kibera and the History of "Mau Mau."* MA thesis, University of Colorado, 1997.

[Gikandi]

Kimenye, Barbara (b. 1930) Ugandan writer of children's literature. Born in England, Kimenye was educated in Yorkshire and trained as a nurse in London. She started her writing career in East Africa, where she was best known for her *Moses* series, which depicts the adventures of a schoolboy. She worked as a private secretary for the Kabaka (king) of Buganda in the 1950s and early 1960s and later as a journalist for the now defunct Ugandan newspaper *The Nation*. Her other children's books include *The Smugglers* (1966), *Kayo's House* (1995), *The Gemstone Affair* (1978), *The Scoop* (1978), *The Mating Game* (1992), and *The Money Game* (1992). She has also written two volumes of lighthearted short stories that examine the conflict between modern ways and the institutions of traditional rule and power: *Kalasanda* appeared in 1965; *Kalasanda Revisited*, a year later. One of the stories from the *Kalasanda* series, "The Battle of the Sacred Tree," was turned into a feature film. Kimenye has also produced a series of fictional works intended to aid in the teaching of English in schools, including *Prettyboy, Beware* (1997) and *The Beauty Queen* (1997).

PRIMARY TEXTS

Kimenye, Barbara. *The Smugglers*. London: T. Nelson, 1966.

———. *The Gemstone Affair*. Sunbury-on-Thames, Middlesex: Nelson Africa, 1978.

———. *The Scoop*. Sunbury-on-Thames, Middlesex: Nelson Africa, 1978.

———. *Moses and the School Farm*. Nairobi: Oxford University Press, 1989.

———. *Moses and the Man from Mars*. Nairobi: Heinemann Kenya, 1991.

———. *Moses in a Mess*. Nairobi: Heinemann Kenya, 1991.

———. *The Mating Game*. London: Macmillan, 1992.

———. *The Money Game*. Oxford: Heinemann, 1992.

———. *Kayo's House*. London: Macmillan, 1995.

———. *The Beauty Queen*. Nairobi: East African Educational Publishers, 1997.

———. *Prettyboy, Beware*. Nairobi: East African Educational Publishers, 1997.

REFERENCES

Nazareth, Peter. "The Social Responsibility of the East African Writer." *Callaloo* 8, no. 10 (1980): 87–105.

Schmidt, Nancy J. "The Writer as Teacher: A Comparison of the African Adventure Stories of G. A. Henty, Rene Guillot, and Barbara Kimenye." *African Studies Review* 19, no. 2 (1976): 69–80.

[Mwangi]

Kiriamiti, John (b. 1950) Kenyan writer of popular fiction. Since he first appeared on the scene in the 1980s, Kiriamiti's novels of crime and urban life have been bestsellers in Africa. His first novel, *My Life in Crime* (1984), is a fictional autobiography of a professional robber, largely based on Kiriamiti's experiences as a bank robber and jailbird. The author was imprisoned in 1970 for committing a robbery and was released in

1984. Although largely autobiographical—and indeed it claims in the preface to be a truthful account—*My Life in Crime* is laced with fictional details and captures the crime wave that rocked East Africa, especially Kenya and Uganda, in the 1960s and 1970s. Its sequel, *My Life with a Criminal: Milly's Story* (1989), retells the story of the robber from the perspective of his fiancée, while *Son of Fate* (1994) narrates the difficulties the main character has adjusting to rural life after his release from prison. He returns to the city, where he relapses into crime and becomes a hunted person, until he saves a rich man from the jaws of a python. Its sequel, *The Sinister Trophy* (1999), is about the hunt for the main character, who is considered a trophy because of the price on his head.

Like his first novel, Kiriamiti's *My Life in Prison* (2004) narrates in an autobiographical voice, vouchsafed in the preface and in the story as the narrator's own, the writer's experiences in prison for violent robbery. Insisting on its realism just as his other novels do, it explains the reception of the author's first work by the jailers and hints in a paratextual statement that prison conditions might have changed as a result of the reforms initiated by the Narc government. The story then reveals the dehumanizing conditions in Kenyan prisons, where the warders are as brutalized as the prisoners and are as addicted to their lowly jobs as the prisoners are to crime: "I could see from the warder's face that his life wasn't a picnic. I felt I would rather be employed as a grave digger than look for a job as a warder. I never met a warder who is proud of his work in all the years I have been with them." While Kiriamiti's earlier fiction at times seemed to glorify crime through its breathtaking and detailed descriptions of swashbuckling encounters, his later fiction has a contrite ring to it. His fiction is lighthearted but—if only unconsciously—also reveals the gross abuse of human rights, corruption of the Kenyan police, and the alienating effects of crime.

PRIMARY TEXTS

Kiriamiti, John. *My Life in Crime*. Nairobi: Heinemann Educational Books, 1984.

——. *My Life with a Criminal: Milly's Story*. Nairobi: Spear Books, 1989.

——. *Son of Fate*. Nairobi: Spear Books, 1994.

——. *The Sinister Trophy*. Nairobi: Spear Books, 1999.

——. *My Life in Prison*. Nairobi: Spear Books, 2004.

[Mwangi]

Kulet, Henry ole (b. 1946) Kenyan popular novelist. Kulet's writing expresses and sometimes questions the identity of the traditional Maasai community in postindependence East Africa. He combines autobiography with history and politics to depict a society both in need of change and self-preservation. Kulet admires the empire-building narratives of H. Rider Haggard, whose *Allan Quatermain* is echoed powerfully in Kulet's first novel, *Is It Possible?* (1971), the story of the young man Lerionka, whose first name, Henry, is shared by both the author and the protagonist of Haggard's story. Lerionka receives a Western education and becomes one of the modern men in his conservative society. Written in an autobiographical narrative mode, the novel expresses and at the same time contests the possibilities of combining African traditions with Western modernity. The central dilemma in the novel is posed by the narrator's father: "How do you expect a man to be able to hold the heavy spear in one hand, the stick in the other, and the books at the same time? It is impossible. Impossible, I say." The novel depicts the role of the school as a tool of alienation, but it also ponders how modern education can be made integral to the needs of the culturally proud community.

Kulet's second novel, *To Become a Man* (1971), is also the story of an only son who is caught at the crossroads of culture and modernity. Formal education, office employment, and circumcision in hospitals are presented vis-à-vis the traditional acts of expressing one's manhood. According to the Maasai, all the cattle in the world are their property, and one affirms one's manhood by raiding other communities for cattle. Give a choice between one hundred modern houses and a sick cow, Ole Merreshho, a village elder, would "definitely and with pride take the sick cow." In the society presented in the novel, modern laws punish Maasai men who raided other communities for cattle. Leshao, the main character, tries to negotiate what manhood means in the contemporary world before he accepts the traditional definition and returns, crippled, to his family, to face a prison sentence. He is lucky to be alive, but he is not a man; the novel, through Leshao's father, asks as the story ends, "What's a man without a leg?" The narrative seems to suggest that one does not have to harass other communities to be a man.

Daughter of Maa (1987) presents an old theme in African literature—the competition between an old man and an educated upstart for a beautiful educated girl. *Moran No More* (1990) bemoans the corruption eating at the vitality of postindependence Kenya, while celebrating the new possibilities offered by modern living. *The Hunter* (1986) narrates the story of a renegade Maasai man, Richmond Sipaya, who is the epitome of all that is evil in his society. In an evil/virtuous dichotomy, Sipaya, who is Christian, is contrasted with Leseiyo, a traditional Maasai now living in the city after refusing to attend high school. Modernity is shown to be inevitable, but the text seems to argue for the respect of Maasai culture as

well. While Kulet's early novels *To Become a Man* and *Moran No More* seem to question some of the fundamental Maasai beliefs, his later works, such as *Bandits of Kibi* (1990), oppose the ethnocentrism that plagued Kenya in the 1990s and resulted in vicious communal clashes in 1992.

PRIMARY TEXTS

Kulet, Henry ole. *To Become a Man.* Nairobi: Longman Kenya, 1971.
——. *The Hunter.* Nairobi: Longman Kenya, 1985.
——. *Daughter of Maa.* Nairobi: Longman Kenya, 1987.
——. *Bandits of Kibi.* Nairobi: Longhorn Publishers, 1990.
——. *Moran No More.* Nairobi: Longman Kenya, 1990.

REFERENCES

Dorsey, David. "The Silence of a Maasai Novel: Kulet's *Is It Possible?*" *Alif: Journal of Comparative Poetics* 17 (1997): 22–42.
Mwangi, Evan. "I to I in the Narrative Mirror: Fictional Autobiography and the Problem of Maasai Identity in Henry Ole Kulet's Writings." *English Studies in Africa* 44, no. 1, (2001): 13–30.

[Mwangi]

Kyomuhendo, Goretti (b. 1965) Ugandan writer, editor, and publisher. Kyomuhendo was the first Ugandan female writer to participate in the International Writing Program at the University of Iowa in 1997. She was a founding member and coordinator of Femrite, a leading women writers' organization in East Africa; she is an Honorary Fellow of Creative Writing at the University of Iowa. Her first novel, *The First Daughter* (1996), is a story about growing up in rural Africa, and it explores the problems girls experience in a polygamous family with few chances to improve their social condition. It celebrates the resilience of the women who are constantly working to overcome patriarchal domination and gender discrimination. *Secrets No More* (1999) portrays the plight of Rwandese refugees and their resilience in exile. Weaving together adventure and political violence, the story revolves around the life of Marina, a refugee who has been rendered powerless by civil war and patriarchy but still manages to survive and exert her own power in a society where she is considered marginal. *Whispers from Vera* (2002) is the fictional first-person confessional account of a modern, emancipated African woman, describing and discussing her relationships with men. Kyomuhendo has also written children's books, the most acclaimed of which is *Different World* (1997).

PRIMARY TEXTS

Kyomuhendo, Goretti. *The First Daughter.* Kampala: Fountain, 1996.

——. *Different World.* Kampala: Monitor, 1997.

——. *Secrets No More.* Kampala: Femrite, 1999.

——. *Whispers from Vera.* Kampala: Monitor, 2002.

[Mwangi]

Language Question The language question is perhaps one of the most controversial issues in African literature, regardless of region. It revolves around two simple questions, both with wide political and cultural ramifications: What is the ideal language for producing an African literature? And can literatures written in European languages be considered African? This contentious debate has its origins in East Africa. Obi Wali, a young Nigerian writer and critic, startled participants at the historic 1962 Makerere Conference on African Literature by asserting that writing in European languages represented the "dead end" of African literature. Wali's claim was that genuine African literature could only be written in African languages. More importantly, he argued that only literature in African languages could enable "a truly African sensibility." This claim was startling because although there was a long history of writing in African languages, especially in East Africa, none of the leading writers in that tradition had been invited to the Makerere conference. It was taken for granted that genuine African literature could be and was produced in European languages. Indeed, this was the claim supported by the major figures invited to the conference, including Chinua Achebe, Ngugi was Thiong'o, and Ezekiel Mphahlele.

So powerful was the claim that European languages were perfectly capable of carrying what Achebe called "the weight of my African experience" and that these languages had become transformed "to suit new African surroundings" that for two decades after Wali's challenge the issue of language was sidelined in critical debates, and two separate and not always equal traditions of literature were consolidated on the continent, one in European languages, the other in African ones. This continued until 1978, when Ngugi, himself a staunch supporter of European-language writing in the 1960s, made his decisive break with writing in English and declared, in a series of essays published in *Writers in Politics* and *Decolonising the Mind*, that the literature produced by Africans in European languages belonged to an "Afro-European" literature tradition. Ngugi argued that literature could only be part of a liberating African perspective and African sensibility if it was written in African languages. This claim was to generate heated debates and deep divisions among

African writers and critics, not simply because it went to the heart of the role of language in the shaping of the literary imagination, but because it called attention to the sensitive nature of the politics of language in Africa. Why did the language question seem to generate the most heated debates in East Africa than almost anywhere else on the continent?

Overall, the debates on language in Africa reflect the complex linguistic geography of the continent. Hundreds of languages are spoken in each country in the region, but these languages exist in unequal and uneven relationships. In addition, when the colonial powers divided the region among themselves in the late 1880s, they did so without consideration of the autonomy or integrity of linguistic groups, so it was not unusual for people speaking a common language to find themselves in different countries. The Somali-speaking population of the horn of Africa found itself belonging to two Somalias (one Italian, the other, British), French-controlled Djibouti, Kenya, and Ethiopia. For these reasons among others, the language question has been central to issues of social identity in Africa and is often tied up with the complex politics of colonialism and nationalism.

Furthermore, colonial governments in the region had ambivalent language policies that affected the process of social and cultural change. They promoted the colonial language as the bearer of superior culture and civilization, yet they confined it to a small elite, leaving the majority of the population to acquire literacy in their vernaculars or panregional languages like Swahili. African nationalists and postcolonial governments inherited this ambivalence and responded to it in diverse ways. In the case of Kenya and Uganda, nationalists and the postcolonial elite sought the expansion of European languages as a gateway to modernity; in Tanzania, the promotion of Swahili

as a national language was considered central to the process of decolonization and development, a point affirmed in the Arusha Declaration of 1967. Somewhere in this linguistic geography, African languages continued to be used by the populace without any official status except as agents of elementary or adult education.

The language situation was made even more complex by the fact that African languages were often seen as markers of ethnic or regional differences. There were often unspoken fears that the promotion of cultural work in one local language would be detrimental to the project of national unity. Indeed, the strongest reactions against Ngugi's turn to Gikuyu were not so much that he had given up English, but that writing in Gikuyu would enforce ethnic chauvinism or political hegemony. The claim that authors could invent ethnicities was a dubious one, but, nevertheless, it shaped the tempo of the language debate in Kenya. In Somalia, on the other hand, writers like Nurrudin Farah turned to writing in English in order to undermine the authority of the Somali language, which, these writers felt, enforced retrograde, clannish traditions and the military dictatorship of Siad Barre, which had its own protonationalist notion of Somalia and Somaliness.

Ironically, the British colonial government in the East African territories had been a major promoter of literature in African languages, through the East African Literature Bureau. As a consequence, in the colonial period English was a language with social prestige but no literature. In reaction against the ideologies of vernacularism favored by the colonial government, most of the new publishing houses and universities that flowered after decolonization tended to privilege writing and publishing in English, leading to a remarkable renaissance in English literature in the 1960s, 1970s, and after, in Kenya and Uganda. The one exception was in Tanzania, where English had been subordinated to Swahili. A literary tradition in English was almost entirely absent there. Although a powerful tradition of writing in African languages such as Swahili, Somali, and Amharic went back several centuries, this literature was marginalized in regional literary histories. Conspicuously absent from the Makerere conference of 1962, to cite one telling example, was the region's most famous poet, Shabaan Roberts, who wrote in Swahili. East African literature thus entered the global map as literature in English. But the debate on language did not disappear. It simmered on the edges of critical debates until it was rekindled by Ngugi's 1978 decision to write in Gikuyu.

The reignited debate on language took three forms. First, there continued the argument that the question of language was not simply about linguistic choice, but that it went to the heart of the identity of African literature: it was about the epistemological or thematic concerns of this literature and its intended audience. If the goal of literature was to intervene in debates about the process of political and cultural change, as many of the leading authors from the region insisted, then its social mission was constricted by the simple fact that it was only addressed to and consumed by a tiny minority, those privileged enough to know English. Second, there was a strong nationalist argument that since language was the mark of national belonging, true selfhood, and proper consciousness, only the use of an African language would liberate writers from the colonial complex. In 1962, Obi Wali had made the explicit connection between African languages and an "African sensibility"; twenty years later, Ngugi would associate these languages with the most essential forms of identity. Third, the language question was not simply determined by the opposition between English and African languages. In East Africa, it was a three-way debate between the proponents of English as the universal language of culture, old and new supporters of African languages, and promoters of pan-African languages such as Swahili. Not surprisingly, the structure of the language debate reflected competing political visions on the national and regional level. In Ethiopia and Somalia, the authority of two African languages (Amharic and Somali) was so strong that it was barely contested. In fact, in those two countries the African languages were associated with the feudal order or the military dictatorships that succeeded it. In Ethiopia and Somalia, writing in English was peripheral to the literary culture; the writers in English were a tiny fragment of the whole. In Uganda, where literary culture had for almost fifty years revolved around Makerere University College, the centrality of English was rarely questioned, except by writers in exile such as Okot p'Bitek.

In Tanzania, on the other hand, the authority of Swahili as the national language was established as official doctrine in the Arusha Declaration of 1967. It was not surprising that some of the most vocal advocates for Swahili as a panregional language, scholars such as Gabriel Ruhumbika and Joseph Mbele, were from Tanzania. They opposed both the privileging of English, the colonial language, and the privileging of vernaculars, which they dismissed as the idioms of narrow ethnicities. In Kenya, there was an almost even split between the advocates of English (supported by a section of the political elite), practitioners of Swahili literature, and the supporters of the vernaculars, which Ngugi came to call the language of individual nationalities. And because Ngugi was at the time considered to be an enemy of the ruling elite, his views on language in the 1980s were often a reflection of the struggle between the conservative one-party state and its radical opponents.

Still, Ngugi's "conversion" to the vernacular in the late 1970s represented the most radical position in Kenyan debates about language, and was thus seen as disturbing the status quo. In his manifesto on language, *Decolonising the Mind*, Ngugi's main argument was that the choice of language was central to social understanding and psychological stability; language was not merely a mode of communication but the bearer of fundamental cultural values. He argued that a literature produced in European languages could not be considered part of the African tradition, since it perpetuated the unquestioned logic of colonial traditions and assumptions. Only African languages could be considered to represent the struggle of African peoples against imperialism. Concluding that European languages impoverished African literature, Ngugi posited his turn to Gikuyu as part and parcel of the struggle to decolonize the African mind.

But this turn to Gikuyu, and the debates surrounding it, did not resolve some of the structural problems that had plagued the search for an African literary tradition at the time of the Makerere Conference and Obi Wali's challenge: Who were the readers of African literature? What made it distinctive from other forms of writing? And could the choice of language alone transform the genres and conventions that African writers had inherited from Europe both through their colonial education and as members of the global community? What was evident from a reading of Ngugi's Gikuyu novels such as *Caitaani Mutharaba-ini* (*Devil on the Cross*) and *Matigari* is that while the vernacular had not helped him escape from the tradition of the European novel, it had given him access to hitherto neglected resources of oral and popular expression.

At the same time, for Ngugi, in exile, to write in Gikuyu also meant being distanced from his literary sources and his audience. The gap between the writer and his context was most evident in *Murogi wa Kagogo*, a fable about the politics of dictatorship in Kenya, whose informing context is metropolitan American debates on postcolonialness and hybrid identities. Finally, students of literary language in East Africa have to consider how English itself has been transformed through its use in postcolonial spaces. One of the most interesting linguistic phenomena in the region, which has yet to be registered in its literature but is the key to musical forms, is the emergence of Sheng, a combination of English, Swahili, and ethnic languages popular with urban youth.

REFERENCES

Achebe, Chinua. "The African Writer and the English Language." In *Morning Yet on Creation Day*, 55–62. London: Heinemann, 1975.

Bjornson, Richard. "The Language Question." Special issue of *Research in African Literatures* 23, no. 1 (Spring 1992).

Ngugi wa Thiong'o. *Decolonising the Mind: The Politics of Language in African Literature*. London: James Currey, 1986.

Wali, Obi. "The Dead End of African Literature." *Transition* 3, no. 10 (1963): 13–14.

[Gikandi]

Lihamba, Amandina (b. 1944) Tanzanian actress, playwright, film producer, educator, and university administrator. Educated at Yale University in the United States and the University of Leeds in the United Kingdom, Lihamba has served as the Dean of the Faculty of Arts and Social Sciences at the University of Dar es Salaam. She is renowned for her work in culture, gender, women, youth and children, and development issues. She has acted as a consultant to organizations and institutions including UNICEF, various international development agencies, the Tanzania National Arts Council, the Ministry of Education and

Culture, the Forum for African Education-alists, the Popular Theatre Alliance, and the Tanzania Commission for Sciences and Technology.

Lihamba has been a pioneer practitioner of theater for community development, seeking to integrate African performance into economic and social development ef-forts, in order to enable marginalized com-munities and children to have a platform through which they can express themselves and discuss issues affecting both their and their countries' development. In programs that have been replicated in Kenya, Zim-babwe, Zambia, and Ethiopia, Lihamba has lobbied the Tanzanian government to inte-grate children's theater into the school pro-grams, to facilitate locally relevant learning and help students develop leadership skills. The success of her community-theater methodology has been registered in projects implemented in rural areas where women are not allowed to speak in public and in campaigns to combat the spread of HIV/AIDS. Her article "Health and the Afri-can Theatre" explores the representation in performance and theater of contrasting ap-proaches to the understanding of disease-causality explanations. She examines the at-titudes toward health, disease, and cure manifested in traditional and contemporary African performances. Her "Politics and Theatre in Tanzania After the Arusha Decla-ration, 1967–1984" is a detailed examination of the transformations of theater and per-formance practices to promote and contest nationalist ideology.

As a creative writer, Lihamba works mostly in Swahili. Her play *Mkutano wa Pili wa Ndege* (*The Second Conference of Birds*, 1991) dramatizes the disillusionment with *ujamaa* socialist nationalism adopted by the Tanzanian government since the 1960s. Her other major play, *Harakati za Ukombozi* (*The Struggle for Liberation*, 1977), was coau-thored with Penina Mhando and May M. Balisidya. Though sponsored by the socialist Tanzanian government, the play satirizes postcolonial leaders who mouth socialist mantras on political platforms but do not practice what they preach.

Lihamba is also a prominent figure in East African film, and her credits include performing in, directing, and producing *Arusi ya Mariamu* (*Mariamu's Wedding*, 1985), *Maangamizi: The Ancient One* (2001), *Uhai Bongo* (*Bongo Life*), *City Fishers*, *Khalfani Khalfani*, and *Sobi*. She played a stellar role as Samehe in *Maangamizi: The Ancient One*, a film about an African-American woman psychiatrist who secures an appointment at a Tanzanian mental hos-pital and gets an opportunity to delve into the past of a withdrawn patient and redis-cover, through the patient's communication with ancestral spirits, the interconnections between Africa and the black diaspora.

PRIMARY TEXTS

Lihamba, Amandina. *Mkutano wa Pili wa Ndege* [*The Second Conference of Birds*]. Dar es Salaam: Dar es Salaam University Press, 1992.

Lihamba, Amandina, Penina Mhando, and May M. Balisidya. *Harakati za Ukombozi* [*Struggle for Liberation*]. Dar es Salaam: Tanzania Publishing House, 1982.

CRITICISM

Lihamba, Amandina. "Politics and Theatre in Tanzania After the Arusha Declara-tion, 1967–1984." PhD diss., University of Leeds, 1985.

——. "Women's Peace Building and Con-flict Resolution Skills, Morogoro Region, Tanzania." In *Women and Peace in Africa*, 111–131. Paris: UNESCO Workshops, 2003.

[Mwangi]

Likimani, Muthoni Gachanja (b. 1940)
Kenyan novelist, poet, nutritionist, welfare

officer, teacher, broadcaster, and women's rights activist. Likimani was educated in Kahuhia Mission in Kenya and in Britain, and her writing reflects the tensions and possibilities between Western and African cultural practices. Her novel *They Shall Be Chastised* (1974) examines the conflict between African traditional culture and missionary practices. While criticizing the missionaries for their disregard for Gikuyu culture, the novel also casts a disapproving gaze at some traditional practices, though it offers what has been read by some critics (such as Tobe Levin) as a tacit apologia for female genital mutilation. While autobiographical, *Passbook Number F. 47927: Women and Mau Mau in Kenya* (1985) highlights women's contributions to the nationalist struggle for independence against British colonialism in the 1950s. Her narrative poem *What Does a Man Want?* (1974) is a light-hearted critique of male privilege. Men are portrayed as passing themselves off as mysterious and inaccessible, pretences that can lead a woman to despair and apathy. The poem explores ways in which women can come to terms with ubiquitous male unfaithfulness and domestic violence without relapsing into prostitution or self-pity. She has represented Kenyan women at major international conferences, including the United Nations Decade for Women in 1985, and has written political essays on women's development efforts. In 1994, she was honored with the National Council of Women of Kenya Award for her role in advancing women's rights in Kenya.

PRIMARY TEXTS

Likimani, Muthoni Gachanja. *They Shall Be Chastised*. Nairobi: East African Literature Bureau, 1974.

——. *What Does a Man Want?* Nairobi: Kenya Literature Bureau, 1974.

——. *Passbook Number F. 47927: Women and Mau Mau in Kenya*. Houndmills: Macmillan, 1985.

REFERENCES

Clough, Marshall S. *Mau Mau Memoirs: History, Memory, and Politics*. Boulder, Colo.: Lynne Rienner, 1998.

Kurtz, J. Roger. *Urban Obsessions, Urban Fears: The Postcolonial Kenyan Novel*. Trenton, N.J.: Africa World Press, 1998.

Levin, Tobe. "Female Genital Mutilation and Human Rights." *Comparative American Studies* 1, no. 3 (2003): 285–316.

Peterson, Derek R. *Creative Writing: Translation, Bookkeeping, and the Work of Imagination in Colonial Kenya*. Portsmouth, N.H.: Heinemann, 2004.

[Mwangi]

Literary Theory and Criticism Literary theory and criticism is dual in nature, reaching back to the traditional aesthetics of precolonial Africa and adapting Western theories of literary evaluation. So central is colonialism as a discursive reference point in East African culture that, while emphasizing the independence of the African value system, the various schools of literary criticism and theory that have emerged from the region are all haunted by colonial modernity and its consequences. Because of its grounding in precolonial and oral literary standards of evaluation that insisted on the moral component of art and because of the influence of the Leavisite "Great Tradition" offered in East African universities founded on the British model, East African theory and criticism is marked by an insistence on the educative value of art.

Although art for art's sake exists in both precolonial and postcolonial traditions, it is traditionally looked down upon in favor of more politically engaged and morally poignant cultural production. Particularly critical of popular literature, which he views as art for art's sake, is Chris Wanjala, in *For Home and Freedom* and *Season of Harvest*. Wanjala employs a markedly Leavisite approach that subscribes to a high/low hierarchy of art. While there are various inflections in the schools of criticism, there seems to be a consensus about the necessity for the political and moral intervention of art from the region to help heal the wounds created by colonial subjugation and its consequences.

One of the earliest schools of criticism follows the "cultural revolution" trajectory founded by Ugandan poet Okot p'Bitek, whose series of essays published in his *Africa's Cultural Revolution* (1973) have been foundational in attempting to establish an aesthetics that reinstates precolonial traditional artistic production and procedures of evaluation. Following Negritude principles articulated by Francophones Aime Cesaire and Leopold Sedar Senghor since the 1930s, Okot p'Bitek, in an Anglophone context, works to recover the precolonial ethnic creative practices and critical standards. Insisting on ethnomethodological approaches to literature, Okot p'Bitek not only calls upon writers to draw on the precolonial practices of East African communities, but he also argues that one cannot analyze a literary work unless one is fully familiar with the culture of the community from which the work comes. Okot p'Bitek proposes that it is only critics who have participated in the rituals and daily activities of particular East African communities who can evaluate "how effective the song or dance is; how the decoration, the architecture, the plan of the village has contributed to the feast of life; how these have made life meaningful." Aligning himself with Romantic theorists, Okot p'Bitek deemphasizes the place of academics in the production of good art and criticism and tries to reestablish spontaneous response to art, as was the case in live folk literary performances. In "What is Literature?" he argues that formal training in literary criticism does not necessary make one a good critic: "Literature must not be allowed to degenerate into a quest of 'knowledge,' to be attained through pains. The false belief that a certificate in literature is a necessary qualification for the enjoyment of literature must be rejected, together with other false assumptions that the ability to quote Homer or Shakespeare is a mark of 'education' or refinement." In *Artist the Ruler*, a series of essays on African culture, Okot p'Bitek invokes Percy Bysshe Shelley's notion of artists as legislators to emphasize the critical role of the artist in modern society, but he rejects Jean-Jacques Rousseau's existentialist argument that man is born free. For Okot p'Bitek, the artist is inextricably tied to the society from birth and has to reflect the values of the community.

While agreeing with Okot p'Bitek on the importance of traditions and culture, Ngugi wa Thiong'o (in the introduction to Okot p'Bitek's *Africa's Cultural Revolution*) supports a Marxist-inflected approach to culture and literature. Citing Kenyatta's *Facing Mount Kenya*, Ngugi argues that the reason East Africans have abandoned their culture is because of political and economic dispossession by colonialism. He develops this argument further in *Homecoming*, where he argues:

> Literature does not grow or even develop in a vacuum; it is given impetus, shape, direction and even area of concern by social, political and economic forces in a particular society. The relationship between creative literature and these other forces cannot be ignored, especially in Africa, where modern literature has grown against the gory background of European imperialism and its changing manifestations: slavery, colonialism and neocolonialism. Our culture over the last hundred years has developed against the same stunting dwarfing background. (xv)

Ngugi and a number of critics and theorists such as Grant Kamenju and Leonard Kibera have used Frantz Fanon's *Black Skin, White*

Masks to theorize the destructive nature of colonialism and Fanon's *The Wretched of the Earth* to come to terms with the betrayal of constitutional independence in Africa. These are themes with which the literature itself was grappling. Kenyan critic Grant Kamenju, operating from Dar es Salaam, also emphasizes a Marxist approach to African literature. However, Ngugi deemphasized Fanon's more personalized experience of trauma in favor of a communitarian understanding of the effects of colonialism. Peter Nazareth's criticism in *The Third World Writer: His Social Responsibility and Literature and Society in East Africa* and *Literature and Society in Modern Africa* combines historical approaches with sociological and moral analyses of the literature. He underscores "social responsibility" as an imperative in African writing and states that even literature produced outside of Marxist aesthetics qualifies for a Marxist reading.

On the other end of the spectrum, Taban Lo Liyong adopts an existentialist approach to literary criticism in his *The Last Word* and encourages more experimental writing. While fellow critics endorsed the unambiguous presentation of political issues, Lo Liyong prioritized stylistic innovation, and he wrote poetry and short stories that, compared to contemporaneous literary production, were solipsistic. Theorists in the 1960s and 1970s emphasized pan-Africanist ideals espoused by Negritude. Following Ngugi's *Homecoming*, a collection of essays on African and Caribbean literature, comparative work on literatures throughout the African diaspora emphasized the shared values among people of African descent. However, Lo Liyong not only dismissed the veracity of Negritude but also declared African Americans non-Africans.

Criticism since the 1980s has been more heterogeneous, with critics applying various theories in local contexts. At the same time, academics avoided government reprisal by adopting formalistic approaches. Henry Indangasi's stylistic approach gained favor because, while emphasizing the formal and structural qualities of art, it also highlighted its moral and thematic content. While maintaining a Leavisite posture, Chris Wanjala applied a Hegelian approach to the study of alienation. The 1980s also saw the introduction of feminist approaches. Kavetsa Adagala examined Ngugi's female character Wanja in *Petals of Blood* from a Marxist perspective. Delivered in praise of Ngugi's gender consciousness at a time when Ngugi was a vilified subject in Kenya, Adagala's essay is radical in perspective but fails to see the blind spots in Ngugi's portrayal of women, a subject taken up by Elleke Boehmer, Florence Stratton, and Brendon Nicholls, among others. In the 1990s, critics examined the stereotypes of women in male novels and traditional oral literature while at the same time celebrating female agency in novels by both men and women. The critics seemed cautious about fully endorsing Western feminism.

The poststructuralist wave entered East Africa in the 1980s and 1990s, but the critics tenaciously held on to the notion of close readings that were politically engaged as opposed to the solipsism associated with postmodern theory; there remained an emphasis on considering the political and social referent when analyzing the literature. Peter Amuka studied East African oral literature from a deconstructionist perspective, but emphasized the local values and interpretations signaled by the artists. Indangasi also read Ngugi wa Thiong'o using reader-response criticism to show that Ngugi's "ideal reader" is multiple and in flux.

The arrival of poststructuralist theory, which disrupts binary hierarchies, also saw the rise of interest in popular culture, which had previously been relegated to the realm of the nonserious. Critics used different aspects of poststructuralism to study the postcolonial condition in the region as presented in popular art, especially the use of popular culture to construct and deconstruct national and gender identities. Among others, James Ogude, Joyce Nyairo, Mwenda Ntaragwi, Werner Graebner, Kelly Michelle Askew, Kimani Njogu, Douglas B. Paterson, Atieno-Odhiambo, Frank Gunderson, and Gregory F. Barz discussed popular music and culture as a productive site where political consciousness was shaped and dominant identities and ideologies challenged.

REFERENCES

Adagala, Kavetsa. "Wanja of *Petals of Blood*: A Study of the Women Question and Imperialism in Kenya." Seminar presentation, University of Nairobi, April 30, 1981.

p'Bitek, Okot. *Africa's Cultural Revolution*. Nairobi: Macmillan, 1973.

——. *Artist the Ruler. Essays on Art, Culture, and Values*. Nairobi: East African Educational Publishers, 1986.

Chesaina, Ciarunji. *Perspectives on Women in African Literature*. Nairobi: Impact, 1994.

Lo Liyong, Taban. *The Last Word: Cultural Synthesism*. Nairobi: East African Publishing House, 1969.

Nazareth, Peter. *Literature and Society in Modern Africa: Essays on Literature*. Nairobi: East African Literature Bureau, 1972.

——. *The Third World Writer: His Social Responsibility*. Nairobi: Kenya Literature Bureau, 1978.

Ngugi wa Thiong'o. *Writers in Politics*. Nairobi: East African Educational Publishers, 1981.

——. *Decolonising the Mind: The Politics of Language in African Literature*. Nairobi: East African Educational Publishers, 1986.

Wanjala, Chris L. *The Season of Harvest: Some Notes on East African Literature*. Nairobi: Kenya Literature Bureau, 1978.

——. *For Home and Freedom*. Nairobi: East African Publishing House, 1980.

——. "The Growth of a Literary Tradition in East Africa." Inaugural lecture, University of Nairobi, 2003.

[Mwangi]

Lo Liyong, Taban (b. 1938) Ugandan poet, essayist, and academic. Considered one of the most controversial and iconoclastic figures in East African writing, Taban Lo Liyong was born in a Lwo family in the southern Sudan and grew up in northern Uganda. He was educated at Gulu High School and later attended the Sir Samuel Barker School, where he was a student of the poet Okot p'Bitek. After high school, Taban, as he is popularly known, studied at Howard University in the United States. It was while he was a student at Howard that Lo Liyong began to reflect on the place of East African literature in the emerging field of African letters, a process that led him to write and publish "Can We Correct Literary Barrenness in East Africa?" This was a powerful and polemic essay that was to shock writers in the region out of their complacency. Later, Lo Liyong studied at the famous writers' workshop at the University of Iowa, where he was the first African to be awarded an MFA degree in creative writing. In the late 1960s, Lo Liyong joined the University of Nairobi, where he initially worked as a researcher in the Institute of Cultural Studies, specializing in the oral traditions of the Lwo. In 1968, he joined the English department at the University of Nairobi where, together with his African colleagues Ngugi wa Thiong'o and Owuor Anyumba, he argued for the abolition of the English department and the establishment of a "Department of Literature," which would have a primary focus on the oral and written literatures of the African peoples. In 1969, Lo Liyong was the first teacher of a course in

African oral literature, and one of his most influential texts, *Popular Culture of East Africa*, was a collection of materials submitted by his students, many of whom would later occupy influential positions as teachers and publishers in East Africa. In the mid-1970s, Lo Liyong was a lecturer at the University of Papua New Guinea. He taught at universities in Australia and Japan before moving to South Africa in the late 1980s to teach at the University of Venda.

In general, Lo Liyong's essays and poems are notable for his deployment of the techniques and arguments of the international avant-garde. He has cast himself as the cultural gadfly of the region, casting aspersions at all the major players in the cultural debates that have characterized the emergence of postcolonial culture. Lo Liyong advocates a politics of culture driven by a self-conscious rejection of both political and poetic conventions; he has posited writing as a form of blasphemy against established cultural institutions. Often aphoristic in character, Lo Liyong's poetry frequently functions as a metacommentary on the desire to produce a form of writing that is defined by its irreverence toward the canon of both Western and African letters. In both his poems and essays, he has presented his task as that of a superman rejecting the established authority of culture and language. At the center of Lo Liyong's poetics is the myth of the poet as superman, the Nietzschean character who has confronted the limits of society and transcended them, driven by the belief in the rational will of the singular individual. This philosophy of life—of the triumph of the soul over conventions of religion and society—is summed up in Lo Liyong's preface to *The Uniformed Man* (1971), a collection of essays: "Nature and culture are broken; art which mirrors them can only correctly register broken images." In this content, the work of art is not the site of a return to tradition or an embrace of moder-

nity, but is rather the contradictory register of the ways that culture and nature have become separated or broken in the modern period. Lo Liyong's works thus valorize the fragmentary and incomplete, the repetitive and indeterminate. At the same time, however, his works are powerfully allusive, drawing upon the authority of the European canon he loves to deride and informed by a keen sense of the very postcolonial political movements such as Negritude and pan-Africanism he has set out to deconstruct.

But perhaps a better way to think about Lo Liyong's work is to approach it according to the key periods in which it emerged: the late 1960s, early 1970s, and the 1990s, when he returned to writing after a long hiatus. There is a distinctiveness, for example, to the cluster of poems and essays published in the late 1960s, when Lo Liyong positioned himself as both the defender of the interests and character of the African against American prejudices and as a powerful critic of the ideologies of Africanness popular in the period. Quite often, works from this period seek to shift from one vector to another, from a defense of Africanism to its radical deconstruction. *Fixions* (1969) and *Eating Chiefs* (1971), for example, display Lo Liyong as the defender of African cultures, recuperating, transmitting, and interpreting folktales and songs. But in the collections of essays from the same period, most notably *The Last Word* (1969), *The Uniformed Man* (1971), and *Meditations in Limbo* (1970), Lo Liyong's harsh satire is directed against the claims of the canon of African letters and the whole project of cultural nationalism.

The same pattern is repeated in his poems from the same period. For example, the poems collected in *Frantz Fanon's Uneven Ribs* were part of Lo Liyong's subversive project, namely, a systematic misreading of Western history and its canon in order to create a space for the African's voice. But the process was reversed in *Ballads of Underde-*

velopment (1976), where Lo Liyong undermined the philosophical and poetic basis of an African tradition. Finally, a second phase in Lo Liyong's creative output is evident in the poems published after his return to Africa in the 1980s. He still retains his satirical voice, but the aphorisms have almost disappeared from his poetry and a more lyrical note seems to mark his engagement with the crisis of postcolonialism, often seen, as in *Carrying Knowledge up a Palm Tree* and *The Cows of Shamba*, from the vantage point of fifty years of experience, in which an engagement with the problems of Africa is mediated through the prism of home, exile, and return.

PRIMARY TEXTS

Lo Liyong, Taban. *Fixions, and Other Stories.* London: Heinemann Educational, 1969.

——. *The Last Word: Cultural Synthesism.* Nairobi: East African Publishing House, 1969.

——. *Eating Chiefs: Lwo Culture from Lolwe to Malkal.* London: Heinemann Educational, 1970.

——. *Frantz Fanon's Uneven Ribs: With Poems, More and More.* London: Heinemann Educational, 1971.

——. *Another Nigger Dead: Poems.* London: Heinemann Educational, 1972.

——. *Popular Culture of East Africa: Oral Literature.* Nairobi: Longman, 1972.

——. *Thirteen Offensives Against Our Enemies.* Nairobi: East African Literature Bureau, 1973.

——. *Another Last Word.* Nairobi: Heinemann Kenya, 1990.

——. *Culture Is Rutan.* Nairobi: Longman Kenya, 1991.

——. *The Cows of Shambat: Sudanese Poems.* Harare: Zimbabwe Publishing House, 1992.

——. *Words That Melt a Mountain.* Nairobi: East African Educational Publishers, 1996.

——. *Carrying Knowledge up a Palm Tree: Poetry.* Trenton, N.J.: Africa World Press, 1997.

TRANSLATIONS

Lo Liyong, Taban, trans. *The Defense of Lawino,* a new translation of Okot p'Bitek's *Song of Lawino.* Kampala: Fountain Publishers, 2001.

REFERENCES

Goodwin, K. L. *Understanding African Poetry: A Study of Ten Poets.* Heinemann Educational Books, 1982.

Nazareth, Peter. "Bibliyongraphy, or Six Tabans in Search of an Author." In *The Writing of East and Central Africa,* edited by G. D. Killam, 159–176. London: Heinemann, 1985.

[Gikandi]

Lubega, Bonnie (b. 1929) Ugandan novelist, author of children's literature, and lexicographer. Born in the Buganda province of Uganda, Lubega received his education in the region and qualified as a teacher. In the mid-1950s, he worked for a number of newspapers in Kampala and published his own pictorial magazine, *Ssanyu.* He later studied journalism in Germany and worked as a script writer and radio presenter. His works in English include two novels, *The Burning Bush* (1970) and *The Outcasts* (1971), and two works of children's literature, *The Great Animal Land* (1971) and *Cry, Jungle Children* (1974). He is also the author of a highly regarded Luganda semantic dictionary.

PRIMARY TEXTS

Lubega, Bonnie. *The Burning Bush.* Nairobi: East African Literature Bureau, 1970.

——. *The Great Animal Land.* Nairobi: East African Literature Bureau, 1971.

——. *The Outcasts.* London: Heinemann, 1971.

——. *Pot of Honey*. Nairobi: East African Literature Bureau, 1974.

——. *Cry, Jungle Children*. Kampala: East African Literature Bureau, 1974.

——. *Four-Language Easy Communication Pocket Book: Luganda, English, Kiswahili, German*. Kampala: Pan Africa Books, 1997.

[Mwangi]

Lubwa-p'Chong, Cliff (1946–1997) Ugandan playwright and poet. Born in Gulu in northern Uganda and educated at National Teachers College, Kyambogo, Lubwa taught for several years before entering Makerere University College, where he studied literature and linguistics. His work explores the cultures of Ugandan traditional communities at the moment of change from colonialism to postcolonialism. He was also active in the editing of journals that promoted African literature. At the National Teachers College, he founded and edited the magazine *Nanga*. He was also an editor of *Dhana*, the Makerere literary magazine. A prolific dramatist, most of his plays were performed on stage but were not ever published in book form. His play *Generosity Kills* (1975) dramatizes a famous traditional saying of that title. *The Last Safari* (1975) and *Words of My Groaning* (1976) revolve around the disillusionment that defines life in independent Africa, while *The Minister's Wife* (1982) examines the abuse of power in postindependence Africa. His other plays include *The Bishop's Daughter* (1988), *Do Not Uproot the Pumpkin* (1987), *Kinsmen and Kinswomen* (1988), and *The Madman* (1989). Lubwa taught literature and drama at National Teachers College until his death in 1997.

PRIMARY TEXTS

Lubwa-p'Chong, Cliff. *Generosity Kills*. Nairobi: Longman, 1975.

——. *The Last Safari*. Nairobi: Longman, 1975.

——. *Words of My Groaning*. Nairobi: East African Literature Bureau, 1976.

——. *The Minister's Wife*. Unpublished. 1982.

——. *Do Not Uproot the Pumpkin*. Unpublished. 1987.

——. *The Bishop's Daughter*. Unpublished. 1988.

——. *Kinsmen and Kinswomen*. Unpublished. 1988.

——. *The Madman*. Unpublished. 1989.

[Mwangi]

Macgoye, Marjorie Oludhe (b. 1928) Kenyan novelist, essayist, and poet. Considered to be one of East Africa's most prolific women writers, Macgoye was born Marjorie King in Southampton, England, to a working-class family; she moved to Kenya in 1954. She married a Kenyan doctor in 1960—a time when interracial marriages were rare—and has used her mixed-race family as the background for her major works in both prose and poetry.

In her literary works, Macgoye weaves local idioms and historical references into her narratives to comment on historical and political events in Kenya—especially their effects on gender dynamics in East Africa—and depict the challenges of forging new identities in places that would be traditionally hostile because of painful events and memories. The problem of forging new identities is a key theme in Macgoye's earliest fiction: *Growing Up at Lina School* (1971) is a story based on the childhood of a Kenyan girl, while *Murder in Majengo* (1977) is concerned with the aggressiveness and destructive individualism associated with life in East African towns. The question of identity is also a central theme in her poetry. *Song of Nyarloka and Other Poems* (1977) is a collection that presents the hybridity of East African societies. The title poem, "Song of Nyarloka" (Nyarloka in Luo means the "one from abroad"), explores the possibilities of interracial integration in East African society, examining with rare poignancy the challenges of crossing over from a European ancestry to a new African reality and identity. Articulated from Nyarloka's point of view but interwoven with the communal "we" of the community, the epic poem dramatizes a young woman's entry into a new home in Africa and her views, both as insider and outsider, of the changing society. In the poem, the persona grows as the poem proceeds, with the naïve voice at the beginning of the poem eventually growing in confidence to a point where she can criticize some of the practices of her adopted home society. The poem discusses historical events, such as the 1969 visit by Jomo Kenyatta to Kisumu, which ended in bloodshed because of the ethnic and ideological differences in the new Kenyan nation. In "Song of Kisumu," Nyarloka is moved by the brutal extermination of innocent children by a regime that will apparently do anything to maintain power:

> Aiee, he does not answer . . .
> Sleep Anoor my son.
> Lie quietly, my baby Ochieng',
> Hush, they hear you fidget
> As though those little graves did not
>   content you.

Using sarcasm and apostrophe, the poem uses the figures of the dead children to criticize the postcolonial regime and its paranoia. But perhaps aware of her outsider status, Nyarloka has to speak to the government in circumlocutory metaphors.

If the poems in *Song of Nyarloka and Other Poems* express the major historical events in Kenya, Macgoye's most famous novel, *Coming to Birth* (1986), is constructed as a Bildungsroman in which the main character's life parallels the history of the Kenyan nation in profound ways. The novel, which won the Sinclair Prize for Literature in 1986, traces the life of Paulina Were as she grows up in tandem with the formation of the Kenyan nation from the mid-1950s to the late 1970s. The narrative moves from Paulina's coming of age through her painful marriage and difficult life in Nairobi. The key moments in her life coincide with major events in Kenya's history, such as the state of emergency declared by the British colonial government in the 1950s, independence in 1963, the assassination of politician Tom Mboya in 1969, and the detention without trial of writer Ngugi wa Thiong'o. Using a series of miscarriages to symbolize the problems and challenges of Kenya's nationhood, the story begins with despair but ends cautiously optimistic, with Paulina expecting a baby. More hope is suggested by the narrative style of the novel: the story opens on notes of uncertainty and unreliability but moves to a more confident and deliberate vocabulary and grammar as it reaches the end.

The Present Moment (1987) is an accomplished portrait of Kenyan women over six decades. It particularly presents the contradictions and ambiguities that mark memories of the Mau Mau liberation struggle. Told through the voices of seven women protagonists, the story contrasts the story of Wairimu and her memory of the liberation war against other voices, like that of Priscilla, who would prefer that the movement be forgotten. *The Present Moment* is the first East African polyphonic novel in which the major characters are women. This is important because it helps Macgoye recover agency and voices suppressed by misogyny, colonialism, and neocolonialism. *Street Life*

(1987), *Victoria and Murder in Majengo* (1993), and *Homing In* (1994) examine life in the city. *Chira* (1996) treats the theme of the AIDS scourge against the background of general political and social degeneration. Through the characters Gabriel Otieno, a Luo man in his thirties, and Helen, a Kenyan Luo born and bred in Tanzania, Macgoye revisits the theme of changing gender roles and the ambiguities wrought by urbanization in the age of AIDS. Many of the characters with whom the protagonists interact are associated with "chira," a "wasting disease" that emaciates them. At the same time, Helen cannot be accepted in Kenya because of her Tanzanian ties, and she must renegotiate her identity in a city that does not easily accept foreigners. Otieno, meanwhile, has to contend with changing notions of masculinity. Her other books include *Make It Sing*, a collection of poetry, and *A Farm Called Kishinev*, a novel about the 1903 British offer of parts of East Africa to Jews escaping persecution in Eastern Europe.

PRIMARY TEXTS

Macgoye, Marjorie Oludhe. *Growing Up at Lina School.* Nairobi: East African Publishing House, 1971.
——. *Murder in Majengo.* Nairobi: Oxford University Press, 1977.
——. *Song of Nyarloka and Other Poems.* Nairobi: Oxford University Press, 1977.
——. *Coming to Birth.* Nairobi: East African Educational Publishers, 1986.
——. *The Story of Kenya: A Nation in the Making.* Nairobi: Oxford University Press, 1986.
——. *The Present Moment.* Nairobi: East African Educational Publishers, 1987.
——. *Street Life.* Nairobi: East African Educational Publishers, 1987.
——. *Victoria and Murder in Majengo.* London: Macmillan, 1993.
——. *Homing In.* Nairobi: East African Educational Publishers, 1994.

——. *Chira.* Nairobi: East African Educational Publishers, 1996.
——. *Moral Issues in Kenya: A Personal View.* Nairobi: Uzima Press, 1996.
——. *Make It Sing and Other Poems.* Nairobi: East African Educational Publishers, 1998.
——. *A Farm Called Kishinev.* Nairobi: East African Educational Publishers, 2005.

REFERENCES

Hay, Jean. "Historical Context." Introduction to *The Present Moment*, by Marjorie Oludhe Macgoye. New York: Feminist Press, 2000.
Kibera, Valerie. "Adopted Motherlands: The Novels of Marjorie Macgoye and Bessie Head." In *Motherlands: Black Women's Writing from Africa, the Caribbean, and South Asia*, edited by Susheila Nasta, 310–329. New Brunswick, N.J.: Rutgers University Press, 1992.
Kurtz, Roger J. "Crossing Over: Identity and Change in Marjorie Oludhe Macgoye's Song of Nyarloka." *Research in African Literatures* 33, no. 2 (2002): 100–118.
——. *Nyarloka's Gift: The Writing of Marjorie Oludhe Macgoye.* Nairobi: Mvule, 2005.
Simatei, Tirop Peter. *The Novel and the Politics of Nation Building in East Africa.* Bayreuth: Bayreuth University Press; London: Global, 2001.

[Mwangi]

Maillu, David Gian (b. 1939) Kenyan popular writer. With an extensive canon of about fifty books, Maillu is undoubtedly East Africa's most prolific writer, and though his works cover a variety of issues covering a considerable stretch of time in the history of modern Kenya, his works have not been taken seriously by the academy because of their sexual explicitness. What makes Maillu stand out among his literary contemporaries is his frank approach to intimate issues and an obsession with the prurient aspects of life. Although the unrecorded date of his birth remains uncertain to him, Maillu has made October 19, 1939, his birthday. This invented aspect of his life is reflected in his writing, where birthdays are "fixed" in retrospect by characters reconstructing a fictionalized account of their lives. Born as what he has described as "extra-ordinarily dark" to Joseph Mulandi and Esther Kavuli, the writer was given the name Maillu, which is a derivative of the Kikamba word for "black" or "dark." He was later baptized David by a Salvation Army minister. His middle name Gian is a "secret invention," which he suppresses by using only its initial letter *G* because, as he says, "it sounds better that way."

In 1971, Maillu married Hannelore Kuthmann, a German expatriate who had come to Kenya in 1967 to work for the National Council of Churches of Kenya. This fact is important because interracial relationships haunt Maillu's narratives; the conflict between European and African cultures are the source of tension in the structure of his works. An ardent letter writer, Maillu ran a weekly epistolary column called "Dear One" in the Nairobi *Sunday Times* in the mid-1980s. His novels use the epistolary technique by mixing third-person narration with letters between characters, a technique that produces a multiplicity of voices in the texts. In fact, *Dear Monika* and *Dear Daughter*, Maillu's most famous works, are epistolary novellas each containing a letter and a reply to it. But even before the publication of *Broken Drum*, Maillu had established himself as the most popular writer in Kenya. For instance, his first literary work was published in the late 1960s in *Risk*, a magazine based in Geneva. But it was his 1973 thrillers *Unfit for Human Consumption* and *My Dear Bottle* that catapulted Maillu to instant fame as a writer and publisher. While the former

was in prose, the latter was a long narrative poem written in irregular verse. *After 4:30* followed in 1974, and an epic verse narrative, *The Kommon Man*, appeared in three volumes during 1975 and 1976. All these books were published by the author's publishing firm, Comb Books, and were highly popular, selling tens of thousands of copies.

Maillu claims that he writes his novels after rigorous research into what the reading public desires in a book, settling on the most common yet entertaining subjects in the East African cultural scene. *My Dear Bottle* is an apostrophe to alcohol, to which the main character, the speaking persona, has turned to for an escape from the hard life in the city. Echoing Okot p'Bitek's *Song of Lawino*—but without the complexity of the latter—Maillu's *After 4:30* is a long poem by a prostitute who has been forced into the trade by difficult economic conditions and the insatiable habits of her bosses. *The Kommon Man* is the testimony of an average Kenyan caught in an extremely difficult sociopolitical climate. It exposes the infidelity, despair, corruption, and inefficiency in the modern East African bureaucracy. *No!* is a melodramatic story about a man who sleeps with the wife of his junior employee. When they were published, all these works were condemned for what was seen their sexual explicitness, earning Maillu the dubious distinction as the father of African pornography. His books were even banned in Tanzania in the 1970s.

After the collapse of Comb Books in the 1970s, Maillu formed David Maillu Publishers, which brought out *Kadosa* in 1979 and *Hit of Love/Wendo Ndikilo* in 1980. However, David Maillu Publishers lasted only a brief time, and it was soon replaced by Bookwise, which brought out the author's *Looking for Mother* in 1980. Macmillan, a more established press, started publishing his novels in 1980 in its popular "Pacesetters" series, and Maillu's fiction began to grow in scope.

Benni Kamba 009 in the Equatorial Assignment is a pan-Africanist novel about a spy fighting an imperialist force trying to recolonize Africa. *For Mbatha and Rabeka* is a love story addressing the poor/rich, rural/urban polarities that inform Kenya's socioeconomic structure. *P.O. Box I Love You Via My Heart* (1989) deals with the role of racism in human relations.

Maillu has experimented in linguistic code-switching, an urban phenomenon in East Africa since the 1970s, which entails the use of a mixture English, Swahili, and other indigenous languages. *Without Kiinua Mgongo* (*Without a Bribe*), for example, is narrated by an urbanized and multilingual housekeeper using a mixture of different languages. Using this bilingual strategy, the novel manages to decry the corruption that is eating into the socioeconomic fabric of the country in a humorous, seemingly non-serious, way. *Anayekukeep* (*He Who Pays for Your Upkeep*), published a year later in 1990, is also written using a similar strategy. The two novels successfully simulate a modern urban setting in which the characters and the narrator mix standard English with Kiswahili and other local languages to interact with one another in an informal, "unauthorized" manner. The novels use Kiswahili syntax but borrow their vocabulary from different languages including English. The ability of the author to imitate the exact speech habits of urban Kenyans helps to capture the rhythms of urban life while representing the grave problems with which the modern Kenyan grapples.

Broken Drum (1991) is Maillu's most ambitious work. Set in the early 1980s but going back in time (through the exploration of its characters' memory) over two hundred years, it revolves around Boniface Ngewa, a well-traveled African man and his riotous modern black wife, Vikirose, and her European potential co-wife, Sheila. The main characters believe in different values, leading to marital anxiety around which the narrative discusses race, cultural conflict, and sexuality in traditional and modern Africa. In *The Government's Daughter* (1996), Maillu explored gender relations in Kenya, telling the story of Tamia, a twelve-year-old orphan in a nomadic community threatened with forced marriage. Discovered by tourists in a game reserve, Tamia is taken to a police station in Nairobi, where she meets a female administrator. The administrator saves her from the forced marriage and orders that she be taken to school. Tamia does well in school and comes to be respected in her village as "the government's daughter." *The Survivors* (2002) is a fable exploring human struggles to master nature and colonize other societies. Through a seemingly straightforward narrative about insects, Maillu raises fundamental questions about self-generation, the splintering of identities, the clash of civilizations, the constitution of history, and race politics.

Maillu has also written nonfiction works. These include *Our Kind of Polygamy* (1988) and *The Principles of Nyayo Philosophy*, which Maillu Publishing House brought out a year later. He has made numerous contributions to the field of children's literature. In 1972, his first book, a collection of children's stories entitled *Kisalu and His Fruit Garden and Other Stories* was published by the now defunct East African Publishing House and has been reissued several times since then. Two other children's stories, *Journey Into Fairyland* and *The Lion and the Hare*, were published in 1992. His other children's books include *Precious Blood* (2005) and *Julius Nyerere: Father of Ujamaa* (2005).

PRIMARY TEXTS

Maillu, David Gian. *My Dear Bottle.* Nairobi: Comb Books, 1973.

——. *Unfit for Human Consumption.* Nairobi: Comb Books, 1973.

——. *After 4:30.* Nairobi: Comb Books, 1974.

——. *Troubles.* Nairobi: Comb Books, 1974.

——. *Dear Monika.* Nairobi: Comb Books, 1975.

——. *Dear Daughter.* Nairobi: Comb Books, 1976.

——. *Benni Kamba 009 in the Equatorial Assignment.* Nairobi: Macmillan Publishers, 1980.

——. *Hit of Love—Wendo Ndikilo.* Machakos: Maillu Publishers, 1980.

——. *Looking for Mother.* Nairobi: Bookwise, 1980.

——. *The Ayah.* Nairobi: Heinemann Kenya, 1986.

——. *Untouchable.* Nairobi: Maillu Publishing House, 1987.

——. *Our Kind of Polygamy.* Nairobi: Heinemann Kenya, 1988.

——. *Thorns of Life.* Nairobi: Macmillan Publishers, 1988.

——. *Anayekukeep.* Nairobi: Maillu Publishing House, 1989.

——. *My Dear Mariana: Kumya Ivu.* Nairobi: Maillu Publishing House, 1989.

——. *Without Kiinua Mgongo.* Nairobi: Maillu Publishing House, 1989.

——. *Broken Drum.* Nairobi: Jomo Kenyatta Foundation and Maillu Publishing, 1991.

——. *P.O. Box I Love You Via My Heart.* Nairobi: Maillu Publishers, 1991.

——. *Journey Into Fairyland.* Nairobi: Jomo Kenyatta Foundation, 1992.

——. *The Lion and the Hare.* Nairobi: Jomo Kenyatta Foundation, 1992.

——. *Kisalu and His Fruit Garden, and Other Stories.* Nairobi: Heinemann Kenya, 1993.

——. *Julius Nyerere: Father of Ujamaa.* Nairobi: Sasa Sema, 2005.

——. *Precious Blood.* Nairobi: Phoenix, 2005.

REFERENCES

Kurtz, Roger John, and Robert M. Kurtz. "Language and Ideology in Postcolonial Kenyan Literature: The Case of David Maillu's Macaronic Fiction." In *Readings in African Popular Fiction*, edited by Stephanie Newell, 124–128. Bloomington: Indiana University Press, 2002.

Lindfors, Bernth. "East African Popular Literature." *Journal of Popular Culture* 13 (1979): 106–115.

——. "A Basic Anatomy of East African Literature in English." *New Literature Review* 8 (1980): 8–14.

——. *Mazungumzo: Interviews with East African Writers, Publishers, and Scholars.* Athens: Ohio University Press, 1990.

——. "The New David Maillu." In *Popular Literatures in English*, edited by Bernth Lindfors, 87–100. Trenton, N.J.: Africa World Press, 1991.

Mwongera, Elizabeth, and Richard Arden. "Approaches and Techniques in Teaching Literature to Secondary School Students." In the proceedings of the conference entitled "The Role of Language and Literature in Schools." British Council, Nairobi. February 25–27, 1991.

Wanjala, Chris (Lukorito). *The Season of Harvest: Some Notes on East African Literature.* Nairobi: Kenya Literature Bureau, 1978.

——. *For Home and Freedom.* Nairobi: East African Publishing House, 1980.

[Mwangi]

Nagenda, John (b. 1938) Ugandan poet, novelist, and journalist. Born in Gahini, Rwanda, the son of Ugandan missionaries, Nagenda was educated at Kiwanda Primary School, Busoga College, Mwiri, and King's College, Budo, before joining Makerere University College, from where he graduated with a BA honors degree in English in 1962. At Makerere, Nagenda served as the editor of *Penpoint*, the university literary magazine. He has worked as an editor for Oxford University Press in Nairobi (1962–1964); a radio and television producer in London, New York, and Kampala; a member of Uganda Human Rights Commission (1986–1995); and as a senior presidential adviser in Uganda. Writing in both Luganda and English, Nagenda's novels and poems are primarily concerned with the tensions between rural and urban life and are often pervaded by biblical allegories and reflect a serious moral vision. His novel *The Seasons of Thomas Tebo* is an allegory of the political violence suffered by the Ugandan people at the hands of several successive regimes. It showcases the hardiness of a population that does not give up hope in the face of political and social horror. Its main character, Tebo, is a young, precocious politician who refuses to give in to the rottenness that surrounds him in postcolonial Uganda. Nagenda's other major works include *Mukasa* (1973), a children's book that won the Coretta Award in the 1970s, and poems in anthologies such as *Origin East Africa*, edited by David Cook and David Rubadiri.

PRIMARY TEXTS

Nagenda, John. *Mukasa*. New York: Macmillan, 1973.

———. *The Seasons of Thomas Tebo*. London: Heinemann, 1986.

[Mwangi]

Nation and Nationalism   East African nations were forged by colonialism and Western imperialism; it was the colonial powers that drew up the boundaries that define these countries today. Within these boundaries, some ethnic communities were put together as a nation while others, such as the Maasai and the Somali, were split across different nations. The Maasai straddle the Tanzanian and Kenyan border, while the Somali occupy Kenya, Somalia, Ethiopia, and Djibouti. There is another paradox to the narrative of nation making in East Africa: nationalism in the region has been structured by the struggle against the very colonial institutions that gave rise to the modern nations in the region, and it has been driven by what is conceived to be a struggle against the ethnic identities that preceded colonialism. According to Kenyan nationalist Tom Mboya, nationalism is the force that binds the different ethnic communities "against racialism and against tribalism," an idea emphasized by Ngugi wa Thiong'o when he insists that "to live on the level of race or tribe is to be less than whole" (*Homecoming*, 23).

Made up of diverse ethnic communities drawn from people of Bantu, Nilotic, Nilo-Hamitic, and Sudanic descent, all with different languages and different cultures, each East African nation struggles to forge a sense of a homogenous community against the pressures of historical experience and the realities of everyday life. How the nation is imagined is sometimes at odds with everyday experiences that are not always limited by national boundaries. For this reason, the search for national identity within and outside the territorial boundaries of the East African states has preoccupied the region's literature since its inception in the 1950s and up to the period of national formation in the 1960s and 1970s. East African literature tried to imagine nations within the state and develop a sense of nationhood that could span the various countries as a protest against colonialism and its divide-and-rule policy of fragmenting the East African communities.

In a reaction against the colonial experience, writing from the region has continued to be preoccupied with its indigenous sources and has attempted to break from the colonial grammar by infusing its narratives, poetry, and drama with local idioms and settings. Some East African writings, such as Abdulrazak Gurnah's novel *Paradise* (a reversed version of Joseph Conrad's *Heart of Darkness*), are direct rewritings of the European colonial canon. More often, however, pioneer writing engages the reader in a reconstruction of the past that colonialism destroyed. The writers see themselves as cultural nationalists with a duty to deconstruct the colonial constructions of their societies and reconstruct them as ideal nations. Ngugi wa Thiong'o's *The River Between*, Okot p'Bitek's *Song of Lawino*, Samuel Kyeng's *Echoes from the Two Worlds*, and Henry ole Kulet's *Is It Possible?* explore the confusion caused by colonialism and seek ways of reintegrating modernity into traditional belief systems.

The struggle for independence is praised and immortalized by novels, plays, and poetry that invoke the names of national heroes as a way of creating confidence in the new nations. Tanzanian Ebrahim Hussein's *Kinjekitile* explores the Maji Maji rebellion (1905–1907) in Tanzania against German colonialism. His compatriot Ismael Mbise's novel *Blood on Our Land* (1974) presents the importance of land in the anticolonial struggle by documenting a legal suit the Meru community of Tanzania filed at the United Nations against the colonial powers. Ngugi's *The River Between*, *Weep Not, Child*, and *A Grain of Wheat* draw images from figures such as Kimathi, the Mau Mau freedom fighter; Kenyatta, the founding father of the nation; and Waiyaki, one of the pioneering opponents of colonial rule, to structure meanings on the importance of struggle and the urgency of consolidating independence.

But the nationalist euphoria that characterized East Africa in the early 1960s had, by the end of the decade, been replaced by a sense of disillusionment with the new political order. What came to be known as "flag freedom" was not yielding much satisfaction for the people after all, and it seemed that the new leaders were no different from the colonialists they had replaced. The theme of betrayal and disillusionment dominates the literature emerging from East Africa in the late 1960s and through the 1970s to the turn of the century. Ngugi's *A Grain of Wheat*, Francis Imbuga's *Betrayal in the City*, and John Ruganda's *The Burdens* are some of the works pervaded with a strong sense of disenchantment.

But even the art of disillusionment was nationalistic in the sense that it was bemoaning the failure to achieve nationalistic desires, and it suggested alternative possibilities for achieving nationhood. The past was invoked to remind the readers of the struggles for independence and the need to protect sovereignty from neocolonialists and local henchmen. In her second novel, *The Graduate*, Grace Ogot relates the story of a male Luo protagonist, Jakoyo, who, after studying in America, returns to Kenya only to find that the civil service is dominated by Europeans. In flashbacks, Ogot's novel narrates the struggles by individuals and communities to eject expatriates who are frustrating qualified locals from getting jobs.

To textualize national desires, East African literatures have often figured the nation as a family, used prostitution as a metaphor for a country mortgaged by its elites to Western neocolonialism, and rape as the symbol of the nation's defilement by its irresponsible leaders. Such tropes occupy significant discursive positions in the writings of Nuruddin Farah, Okot p'Bitek, John Ruganda, and Ngugi wa Thiong'o, and to some extent Francis Imbuga and Grace Ogot. For example, in Ngugi's *Petals of Blood*, Wanja functions as the prostitute, a figure of the woman-as-nation, an eroticized member of a kinship network of children-citizens. Eroticizing Wanja, the beloved nation/country, as a loved woman's body leads to associating sexual danger with the transgression of national boundaries. She is made the victim of a German who forces her to have sex with his dog, signifying that the nation is under attack from foreigners who will even stoop to bestiality. She is further raped by a former lover, Kimeria, in a scene that reminds readers of the collusion between the local elite and foreigners in the fleecing of the nation.

To a large extent, nationalistic literatures deployed realism as a mode of representation in which there would be a close correspondence between the artistic work and the society it sought to represent. Globalization and the unstable political and economic conditions in the East Africa of the 1980s catalyzed movements of East African intellectuals to different parts of the world as scholars or exiles, especially to Western Europe and North America. Although literatures of regional migration had already established themselves with texts such as Grace Ogot's *Land Without Thunder* and *The Promised Land,* the movement to racially different worlds produced a literature that was more conscious of migratory conditions.

From the 1980s onward, there was great discontent with the nation as the discursive reference point for the consolidation and maintenance of identities, prompting a radical exploration of gendered, transnational, and subnational carriers of nationality. The 1980s also saw the emergency of subgenres that represented what was construed to be history and realism as a creation of the colonial and neocolonial elites. Even when presenting the everyday reality of the postcolonial nation, these narratives often disavowed realism by claiming to be set in no specific country and at no particular time in history. These literatures use multiple narrative voices and a mixture of genres to contest the notion of a singular nation. During this period, East African writers adapted

foreign literary traditions for local audiences and readers to enhance nationhood and celebrate the resilience of the nation in the face of adversity. Ugandan poet and playwright Rose Mbowa, for example, wrote and produced *Mother Uganda and Her Children* (1987), a Luganda adaptation of Bertolt Brecht's *Mother Courage and Her Children,* as a tribute to Ugandans for holding together despite linguistic and cultural diversity and the devastation by poor military governance.

During this period, East African nations have had moments of crises because of civil wars, dictatorships, ethnic tensions, and, more recently, AIDS, and writers have responded to these political developments in diverse ways. Ngugi wa Thiong'o started writing novels primarily in his mother tongue, Gikuyu, as a way of subverting the monolithic totalitarian state. By reinscribing the Gikuyu nation, Ngugi's goal was to redefine the meaning of the nation and to reject the national politics of subjugation advocated by the state. In contrast, Nuruddin Farah's *Maps* deconstructed the idea of the nation by showing that the boundaries with which colonial cartography was put in place are arbitrary and fictional.

The same period saw the rise of transnational writing from East Africa. While earlier writing had lamented exile in favor of place, Moyez Vassanji's *The Gunny Sack* and Abdulrazak Gurnah's *Admiring Silence* present exile as a necessary condition of identities in flux. Vassanji's work is set in specific places and traces the history of the Asian communities in East Africa. Using a magical realist mode, an unreliable narrator, slippery references, and oral literature, *The Gunny Sack* chronicles the lives of four generations of the Govind family, from 1885 to the 1970s. Finally, in the 1990s, gender became an important concern of East African writers, as they sought to redefine the nation and its narrative modes, with some texts such as Margaret Ogola's *The River and the Source* treating colonialism and Christian evangelism less harshly than earlier writers, pointing to the ways in which European practices had helped in the liberation of East African women from the constraints of traditional patriarchy.

REFERENCES

Barak, Julie. "Literary Nationalism and Its Intersections with Gender, Class, and Ethnicity." In *Modern Kenya: Social Issues and Perspectives*, 164–195. Lanham, Md.: University Press of America, 2000.

Bhabha, Homi. Introduction to *Nation and Narration*. London: Routledge, 1990.

——. "DissemiNation: Time, Narrative, and the Margins of the Modern Nation." In *Nation and Narration*, 291–323. London: Routledge, 1990.

Esonwanne, Uzo. "The Nation as a Contested Referent." *Research in African Literatures* 24, no. 4 (1993): 49–62.

Mamdani, Mahmood. *Citizen and Subject. Contemporary Africa and the Legacy of Late Colonialism*. Princeton, N.J.: Princeton University Press, 1996.

Simatei, Tirop Peter. *The Novel and the Politics of Nation Building in East Africa*. Bayreuth: Bayreuth University Press; London: Global, 2001.

Yewah, Emmanuel. "The Nation as a Contested Construct." *Research in African Literatures* 32, no. 3 (2001): 45–56.

[Mwangi]

Nazareth, Peter (b. 1940) Ugandan (of Goan and Malaysian ancestry) novelist, dramatist, poet, and critic. Nazareth earned a BA honors degree in English from Makerere University College, Uganda, and then pursued a graduate degree in English at Leeds University as part of a group of distinguished East African writers and critics including Ngugi wa Thiong'o, Pio and El-

vania Zirimu, and Grant Kamenju. On his return to Uganda, Nazareth served as a senior finance officer in the Ugandan Ministry of Finance until 1973, when he accepted a fellowship at Yale University. He later joined the University of Iowa, first as an honorary fellow in the International Writing Program and subsequently as a professor in the African-American Studies Program.

Nazareth is best known for the novel *In a Brown Mantle* (1972), which prophesied dictator Idi Amin's ascension to power and the subsequent expulsion of Asians from Uganda, an expulsion that took place the same year the novel was published. Its successor, *The General Is Up* (1991), presents the Asian migrants' experience in the strife-torn postcolonial African country of Damibia (which resembles Uganda), focusing on the frightening period between the dictator's decree expelling Asians and their departure. Nazareth's plays *The Hospital* and *X* were produced for the BBC in the 1970s. His critical writings include *Literature and Society in Modern Africa* (also published as *An African View of Literature*), *The Third World Writer: His Social Responsibility*, and numerous essays on African, Caribbean, and Asian literature and American popular culture.

FICTION

Nazareth, Peter. *In a Brown Mantle*. Nairobi: East African Literature Bureau, 1972.

——. *The General Is Up*. Toronto: TSAR, 1991.

CRITICISM

Nazareth, Peter. *Literature and Society in Modern Africa*. Nairobi: East African Literature Bureau, 1972. Also published as *An African View of Literature*. Evanston, Ill.: Northwestern University Press, 1974.

——. *The Third World Writer: His Social Responsibility*. Nairobi: Kenya Literature Bureau, 1978.

REFERENCES

Ogunsanwo, Olatubosan. "Art and Artifice in Two Novels of Peter Nazareth." *The Literary Half-Yearly* 31, no. 2 (1990): 91–113.

Savan, Charles. "The Writer as Historian: With Reference to the Novels of Peter Nazareth." *Toronto South Asian Review* 10, no. 1 (1991): 15–24.

Scheckter, John. "Peter Nazareth and the Ugandan Expulsion: Pain, Distance . . ." *Research in African Literatures* 27, no. 2 (1996): 83–93.

Simatei, Tirop Peter. *The Novel and the Politics of Nation Building in East Africa.* Bayreuth: Bayreuth University Press; London: Global, 2001.

[Mwangi]

Ndunguru, Severin N. (b. 1932) Tanzanian novelist. Born in the rural Songea region of Mbinga District, Ndunguru's works are infused with folklore from his home region, but they are also concerned with the conflict between traditional ways of life, self-apprehension, and the challenges and opportunities offered by modernity and modernization. *Divine Providence* (1999) is a story about a restored marriage in which the heroine, Hosana Mwandikaulaya, as morally corrupt as her nation is quickly becoming, is reunited with her upright husband, Richard, after transforming herself into the virtuous Grace Watua. The narrative counterpoises logic and science against coincidence and fate to suggest that however technologically advanced Africa becomes, there are forces beyond human control that orchestrate human destiny. The main characters are scientists who are entangled in each other's fates. More fundamentally, the novel is a critique of the postcolonial state in Africa, where corruption has become the order of the day. *A Wreath for Father Mayer of Masasi* (1997) thematizes the role of missionaries in postindependence East Africa. The novel revolves around the outbreak of a cholera epidemic at a Catholic mission station in Masasi, a murder, and a priest determined to solve the mystery. As in *Divine Providence*, preternatural powers, dreams, and prayers combine with prudent detective work to solve the problem at hand.

PRIMARY TEXTS

Ndunguru, Severin N. *A Wreath for Father Mayer of Masasi.* Dar es Salaam: Mkuki na Nyota, 1997.

——. *Divine Providence.* Dar es Salaam: Mkuki na Nyota, 1999.

[Mwangi]

Neogy, Rajat (1938–1995) Ugandan writer and editor of Asian ancestry. Neogy is best known as the founder of *Transition*, a literary journal that introduced some of the most important African writers to the world and also focused on debates over Africa's social, political, and cultural development in the 1960s. Founded in 1961, the journal nurtured creative writers, philosophers, and critics, publishing a wide range of views held by local scholars and expatriates. Neogy was arrested and detained by Milton Obote's government on October 18, 1968. He was accused of sedition for publishing a letter by a controversial parliamentarian, Abubakar Mayanja, but he was acquitted after six months in detention. Later, it emerged that *Transition* had been funded by an American cultural foundation with links to the CIA. Neogy relocated *Transition* to Ghana in 1970, when his close friend, Kofi Brefa Busia, became prime minister. When Busia was overthrown in a military coup in 1972, Neogy went into exile in the United States. At *Transition*, Neogy brought to public attention works and debates by Ezekiel Mphahlele, Obi Wali, Chinua Achebe, John Pepper Clarke, and Wole Soyinka.

REFERENCES

Benson, Peter. *Black Orpheus, Transition, and Modern Cultural Awakening in Africa.* Berkeley: University of California Press, 1986.

[*Mwangi*]

Newspapers and Mass Media The relationship between literature and the media in East Africa is strong but indirect. Almost of the prominent media personalities in East Africa are graduates of literature departments in the major universities of the region, and they often carry over literary influences and tastes into their media work. Almost all the important writers, including Ngugi wa Thiong'o, Grace Ogot, John Nagenda, Ayeta Anne Wangusa, and Wahome Mutahi, have had stints in the media. Similarly, senior journalists including Ben Mkapa (later to become the president of Tanzania), Kwendo Opanga, Chege Mbitiru, Hilary Ng'weno, and Philip Ochieng' have tried their hand at poetry, drama, and fiction. In addition, East African newspapers have run literary and theater columns that, though informal, have shaped literary debates in their respective countries. According to Bernth Lindfors, Ngugi acquired his skills as an essay writer by contributing to the popular press, while Taban Lo Liyong gained notoriety by engaging his adversaries in the newspapers. At the same time, literary artists contributed to popular newspapers and magazines such as *Drum, Trust, True Love, Flamingo, Baraza, Africa ya Kesho, Africa Nyota, Target, Uhuru,* and *Ngurumo.* The works were later expanded or revised for more prestigious presses. Indeed, some of the finest short stories, literary essays, and poems from East Africa were first published in newspapers. Tanzanian author Agoro Anduru published his earliest stories in Tanzania's weekly newspaper *Sunday News.* In addition, the activities and practices of the media have been the subject of some key East African texts. Ngugi's *Matigari* and John Ruganda's *The Floods* are concerned with the abuse of the media by the postcolonial regime to secure power, while Wahome Mutahi's *Three Days on the Cross* covers the trials of journalists in a repressive state.

In spite of its influence in the shaping of literary culture, the East African press is fairly young and has evolved in relation to the colonial encounter and its aftermath. In colonial Kenya, the European press thrived, presenting diverse views on settler politics. Before the state of emergency in 1952, there were forty to fifty newspapers representing missionary views, on the one hand, or the anticolonial campaigns, on the other. Jomo Kenyatta edited the Kikuyu Central Association's Kikuyu weekly *Muigwithania (The Reconciler),* which was established in May 1928 and printed by an Asian press. It halted publication in 1934, when Kenyatta went to England. *East African Annual* (1930) featured articles illustrated with color photographs. *Catholic Times of East Africa* (published in Mombasa in 1937) carried world news of interest to Catholics. *Colonial Times* came out on Thursdays in Gujarat and Saturdays in English and supported the government line. The *Kenya Weekly* was published in the Rift Valley mainly for the settler community. Vernacular Press published a paper in Kikuyu, two in Swahili, and three in Luo. The *Baraza* weekly newspaper in Swahili and the *Tazama* illustrated magazine had an African audience. *Agikuyu* was started by the colonial government in 1955 to help the Gikuyu, Embu, and Meru communities rebuild their lives after the Mau Mau emergency. *Kenya Today* served as the colonial government's propaganda mouthpiece.

Many of the media outlets established during the colonial period survived decolonization. The East African Standard Group is one of the earliest newspaper publishers in the region. Established in 1902 by an Indian immigrant and bought by British settlers in 1912, its flagship title, *The East African Standard*, is East Africa's oldest newspaper. The newspaper's Sunday editions have printed book reviews and literary pages. More important is the Nation Media Group, which publishes four dailies and a few weeklies in Kenya, Uganda, and Tanzania and also runs a radio and television station. By the beginning of the twenty-first century, it was by far the largest and most successful media house in central and East Africa. Edited by Wangethi Mwangi, a graduate of the literature department of the University of Nairobi, the group's newspapers are known for their support of literary issues in its columns and weekly editions. The Nation Media Group has also sponsored school and colleges drama festivals in Kenya.

The electronic media in Kenya has historically been dominated by the Kenya Broadcasting Corporation (KBC), a government-owned institution. KBC radio and television have drama programs in English, Swahili, and local languages, but literature is consigned to school programs. An exception is the "Books and Bookmen" program started in the 1970s by Chris Wanjala. Although years of mounting public protest forced the government to liberalize the airwaves in the 1990s, resulting in the proliferation of private broadcasting stations, the new outlets have given literature little attention. Out of about twenty FM radio stations and eighty other stations commanding the airwaves by the end of 2003, only Kameme FM had a literature radio program in its exclusively Gikuyu broadcasts. However, Kenyan publishing firms use print and electronic media to advertise their books, especially textbooks.

Across the border in Tanzania, Christian missionaries published their first newspaper, *Habari ya Mwezi* (*Monthly News*), in 1898, but the paper had little effect on the development of media in the country as a whole. The German Protestant Mission produced *Pwani na Bara* in 1910. The missionary presses carried secular news, but their influence remained minimal. It was the defeat of Germany in World War I and the consequent handover of the Tanganyika to the British that created room for the establishment of an English-language press. In 1930, over seventy years after major newspapers started rolling out of Africa, the colonial governor invited the East African Group of Kenya to start a newspaper in Tanzania. *The Tanganyika Standard* was nonpolitical and uncontroversial during the interwar years, but it began to support the British colonial government as agitation for freedom took hold in the 1950s. The colonial government also published *Mambo Leo* (*Daily News*) in Swahili and English to support its ideology. Another colonial government venture was *Baragumu* (*The Trumpet*), which in the 1950s opposed the nationalist Tanganyika African National Union of Julius Nyerere in favor of the more moderate United Tanganyika Party (UTP). Another newspaper, *Mwangaza* (*Light*) was more explicit in its opposition to African nationalism.

When the antinationalist cause supported by these papers failed in the late 1950s, the procolonial government presses reduced their political content. *Baragumu* was sold to East African Newspapers, a private company. Indeed, in the late 1950s the colonial newspapers were superseded by more Africa-oriented media outlets like *Zuhra* (*Venus*), started by Robert Makange in the 1950s. In Zanzibar, *The Zanzibar Voice* favored the political positions of the local Indian population, while *Afrika Kwetu*, printed in Swahili and English, supported the British settlers. By the 1960s, the papers had either ceased publication or were about to collapse. They were replaced by the pro-African *Sauti ya Tanu* (*Voice of Tanu*), *Uhuru* (*Liberty*), *Mwafrika na Taifa* (*The African and the Nation*), *Taifa Leo* (*Daily Nation*), *and Ngurumo* (*Thunder*). With the adoption of the Arusha Declaration in 1968, which declared the establishment of Tanzania as a socialist state, the press was under tremendous pressure to toe the new government line. In fact, Nyerere's government demanded that newspapers serve the interests of the state. In 1968, the Tanzanian government introduced the Newspaper Ordinance Bill, which empowered the president to suspend the operations of a newspaper if he deemed it to be in the national interest. Under the terms of the bill, all media outlets in the county were nationalized and placed under the control of government-appointed editors, a situation that was to continue until the liberal reforms of the 1980s, when the media market was once again opened to private owners.

The situation in Uganda was more complicated. For a long time, the country enjoyed a higher literacy rate than the other East African countries, and this allowed newspapers to thrive. The *Ugandan Herald* (1912) was the first newspaper established in the country. Other European-influenced local-language newspapers included *Matalisi* (founded in 1923) and the *Uganda Argus* (1955), owned by the East African Standard. All these newspapers went through a period of crisis during the civil strife from 1968 to 1986, and many of them were nationalized by the governments or simply closed down. Many journalists were killed or exiled during the rule of Idi Amin from 1972 to 1979. Even in the post-Amin era, newspapers in Uganda continued to experience censorship and governmental interference. The government-owned *New Vision* was privatized in the 1990s, but the government continued to influence its editorial policies, while the independent *Monitor*, which was an impor-tant publisher of literary texts, was constantly threatened with closure by the Museveni government. It was eventually bought by the Kenyan-based Nation Group.

REFERENCES

Ansah, Paul, et al., eds. *Rural Journalism in Africa*. Paris: UNESCO, 1981.

Boas, Nicholls K. "Press and Politics: The Tanzanian Experience." In *The Press and Politics in Africa*, edited by Richard Tamba M'Bayo et al., 269–285. Lewiston: The Edwin Mellen Press, 2000.

Hachten, William A. *Muffled Drums: The News Media in Africa*. Ames: Iowa State University Press, 1971.

——. *The World News Prism: Changing Media in International Communication*. Ames: Iowa State University Press, 1992.

Kitchen, Helen, ed. *The Press in Africa*. Washington, D.C.: Ruth Sloan Associates, 1956.

Lindfors, Bernth. *Loaded Vehicles: Studies in African Literary Media*. Trenton, N.J.: Africa World Press, 1996.

M'Bayo, Richard Tamba, et al., eds. *The Press and Politics in Africa*. Lewiston: The Edwin Mellen Press, 2000.

Myton, Graham. *Communication in Africa*. London: Arnold, 1983.

[Mwangi]

Ngugi wa Thiong'o (b. 1938) Kenya's leading novelist, playwright, activist, and literary theorist, and one of Africa's most important literary figures. Born in Kamiriithu, Limuru, in Kiambu District, central Kenya, Ngugi's early development and education took place around his place of birth, a fact that has influenced his writing. He went to Kamaandura School and Manguuo School near his home for basic education. The former was a Christian-sponsored school and the latter was sponsored by members of the Kikuyu Independent Church, which had broken away from the main Christian denomination in the late 1920s over the issue of traditional cultural practices. From 1954 to 1958, Ngugi was a student at Alliance High School, Kikuyu, where he had been admitted because of his outstanding performance in English. It was at Alliance that Ngugi started writing stories in earnest, influenced by such narratives as *Treasure Island* by Robert Louis Stevenson. As an institution, Alliance, a boys' school started by a grouping of Protestant churches in 1926, was to have a marked influence on Ngugi's life and fiction, and some critics have identified the school as the model for the fictional Siriana High School in Ngugi's first published novel, *Weep Not, Child* (1964), and his political epic, *Petals of Blood* (1977).

Originally named James Ngugi, the Kenyan writer dropped his first name in 1972 as a dramatic gesture of renouncing Christianity, which he saw as being implicated in the colonization of his people. In spite of this renunciation of his Christianity, Ngugi's fiction resonates with Christian impulses in both obvious and subtle ways; Biblical imagery and mythology are woven into his fiction and drama. *The River Between*, for example, draws parallels between Gikuyu myths and religious beliefs to deconstruct the view of Christianity as superior to traditional religions. Ngugi goes to great lengths to find a parallel in the Gikuyu beliefs for the major Christian practices such as the creation myth and baptism. Later works such as *A Grain of Wheat* are also structured around Biblical motifs and references.

Ngugi's works are set in Kenya during the late colonial period, the era of decolonization, and the postcolonial period. In this sense, they are considered to be primary sources for readers' knowledge and experiences of the processes of colonization and decolonization and the themes they have engendered in East African writing. The three short plays in *This Time Tomorrow*

deal with the themes of cultural conflict, dehumanization of Africans by their governments to please foreigners, and the traumatic memories of the fight for independence and the return from war to a betrayed romance. The tension between colonialism and precolonial systems are reflected most powerfully in Ngugi's first novel, *The River Between*, and his play *The Black Hermit*, first performed in 1962. *Weep Not, Child* is the story of a young man's struggle to acquire an education against the backdrop of Mau Mau and colonial terror.

A Grain of Wheat (1967) deals with the struggle for independence and the disillusionment that followed in postindependence Kenya. A revised edition of the novel came out in 1986, in which Ngugi dropped the scene in which a freedom fighter rapes a white woman, changed the number of people killed while protesting the arrest of nationalist Harry Thuku from fifteen to 150, and replaces the "Party" with the "movement." *Secret Lives* (1975) is a collection of short stories that depict colonial and postcolonial Kenya. The play *The Trial of Dedan Kimathi*, cowritten with Micere-Mugo, is a celebration of that legendary Mau Mau fighter. *Petals of Blood* (1977) is a critique of postindependence leadership in Kenya, which had become exploitative and dictatorial. Detained without trial in 1977 as a result of his activism, Ngugi, in *Detained*, narrates his experiences as a political prisoner.

An important moment in Ngugi's career is represented by his decision, reached soon after the completion of *Petals of Blood*, to stop writing in English in favor of Gikuyu, his native tongue. The first work Ngugi wrote in Gikuyu was *Ngaahika Ndeenda* (*I Will Marry When I Want*, coauthored with Ngugi wa Mirii in 1977), a play that dramatizes the exploitation of workers in postindependence Kenya. The play was revolutionary not only because it was the first major play in a local language, but because it experimented with the idea and form of community theater. Ngugi and Ngugi wa Mirii put together the play from stories generated by the peasants themselves, offering only technical support. The license to perform the play was withdrawn, and the Kamiriithu open-air theater where it was performed was razed to the ground by what was suspected to be government forces. Soon after the play was banned and the theater destroyed, Ngugi was arrested and detained without trial. *Maitu Njugira* (*Mother Sing for Me*), produced after Ngugi was released from prison, was an equally radical play, which, like *I Will Marry When I Want*, fused traditional song and dance into its critique of neocolonialism in Kenya.

During the same period, Ngugi started writing novels in Gikuyu, and it is perhaps in this language that he has been most innovative. *Devil on the Cross* was first published in 1980 as *Caitaani Mutharaba-ini*. It tells the story of Wariinga, an innocent girl who is forced into prostitution. It is told by a traditional oral narrator who combines fantasy, exaggeration, humor, and irony to satirize the excesses of the modern African government. Using different narrative perspectives and folklore, the novel presents the stories of workers who have been betrayed by the new political dispensation. The perversion of capitalists is underscored using direct authorial statements and the foul language of the capitalists themselves: "Each man here should go home right now and secure his wife's cunt with a padlock, and then take all the keys to a bank safe, which will keep the keys safe until he is ready to retrieve them, primed by erection." Their abuse of women is shown as being their way of anchoring their masculinity.

Matigari (1986), Ngugi's second novel in Gikuyu, tells the story of an eponymous hero who returns from the guerrilla war for independence to liberate the postindependence nation from neocolonialism. Initially written in Gikuyu and titled *Matigari ma Njiruungi*, the novel is set in an unspecified location, but there are strong allusions to events in contemporary Kenya. After fighting for independence, Matigari leaves the forest to reclaim his home through peaceful means, discovering that it is owned and occupied by descendants of colonialists and oppressors. He is soon arrested for agitating for change but stages a dramatic escape. His search for truth and justice around the country earns him confinement in a mental hospital. He eventually escapes and sets some of symbols of the neocolonial government on fire. In 2004, Ngugi published the first installment of *Murogi wa Kagogo* (*The Wizard of the Crow*), his novel on the descent of the African state into the world of the irrational and absurd.

Ngugi has also written and published some of the most influential essays in African literature. *Homecoming* (1972) is a collection of essays on African and Caribbean literature. It is in the preface to this collection that Ngugi insisted that literature cannot be freed from politics and history. For him, "literature does not grow or develop in a vacuum; it is given impetus, shape, direction, and even area of concern by social, political and economic forces in a particular society." The essays collected in *Writers in Politics* (1981; 1997) address the political imperatives of cultural production, arguing that "only by a return to the roots of our being in the languages and cultures and the heroic histories of the Kenyan people can we rise up to the challenge of helping in the creation of a Kenyan patriotic national culture that will be the envy and pride of Kenyans." *Barrel of a Pen* (1983), written during the first phase of Ngugi's exile in Britain, is a collection of essays whose unifying idea is the need for focused resistance in the face of oppression in neocolonial Kenya.

Perhaps Ngugi's best-known book of essays is *Decolonising the Mind* (1986), where he addresses the question of language in African literature and bids his "farewell to

English." Ngugi's main argument in this collection is that, as the language of empire-building, English in Africa is a "cultural bomb" that perpetuates the repression of the people and their sense of self-worth. He asserts that literature cannot claim to be African if it is transmitted in a non-African language, because "language is thus inseparable from ourselves as a community of human beings with specific form and character, a specific history, a specific relationship in the world." The use of African languages in African literature, asserts Ngugi, would create rapprochement between the literature and its readers and would be a potent tool in freeing Africans from colonial and neocolonial shackles. While cautioning against the blind worship of African traditions, Ngugi invests great value in the culture of local communities. In *Moving the Centre* (1993) and *Penpoints, Gunpoints, and Dreams* (1997), he restated and developed his well-known position on literature as a tool of liberation, underscoring the tension between the state and writing and celebrating the subversive potential of literature and theater in promoting democratic ideals.

In addition to his novels and plays, Ngugi has written verse in Gikuyu, published in *Mutiiri*, the journal of culture that he helped found in the early 1990s. He has also written children's stories in Gikuyu, which have been translated into English as *Njamba Nene and the Flying Bus* and *Njamba Nene and the Pistol. Njamba Nene na Cibu King'ang'i* (*Njamba Nene and Chief Crocodile*) remains untranslated. The stories engage issues raised in Ngugi's adult novels and essays, such as the language question, the fight for independence, and class.

PRIMARY TEXTS

Ngugi wa Thiong'o. *Weep Not, Child.* London: Heinemann, 1964.

———. *The River Between.* London: Heinemann, 1965.

———. *A Grain of Wheat.* London: Heinemann, 1967.

———. *The Black Hermit.* London: Heinemann, 1968.

———. *This Time Tomorrow.* Nairobi: East African Literature Bureau, 1970.

———. *Homecoming: Essays on African and Caribbean Literature, Culture, and Politics.* London: Heinemann, 1972.

———. *Petals of Blood.* London: Heinemann, 1977.

———. *The Trial of Dedan Kimathi.* London: Heinemann, 1977.

———. *Caitaani Mutharaba-Ini.* Nairobi: Heinemann, 1980. Translated as *Devil on the Cross.* London: Heinemann, 1982.

———. *Detained: A Writer's Prison Diary.* Nairobi and London: Heinemann, 1981.

———. *Barrel of a Pen: Resistance to Repression in Neo-colonial Kenya.* Trenton, N.J.: Africa World Press, 1983.

———. *Decolonising the Mind: The Politics of Language in African Literature.* London: James Currey, 1986.

———. *Matigari ma Njiruungi.* Nairobi: Heinemann, 1986. Translated as *Matigari.* Oxford: Heinemann, 1989.

———. *Moving the Centre: The Struggle for Cultural Freedom.* Oxford: James Currey, 1993.

———. *Penpoints, Gunpoints, and Dreams: Towards a Critical Theory of the Arts and the State in Africa.* Oxford: Clarendon Press, 1998.

———. *Murogi wa Kagogo.* Nairobi: East African Educational Publishers, 2004.

Ngugi wa Thiong'o and Ngugi wa Mirii. *Ngaahika Ndeenda: Ithaako Ria Ngerekano.* Nairobi: Heinemann, 1980. Translated as *I Will Marry When I Want.* London: Heinemann, 1982.

REFERENCES

Bjorkman, Ingrid. *Mother, Sing for Me: People's Theatre in Kenya.* London: Zed, 1989.

Cook, David, and Michael Okenimkpe. *Ngugi wa Thiong'o: An Exploration of His Writings*. London: Heinemann, 1983.

Gakwandi, Shatto Arthur. *The Novel and Contemporary Experience in Africa*. New York: Africana Publishing, 1977.

Gikandi, Simon. *Ngugi wa Thiong'o*. London: Cambridge University Press, 2000.

Killam, G. D. *An Introduction to the Writings of Ngugi*. London: Heinemann, 1980.

Lovesey, Oliver. *Ngugi wa Thiong'o*. New York: Twayne Publishers, 2000.

Nazareth, Peter, ed. *Critical Essays on Ngugi wa Thiong'o*. New York: Twayne Publishers, 2000.

Ogude, James. *Ngugi's Novels and African History: Narrating the Nation*. London: Pluto, 1999.

Robson, Clifford B. *Ngugi wa Thiong'o*. London: Macmillan, 1979.

Roscoe, Adrian. *Uhuru's Fire: African Literature East to South*. London: Cambridge University Press, 1977.

[Mwangi]

Ngurukie, Pat Wambui (b. 1948) Kenyan writer of popular fiction, dealing mostly with romantic relationships in an urban setting. Her best-known novel, *I Will Be Your Substitute* (1984), is a story of love and interethnic tensions in East Africa. In the novel, Carol Nyokabi, a Kikuyu, marries Sanjay Patel, an Asian living in Nairobi. Njoroge, an African man, tries to woo her, promising to be her substitute should the Asian husband not live up to her expectations. *Soldier's Wife* (1989) interweaves the theme of love with subtle references to peacekeeping and military activities in Africa. It tells the story of Pam Kanini, a secretary who marries a soldier, Major Jim Mutisya. Five months into their marriage, he is posted on a peacekeeping mission to Rhodesia. When she joins him there, she realizes that he has been unfaithful to her. She leaves him and marries a Nigerian, Brigadier George Okonkwo. *Businessman's Wife* (1991) is the story of Flora Njoki, who is married to a rich Nairobi businessman, Jimmy Njoroge, but is barren. She refuses to take her doctor's advice to reverse her barrenness and starts drinking heavily. She refuses to grant Njoroge a divorce, and he becomes the main suspect when she is found strangled in her bathroom. Like *Soldier's Wife*, *Tough Choices* (1991) is a story based on a second marriage. It tells the story of Florence Mwangi, who goes against her children's advice and remarries. Eventually they have no choice but to agree with her decision.

PRIMARY TEXTS

Ngurukie, Pat Wambui. *I Will Be Your Substitute*. Nairobi: Kenya Literature Bureau, 1984.

——. *Soldier's Wife*. London: Macmillan, 1989.

——. *Businessman's Wife*. Nairobi: Pat Wambui Ngurukie, 1991.

——. *Tough Choices*. London: Macmillan, 1991.

[Mwangi]

Njau, Rebeka (b. 1932) Kenyan novelist, educator, playwright, and poet who also writes under the name Marina Gashe. Educated at Alliance Girls High School and Makerere University College, Njau was one of the founders of Nairobi Girls Secondary School, where she served as headmistress between 1965 and 1966. Her major works explore women's lives and the dilemmas of an educated woman in Africa. *The Scar* (1965) is a one-act tragedy in verse about the disinheritance of African women by patriarchal structures. Considered to be the first play by a Kenyan woman writer, *The Scar* is also one of the earliest texts to condemn female genital mutilation. Its heroine leads women in a poverty-stricken village in fighting the practice, but she is eventually betrayed by an old friend. *In the Round* was performed in 1964 in Uganda but was never published. It revolves around a man accused of being a collaborator with the colonial regime and dramatizes the ambiguities that define ordinary people's reactions to the Mau Mau liberation war. It was banned by the Ugandan government for being subversive.

Njau's first novel, *Alone with the Fig Tree*, won the East African Writing Committee Prize in 1964 and was developed into *Ripples in the Pool*, published ten years later. The novel has been hailed by critics as a precursor of the magical realist texts of Nigerian novelist Ben Okri and the mythological novels of Ngugi wa Thiong'o. The novel is also one of the first in East Africa to contain an overt lesbian theme: Selina, the main woman character, falls in love with her boyfriend's sister, Gaciru, a relationship that is considered by the other characters as deviant. The novel also expresses the political disillusionment that defines the postcolony by satirizing the new class of leaders, represented by Kefa Munene, the member of parliament for the poverty-ridden Kamukua.

The Hypocrite and Other Stories (1977) is a reworking of traditional oral narratives, while *Kenya Women Heroes and Their Mystical Power* (1984) records the contributions of women that have been left out of the historical record. *The Scared Seed* (2003) is a novel about dictatorship and women's oppression in postcolonial Africa. Its heroine, Tesa, is raped by the head of state, who consequently contracts a strange disease after desecrating a women's shrine. The story uses multiple narratives by women who have suffered under the ethnocentric leadership of President Chinusi. Although set in no particular country in Africa, the appearance of proper nouns such as Mt. Nongolot (an anagram of Mt. Longonot) and Olom (an anagram of Molo) suggests that the

story's setting is Moi's Kenya. His government is said to have sponsored ethnic cleansing, another theme of the novel. The narrator presents the destruction by modern regimes of the resourcefulness of women in traditional African societies, and points to the ways women's power can be restored through the demolition of class hierarchies. It is one of the first novels in Africa to depict the role African American women played in the liberation of their continental counterparts.

PRIMARY TEXTS

Njau, Rebeka. *The Scar: A Tragedy in One Act.* Moshi, Tanzania: Kibo Art Gallery, 1965. Originally published in *Transition* 8 (March 1963): 23–28.

——. *Ripples in the Pool.* Nairobi: Transafrica Publishers; London: Heinemann, 1975.

——. *The Hypocrite and Other Stories.* Nairobi: Uzima Press, 1977.

——. *The Sacred Seed.* Nairobi: Books Horizon, 2003.

Njau, Rebeka, and Gideon Mulaki. *Kenya Women Heroes and Their Mystical Power.* Nairobi: Risk Publications, 1984.

REFERENCES

Nelson, Nici. "Representations of Men and Women, City and Town in Kenyan Novels of the 1970s and 1980s." *African Languages and Cultures* 9, no. 2 (1996): 145–168.

[Mwangi]

Novel As a genre, the novel is the youngest literary genre to have developed in East Africa, but it is perhaps the most important in mapping the literary history of the region and its relationship to the rest of the continent and the world. The novel is considered a young genre because, unlike drama and poetry, it has no indigenous tradition to draw upon and is thus not linked directly to precolonial modes of oral representation. East Africa has a long tradition of drama and poetry rooted in both oral traditions and African-language literatures. For example, the tradition of *utendi* in Swahili poetry is almost as old as Swahili culture itself, and it draws on both African oral forms and poetic traditions imported from Arabia and Persia. Similarly, East African theater has relied heavily on traditional forms of dramatic performance that are found in almost every community in the region. The growth of East African drama and poetry, then, has been a continuous process of drawing on those older forms of representation, adapting them to the modern world, and reconciling them to inherited European forms of writing. Indeed, East African theater and poetry have been most successful when they have acquired their identity through the incorporation of oral forms of poetic expression and performance. The novel has not been built on this kind of foundation, for although long narrative forms and epics have thrived in many African cultures, they have not as a rule provided models for a long, sustained prose narrative often built around the experiences of self-conscious subjects— the essence of the novel as a genre. For this reason, the novel has often been described as an alien genre in Africa as a whole.

Yet, in spite of what appears to be its historical belatedness, the novel has acquired incredible authority and cultural capital. It is not by accident that some of the most famous and influential East African writers, such as Ngugi wa Thiong'o, Nurrudin Farah, Abdulrazak Gurnah, and M. G. Vassanji, are novelists. The prominence of the novel as a genre reflects a global rather than local phenomenon, for the genre tends to have the widest readership and to dominate the market in books and ideas. Still, there are some specific reasons why the novel has come to occupy a central position in the cultural history of East Africa and to acquire its currency in literature, history, sociology, and anthropology. While other genres were produced both inside and outside the institutions of colonialism, the novel was the product of the colonial school, mission, and university. The most obvious consequence of the novel's close association with the institution of colonialism was that it had a small audience, made up mostly of the emergent elite that had access to the European language, and thus its structure was often based on borrowed European models. The models of European novelistic discourse that were available to East African writers before World War II—either abridged versions of adventure stories or canonical works by Jane Austen or Charles Dickens—sometimes seemed at odds with East African experiences. This might explain why there are no notable novels in East Africa until after World War II.

It was not until the 1950s, when modern writers were introduced into the curriculum at Makerere University College (at that time, the region's only center of higher education), that the possibility of using fiction to represent East African experiences became real. In fact, the first batch of East African fiction in English produced at Makerere University College in the late 1950s and early 1960s was modeled not on canonical English writers, but on modernists such as Joseph Conrad, D. H. Lawrence, and to some extent James Joyce. In rebelling against the realist novels of the nineteenth century, modernist writers were globally celebrated as linguistic rebels. Nevertheless, what attracted East African writers to modernism was not linguistic experimentation, but its thematic focus on the modern condition of alienation. Modernism was about characters that were defined by their marginal relation to their cultures, nations, and traditions. As colonial subjects, young East African writers understood this condition well. Young East Africans could easily identify their situation with those of the characters of modern fiction in novels by Lawrence and Conrad, for example, because these were subjects who, like them, were defined by a tug-of-war between the autonomous life promised by modernity and the claims of tradition.

Thus, in the short stories produced at Makerere in the late 1950s and 1960s—most of them published in *Penpoint* and later anthologized in *Origin East Africa* (1965)—the primary themes were the tragic conflict generated by the subjects' incomplete relationship to modernity and the deep sense of psychological conflict created by lives divided between geographies, languages, and histories. Almost without exception, the tragic subjects of these short stories are newly converted or educated Africans, trying to find a middle ground between the world they have left behind and the one they have entered. In Jonathan Kariara's short stories "Unto Us a Child is Born" and "The Initiation," both originally published in *Penpoint*, the conflict is represented through the introspective idiom of modernism, as characters reflect on their condition of alienation. In retrospect, these Makerere stories were rehearsals for themes that were to dominate East African fiction in the first decade of independence. For example, Ngugi's "The Village Priest" was an early version of his first written novel, *The River Between*, while the tone of the "The Return" echoes *Weep Not, Child*. The theme of the latter, the story of a former Mau Mau detainee who returns home to discover his world turned upside down, was reworked elaborately in *A Grain of Wheat*.

However, by the time Ngugi worked out into complete novels the issues raised in his Makerere stories, the historical and social context had changed radically. It was the early 1960s, the era of self-government and independence, a period when the ideal of the community of the nation seemed to have been realized, providing the impetus for the emergence of the novel as an important genre in the region. Although published amidst the euphoria that accompanied independence, the novels of the early 1960s carried within them the anxieties of colonialism. Ngugi's first two novels, *Weep Not, Child* and *The River Between*, are about the cultural conflict engendered by the colonial encounter, the alienation of African subjects from their lands and traditions, and the culture of violence associated with decolonization.

These novels were set in specific Kenyan contexts, the 1920s and 1950s, but their form was influenced by the tradition of English modernism. This is evident in their obsessive concern with the lives of alienated individuals trying to reconcile their desire for personal autonomy with the demands of larger communal and collective entities. At this stage in his career, Ngugi did not seem to be interested in incorporating elements of African oral culture into his novels. He seemed content to use the idiom of modernism to invoke simultaneously the local landscape—especially its mythologies and histories—and the tortured lives of individuals at odds with collective interests. *Weep Not, Child* and *The River Between* are certainly novels about larger social movements (Mau Mau and cultural nationalism), but they are also stories about the tenuous existence of individuals deprived of their will by the demands of history. These worlds have now come to be associated with cultural nationalism, but when they were being written in the early 1960s, Ngugi was a vocal advocate of the liberal notion that individual freedom, rather than nationalism, was the real goal of decolonization.

The novels and short stories of Grace Ogot represent the only significant attempt by novelists of this generation to fashion their works after some aspects of African storytelling. In *The Promised Land*, Ogot told the story of a migrant Luo family in Tanzania struggling to improve their lot while holding on to their traditions. The novel did not enter the canon of East African letters when it was first published because it was considered to be too preoccupied with the detritus of ordinary life and lacked the drama that had made Ngugi's work resonate with the new postcolonial reading elite. In retrospect, however, these critics missed the major aspects of Ogot's imagination, especially her desire to incorporate Luo myths and speech patterns in her works.

Although the publication of Okot p'Bitek's long poem *Song of Lawino* was the major literary event of the first decade of independence, the novel continued to be the most influential genre, both because of its privileged position in the culture of the school and because of its close formal and thematic connection to the changing narrative of decolonization. The relation between novel and nation was particularly marked in the mid-1960s, when a new discourse, revolving around what Frantz Fanon had called "the pitfalls of national consciousness," emerged to reflect the growing disillusionment with the political project of decolonization. While up to this point major novelists had positioned their works within the general narrative of decolonization, the twin goals of their works were to imagine a decolonized polity and to recover a usable past.

By 1966, however, it was obvious that the romantic vision of cultural nationalism was not coming to fruition. This situation was aptly summed by Fanon in *The Wretched of the Earth*, where he noted that the new postindependence ruling elites would perpetuate and raise to higher levels the exploitative and repressive practices of the colonial governments they replaced. Major novelists had been reading Fanon and borrowed from him a grammar for representing the failure of the nationalist project. The result was a series of novels revolving around the motif of betrayal and failure. We see this motif in Ngugi's *A Grain of Wheat*, Leonard Kibera's *Voices in the Dark*, Rubadiri's *No Bride Price*, Peter Palangyo's *Dying in the Sun*, and Robert Serumaga's *Return to the Shadows*. In addition to sharing a common theme, these novels drew powerfully on the interiorized language of their disenchanted characters, temporal fragmentation, and the rhetoric of failure much more than novels published only five years earlier.

The concern with the failure of decolonization was to continue dominating the geography of the novel in the 1970s, but there was a sense that the modernist style alone could not capture the full range of possible experience. In the 1970s, then, novels were produced in a variety of subgenres. The most important of these was the popular novel, exemplified by the works of Charles Mangua and David Maillu. Mangua's *Son of Woman* (1971) sold over ten thousand copies in its first six months, an unprecedented and still unmatched record for sales of regional fiction. What accounted for the popularity of this novel was its ability to represent postcolonial failure and disillusionment using the idiom of American popular fiction. This enabled it to reach readers outside the formal institutions of education. Indeed, these works attracted student readers precisely because they went against the mores of school culture.

It was also in this period that a new tradition of urban literature, represented by the novels of Meja Mwangi, first emerged. In his urban novels, especially *Kill Me Quick* and *Going Down River Road*, he captured the grit and poverty of the overcrowded postcolonial city in a style that was halfway between the popular and the serious, attuned to the entrapment of his characters in the cycle of urban poverty but also using their difficult lives as the basis for entertainment. A different mode of representing what social scientists had termed "underdevelopment" would not depict lives of the poor and alienated with deep, sociological sophistication. This was evident in Ngugi's *Petals of Blood*, the works of the Tanzanian novelists Ismael Mbise and Gabriel Ruhumbika, and Nurrudin Farah's first two novels in English, *From a Crooked Rib* and *A Naked Needle*.

It is fair to say that the period from 1964 to 1978 represented the high point of the novel in East Africa. After that, the genre found its numbers diminished by changed historical circumstances and its energies sapped by the crisis of what has come to be known as "postcolonial failure." Beginning in the early 1980s, and perhaps earlier in some countries, the conditions in which culture was produced were affected by economic stagnation or failure, the collapse of social and cultural institutions, political instability, and the impoverishment of the middle class, the traditional readers of novels. This situation affected writing in general in several ways: Economic and political crisis led to the collapse or dispersal of established publishing houses such as the East African Publishing House and the East African Literature Bureau. The crisis in institutions of education such as the universities, many of which were subjected to political violence and underfunding, meant that there was no longer a powerful center for exchanging ideas, a place where serious creative writing, other cultural projects, and criticism could thrive together. The failure of democracy sent many of the region's influential writers into prison or exile. Others were imprisoned by a culture of silence. The list of writers imprisoned or exiled reads like a who's who of East African letters. In even more extreme cases, writers were killed by government forces or died under mysterious circumstances. By the 1990s, the centers of publishing had shifted. The region's major writers were living and being published elsewhere. Ngugi was in the United States; Farah was in Nigeria and then South Africa.

Still, this crisis did affect the nature of novelistic production in unexpected and more positive ways. For one, writers unhappy with the split of the novel between high modernism and documentary realism were quick to argue that a state of crisis demanded a rethinking of the form of the novel itself. Indeed, prominent novelists from the region responded to the state of political crisis by overcoming the binary opposition between modernism and realism. Thus Ngugi's later novels *Devil on the Cross* and *Matigari*, originally published in Gikuyu, were an imaginative melding of modernist scatology, allegory, and social realism, focused simultaneously on the politics of everyday life and the fantastic. In Nurrudin Farah's "dictatorship" trilogy, *Sweet and Sour Milk, Sardines*, and *Close Sesame*, a self-consciously high modernist style, one that privileges interiorized consciousness, is balanced with an acute representation of Somalia under the military dictatorship of Siad Barre.

It was also during the period of crisis that a distinctive feminist tradition in East Africa emerged. Before the 1980s, the majority of women novelists, most prominently Grace Ogot and Rebecca Njau, were not focused on the lives of women except in relation to the changing narrative of cultural nationalism and the crisis of decolonization. In the 1980s, however, women novelists seemed to have come to the realization that the narrative of nationalism, whose pitfalls were so marked in that decade, was gendered, and that women bore the brunt of political and social failure. It was in this context that veteran writers like Marjorie Macgoye started writing fiction in which the story of nationalism (*Coming to Birth*) or the social pathologies of the age, HIV/AIDS and corruption, for example, were narrated from the perspective of women characters (*Chira*). A new generation of women writers such as Margaret Ogola (*The River and the Source*) and Goretti Kyomuhendo (*Secrets No More* and *The First Daughter*) also emerged during this period, often published by cooperatives organized by women's groups such as Femrite in Uganda.

By the end of the 1990s, the East African novel seemed to have developed two distinct traditions. The first one was represented by locally published authors, many of them self-published, whose works focused on specific social problems such as corruption and HIV/AIDS. In this category belong the later works of Meja Mwangi (*The Last Plague*) and Margaret Ogola (*I Swear by Apollo*). In view of the challenges presented by political and economic crisis, these novelists had fallen back on local resources, often producing novels that were allegories of the crisis. Indeed, if these novels have anything in common, it is their intense focus on the contemporary and everyday as the locus of fiction.

A second tradition was represented by authors who had left East Africa and become established as part of the global postcolonial set. In this category belong the works of Abdulrazak Gurnah (for example, *Pilgrimage of Departure* and *Paradise*) and M. G. Vassanji (for example, *The Gunny Sack*, *Uhuru Street*, and *The Book of Secrets*). Gurnah and Vassanji draw heavily on both the authors' East African experiences and the history of the region, but they are also part of the literary canon of Britain and Canada, respectively. An analogous situation is represented by the novels of Nurrudin Farah, which have been circulated and read all over the world. These novels are intensely Somali in their preoccupation but are barely read in Somalia itself, since they were written in exile and in English. By contrast, Ngugi's late novels, including his trilogy *Murogi wa Kagogo* (*The Wizard of the Crow*) was produced in exile but limited to a small Gikuyu reading audience.

REFERENCES

Gikandi, Simon. *Reading the African Novel*. London: James Currey, 1987.

[Gikandi]

Ntiru, Richard Carl (b. 1946) Ugandan poet and editor. Ntiru was born near Kisoro in Kigezi District, in southwestern Uganda. He was educated at Ntare School, in Mbarara in Ankore District. In 1968, he joined Makerere University College, where he studied English and edited the university magazine *Makererean* as well as the campus journal of creative writing *Penpoint*. For many years, Ntiru worked as an editor with publishing companies and research organizations in East Africa, including the now defunct East African Publishing House. He has contributed to East African magazines, produced a radio play, and written a few short stories, but he is known primarily as a poet.

Ntiru's poetry makes references to the works of modern poets like Christopher Okigbo, but it is reminiscent of rural oral poetry, even when it presents modern themes. His first book, a collection of poems entitled *Tensions* (1971), deals with contemporary issues in East Africa. His poetry is driven by a profound awareness of the gap between the rich and the poor in East Africa and the indifference of local elites and the international community to the plight of ordinary people in the region. For example, "The Pauper," widely anthologized in textbooks, addresses the poverty-stricken East African and questions the status quo:

Pauper, pauper, craning your eyes
in all directions, in no direction!
What brutal force, malignant element

dared to forge your piteous fate?
Was it worth the effort, the time?

In the poem, the desperateness of the beggar is underlined by parallel structures that suggest social immobility, despite attempts by the beggar to forge ahead or attract attention. The rhetorical questions in the poem echo African oral poetry. Ntiru uses rhetorical questions to underline the fact that the conditions the majority of the people live in are unjustified and wicked. In "The Pauper," for example, the environment is evoked to emphasize the despair to which the pauper has been reduced:

You limply lean on a leafless tree,
nursing the jiggers that shrivel your
bottom,
like a baby newly born to an old
woman.
What crime, what treason did you
commit,
that you are thus condemned?

While on the surface it may appear that the fate of the beggar is natural, the artist uses images that indicate that his poverty may have a political origin. The use of the word "treason" suggests deliberate neglect of the poor and governmentally engineered poverty. The poem seems to question the unfairness of God, but within the overall context, the preternatural power is a metaphor for the power-wielding policy makers.

While most East Africans evoke the rural landscape to create the impression of a lost Eden posed against the ugliness of modernity, Ntiru uses the rural setting to address contemporary issues such as poverty and drought. In "First Rain," for example, he uses images of rural dilapidation to express the despair that grips the nation in the face of economic failure:

From bewildered heights, heaven
gazed on earth:

She was brown and wizened with
care.
Sallow vegetation lingered motionless
in emptiness,
Cocking her crisp leaves, devoid of
harmony.
And the famished animals limply
trudged,
And slowly stopped with lifeless
uncertainty,
Calmly resigned to their cruel fate.

Even when his poetry is bleakly expressing disillusionment with postindependence politics, there are glimmers of hope. In "First Rain," the drought ends in a scene that recalls a literary masterpiece: "the scene was set: Paradise recreated: / First rains had come to salvage the earth." The alternation between despair and hope is a hallmark of Ntiru's poetry.

PRIMARY TEXTS

Ntiru, Richard Carl. *Tensions*. Nairobi: East African Publishing House, 1971.

REFERENCES

Yesufu, A. Rasheed. "Richard Ntiru's Poetry and the Paradox of Uhuru." *Commonwealth* 8, no. 2 (1986): 94–101.

[Mwangi]

Nyabongo, Prince Akiki K. (1904–1975)
Ugandan autobiographer and folklorist. Born into the Toro royal family, Prince Nyabongo was one of the first Ugandans to be educated abroad. He graduated from Yale University, acquired an MA from Harvard University, and earned a PhD in philosophy from Oxford University. In the 1940s and 1950s, Nyabongo lived and worked abroad, mostly in the United States, where he taught at Tuskegee University and North Carolina A&T University, both historically black colleges. He returned to Uganda after independence and served for many years as the

chairman of the Uganda Town and Country Planning Board. Nyabongo's published works include an autobiographical account of the encounter between Toro and European colonizers, published as *The Story of an African Chief* and as *Africa Answers Back*. In the book, he provided his own subjective experience of what life in Toro was like both before colonialism and after, but he saw the work not simply as the story of everyday life in the kingdom, but also as a generalized African response to what was considered to be the cultural slander that justified colonialism, namely, the claim that African peoples did not have a distinctive culture or history before the European occupation. Nyabongo was also an avid collector of folklore.

PRIMARY TEXTS

Nyabongo Akiki K. *Africa Answers Back*. London: Routledge, 1936.
——. *The Story of an African Chief*. New York: Scribner, 1935.

REFERENCES

Turfan, Barbara. *Some African Critics of East African Society During the 1930s*. London, 1985.

[Gikandi]

Nyerere, Julius Kabarage (1922–1999) Tanzanian statesman, intellectual, and translator. Nyerere was born in Butiama, on the shores of Lake Victoria, in a minor chiefdom of the Zanaki people. He was educated in local Catholic schools in Musoma and, for his secondary education, at Tabora Government School. After high school, he went to Makerere University College, from where he obtained a diploma in teaching. He later was sent to Britain for further education and graduated with an MA from the University of Edinburgh. On his return to colonial Tanganyika in 1952, Nyerere tried to balance his role as a teacher and a nationalist, but he was eventually forced to give up teaching to concentrate on politics. In 1959, he was elected to the Tanganyika Legislative Assembly. In 1960, he became the chief minister of the first autonomous Tanganyika government, was elected prime minister upon the achievement of independence in 1962, and was elected president of Tanzania when mainland Tanganyika formed the union with the islands of Zanzibar and Pemba in 1964.

In addition to his well-known political activities as president of Tanzania, his relentless advocacy of pan-Africanism, and his leadership of the Non-Aligned Movement, Nyerere was a cultural theorist and intellectual, a proponent of African socialism, autonomous education, and self-reliance. His ideals regarding the fields of culture and education occupied a central place in the Arusha Declaration of 1967 and found their way into influential collections of his speeches and essays. Nyerere's ideas and ideals were also influential in the lives of radical African writers in East Africa and the rest of the world. In the 1960s and 1970s, European, American, and West Indian intellectuals converged at the University of Dar es Salaam, of which Nyerere was chancellor. These intellectuals included the Kenyan critic Grant Kamenju, the Guyanese historian Walter Rodney, and the Ghanaian novelist Ayi Kwei Armah. Nyerere was one of the staunchest proponents of writing in Swahili in East Africa, and his major contribution to the literary culture of the region is found in his translations of two of Shakespeare's seminal plays, *The Merchant of Venice* and *Julius Caesar*.

TRANSLATIONS

Julius Kaisari (a Swahili translation of *Julius Caesar*). Dar es Salaam: Oxford University Press, 1969.
Mabepari wa Venisi (a Swahili translation of *The Merchant of Venice*). Dar es Salaam: Oxford University Press, 1969.

ESSAYS

Nyerere, Julius Kabarage. *Freedom and Unity; Uhuru na Umoja: A Selection from Writings and Speeches, 1952–1965*. London: Oxford University Press, 1966.

——. *Freedom and Socialism; Uhuru na Ujamaa: A Selection from Writings and Speeches, 1965–1967*. Dar es Salaam: Oxford University Press, 1968.

——. *Ujamaa: Essays on Socialism*. Dar es Salaam: Oxford University Press, 1968.

——. *Freedom and Development; Uhuru na Maendeleo: A Selection from Writings and Speeches, 1968–1973*. London: Oxford University Press, 1973.

——. *Man and Development*. Dar es Salaam: Oxford University Press, 1974.

——. *The Arusha Declaration Ten Years After*. Dar es Salaam: Government Printer, 1977.

[Gikandi]

Oculi, Okello (b. 1942) Ugandan poet, novelist, political scientist, and literary theorist. Born in Lango in northern Uganda, Oculi was educated at Soroti College, St. Peter's College, Tororo, and St. Mary's College, Kisubi, before attending Makerere University College, from where he graduated with a degree in political science. As an undergraduate, Oculi edited the college newspaper *The Makerean.* He later received an MA in political science from the University of Essex, in the United Kingdom, and a PhD from the University of Wisconsin, Madison. He later taught at Makerere University in Uganda and Ahmadu Bello University in Zaria, Nigeria.

Interested in the intersection of literature and politics, Oculi has drawn on his diverse background to produce long poems that blend different literary traditions but are structured by African images, proverbs, and folk wisdom. Despite borrowing from various backgrounds and experiences, his writings attempt to reassert the dignity of African rural life by criticizing the unabashed imitation of dominant cultures. Although written in English, his creative works use an idiom that approximates rural conversation.

Oculi's first and most famous poem, *The Orphan* (1968), belongs to the "song tradition" initiated by Okot p'Bitek's *Song of Lawino* (1966). Through the figure of an orphan, this long dramatic poem explores the problems of the underprivileged in postcolonial African society. The poem is set in an unnamed East African country, at a crossroads, where the Orphan meets his interlocutors. The poem presents various characters' interpretation of postindependence East Africa, which, like the Orphan, is caught at the crossroads of tradition and modernity, the past and the future. Using a combination of prose and verse, the poem laments the loss of African values and traditions and depicts the hopes of a perfect postindependence nationhood as betrayed or compromised. A village elder advises the Orphan, and to a large extent the reader, to wake up to the painful reality that postcolonial subjects have no option but to remain "perpetual tourists" in a world that is still defined by alienating Western values.

In his first novel, *Prostitute* (1968), Oculi turned to prose to comment on the social problems plaguing postindependence Africa, this time using the figure of a prostitute, Rosa Nakintu, to probe the lives of the ruling elite. In *Malak* (1976) and *Kookolem* (1978), he used the long-poem form to depict the conflict between modernity and tradition in postcolonial Africa during the period of the Idi Amin dictatorship, a subject also taken up in *Kanta Riti* (1972), his second novel. Oculi has also published shorter poems on subjects ranging from death and love to cultural conflict, in prominent anthologies such as David Cook and David Rubadiri's *Poems from East Africa* (1971). In *Song for the Sun in US* (2000), he collected many of his poems, written over a period spanning thirty years and dealing with political themes, tensions between different religions in Africa, and academic charlatanism.

PRIMARY TEXTS

Oculi, Okello. *The Orphan.* Nairobi: East African Publishing House, 1968.

——. *Prostitute.* Nairobi: East African Publishing House, 1968.

——. *Kanta Riti.* Kampala: Uganda Publishing House, 1972.

——. *Malak.* Nairobi: East African Publishing House, 1976.

——. *Kookolem.* Nairobi: East African Publishing House, 1978.

——. *Song for the Sun in US.* Nairobi: East African Educational Publishers, 2000.

[Mwangi]

Ocwinyo, Julius (b. 1961) Ugandan novelist and editor. Ocwinyo was born in Apac District, in northern Uganda, and was educated at local schools in Aboke and Lango before training as a teacher of English and French at the Institute of Teacher Education, Kyambogo. After leaving Kyambogo, Ocwinyo taught at various high schools in northern Uganda before attending Makerere University College, where he specialized in language education. Born on the eve of Ugandan independence, Ocwinyo grew up and came of age in the turbulent years that followed decolonization, including the Idi Amin military dictatorship, the guerilla war waged to overthrow it, and the political turbulence that followed. In *Fate of the Banished* (1997), his first novel, Ocwinyo tells the story

of Apire, a young man whose dreams of education and self-advancement collide with the violence of the guerilla war and its heavy toll on individuals and families.

In *Footprints of the Outsider* (2002), Ocwinyo presents a longer view of the history of Uganda as seen by two sets of characters: a couple of Indians who migrate to northern Uganda to set up a cotton ginnery, thus initiating the process of modernization; and Abudu Olwit, who enters this new world determined to acquire a university education. Although Ocwinyo's novels have not gained international attention, they have resonated with Ugandan readers because of their acute sense of the interplay between violence and the dogged determination for identity in contemporary Ugandan society, especially in the era of the civil war in the north of the country. Ocwinyo's poetry has appeared in anthologies, and he is the author of *The Unfulfilled Dream* (2002).

PRIMARY TEXTS

Ocwinyo, Julius. *Fate of the Banished.* Kampala: Fountain Publishers, 1997.

——. *Footprints of the Outsider.* Kampala: Fountain Publishers, 2002.

——. *The Unfulfilled Dream.* Kampala: Fountain Publishers, 2002.

[Gikandi]

Odinga, Oginga (1911–1994) Kenyan nationalist and autobiographer. Born in Sakwa, in Central Nyanza, Odinga was educated at the Anglican Church School at Maseno and Makerere University College in Uganda, where he trained as a teacher of mathematics. After graduating from Makerere, Odinga taught in several Kenyan schools, but in the 1940s he began to develop an interest in politics. This interest was triggered both by the rising tide of nationalist protest in Kenya at the end of World War II and by Odinga's own disenchantment with what he was later to call "the white hand of authority," represented by missionaries and colonial administrators. Odinga's first foray into politics was through the Luo Thrift Organization, a movement whose goal was to organize trade and the marketing of products in Central Nyanza. It was as a leader of this organization that Odinga visited India in 1953. In 1957, he was elected to the Kenyan Legislative Council to represent Central Nyanza, and it was during this time that he became involved in various constitutional debates on the future of Kenya, emerging as the most radical representative of African interests. Odinga came into international prominence in 1958, when, during a visit to London to attend a Kenyan constitutional conference, he told conservative members of the British Parliament that the nationalists who had been arrested, detained, or killed by the colonial government were the true heroes of the Kenyan struggle for independence. That same year, he declared in the Kenyan Legislative Assembly that Jomo Kenyatta, considered by the colonial government to be the agent of terror and death, was the genuine leader of the Kenyan people.

Ironically, it was under Kenyatta's leadership in the 1960s that Odinga was politically marginalized and persecuted. Although he served as Kenya's vice president during the first three years of independence (1963–1966), he was increasingly associated with the radical wing of the ruling party, KANU, and his connections to socialist governments in Europe and Asia were treated with suspicion by an increasingly conservative postcolonial regime. Frustrated in his efforts to bring about radical political change, Odinga resigned from the government and the ruling party in 1966 and formed the Kenya People's Union. The KPU was banned in 1970, and Odinga was detained without trial until 1976. After his release

from detention, he found it difficult to enter formal politics, but he continued to serve as the leader of an unofficial opposition, and in the late 1980s and early 1990s, as the policies of the government of Kenyatta's successor Daniel arap Moi became more repressive, Odinga lent his weight to oppositional groups, emerging as a leader of FORD-Kenya, under whose umbrella he contested the 1991 presidential elections.

Odinga told the story of his long and remarkable life in *Not Yet Uhuru*, an autobiography published to coincide with his resignation from the first Kenyatta government. Following the established structure of African nationalist autobiography, *Not Yet Uhuru* narrated Odinga's life from early childhood in Sakwa, education at Maseno and Makerere, and his entry into politics. The book focused on the key moments in which the author's personal experiences under colonialism mirrored the general conditions under which Africans lived, the grievances they had against the colonial order, and the role of economic deprivation in the shaping of radical politics. However, Odinga's book was different from the traditional African political autobiography in two major respects: First, instead of presenting a chronology of his life, the author tended to focus on discrete moments in the political history of Kenya, even giving considerable attention to events such as the Mau Mau revolt, which did not affect him at a personal level. Second, while other political autobiographies tended to end with the euphoria surrounding independence, often seen as the moment of arrival of the African self, *Not Yet Uhuru* was written from the vantage point of postcolonial decline and failure. Indeed, Odinga's work was an attempt to trace the process by which the dreams of the nationalist movement that had shaped his life had collapsed. The book, whose foreword was written by Kwame Nkrumah, is now considered to be one of the most astute observations of the anatomy of neocolonialism in Africa.

PRIMARY TEXTS

Odinga, Oginga. *Not Yet Uhuru*. London: Heinemann, 1967.

REFERENCES

Oruka, H. Odera, and Ajuma Oginga Odinga. *Oginga Odinga: His Philosophy and Beliefs*. Nairobi: Initiatives Publishers, 1992.

[Gikandi]

Ogola, Margaret (b. 1958) Kenyan novelist and pediatrician. Ogola's novels are renowned for their celebration of the spirit of womanhood and their subversion of the epic narratives of nationhood. Her first novel, *The River and the Source* (1994), highlights the achievements of three generations of East African women and their struggle against traditional and postcolonial patriarchy. Other themes covered in the story are colonialism, World War I and its effect on African families, physical beauty versus spirituality, and AIDS. Taught in Kenyan schools in the 1990s as a compulsory text, the novel has influenced writing by younger artists. Its sequel, *I Swear by Apollo* (2002), chronicles the life of the grandchildren of the original characters and their search for identity in a rapidly shifting social world.

In what seems to be a response to the critics' view that Ogola is excessively harsh in her treatment of men in her first novel, the sequel focuses on achievements of women in postindependence Kenya but takes pains to offer more expressive space to its male subjects. It captures the dawn of the twenty-first century, as Kenya struggles to rise from the vortex of inefficiency, corruption, AIDS, and filth that has hounded it up to the close of the last century. Published by religious venues, her writing is highly influenced by Catholic Church doctrines and thinly veils an advocacy for the ideas of the Opus Dei movement. *Place of Destiny* (2005) didactically explores the themes of suffering, grief, separation, and reunion, and the contemplation of life, death, and life after death. Woven into the themes is how women can situate themselves in secular sectors without abandoning their core religious values. Told in a multiplicity of voices that nevertheless all reinforce the same idea, the novel demonstrates the inevitability of preternatural powers in ordering human existence. *Educating in Human Love* (coauthored with her husband, George Ogola, in 1999) is a nonfiction discussion of family values and how to teach children about sexual issues within a pro-life Christian context. *Cardinal Otunga: A Gift of Grace* (1999) is a biographical account of a leading African Catholic figure, Cardinal Maurice Michael Otunga (1923–2003).

PRIMARY TEXTS

Ogola, Margaret. *The River and the Source*. Nairobi: Focus Books, 1994.
——. *I Swear by Apollo*. Nairobi: Focus Books, 2002.
——. *Place of Destiny*. Nairobi: Paulines Publications Africa, 2005.
Ogola, Margaret, and George E. Ogola. *Educating in Human Love*. Nairobi: Focus Books, 1999.
Ogola, Margaret, and Margaret Roche. *Cardinal Otunga: A Gift of Grace*. Nairobi: Paulines Publications Africa, 1999.

[Mwangi]

Ogot, Grace Emily Akinyi (b. 1930) Kenyan novelist, short-story writer, and politician. Ogot is considered one of Kenya's leading writers and the first East African woman writer to write in English. Her first short stories were published in 1962 and 1964, and her first novel, *The Promised Land*, appeared in 1966, the same year as Flora Nwapa's better-known *Efuru*. Ogot was born in Central Nyanza, where despite her grandfather's protest that she should not be taken to school because she was female, her father, a church elder, took her to Maseno Junior School, from where she graduated to attend Ngi'ya Girls' School and Butere Girls' High School in western Kenya. She later trained as a nurse in Uganda. Married in 1959 to the historian Bethwel Allan Ogot, she moved with him to London, where she became a radio announcer for the BBC.

On her return to Kenya from London in 1961, Ogot became a community development officer and principal of a Women's Training Centre until 1963, when she became the chief nurse at Makerere University College in Kampala, Uganda. In 1966, she joined Maendeleo ya Wanawake, a national women's movement, and became an executive committee member of the Kenya Council of Women. In the late 1960s and during most of the 1970s, Ogot worked as a broadcaster for the BBC, journalist, midwife, and tutor, besides serving as a public-relations officer with the Air India Corporation of East Africa. She later held various diplomatic positions as Kenya's representative to the United Nations and UNESCO. She has served as a member of parliament and as an assistant minister; she was also a founding member of the Writers' Association of Kenya.

With Ngugi wa Thiong'o, Ogot attended the 1962 African Writers of English Expression conference at Makerere University College, Kampala, Uganda. Indeed, as the only Kenyan delegates at the conference, Ogot and Ngugi have been credited with shaping the direction of Kenyan writing. J. Roger Kurtz has argued that the two novelists established the thematic and stylistic order that other writers would emulate: "Ngugi and Ogot produced the archetypal characters in Kenyan fiction and set out the the-

matic concerns of their generation" (*Urban Obsessions and Urban Fears*, 22).

While Ogot's early writings display the nationalistic fervor that characterized East African writing in the 1960s, they are also deeply sensitive to the ambivalent place of women and their institutions in postcolonial Africa. Although highly influenced by African traditions, her writing subverts cultural practices that stand in the way of women's development. For example, her widely anthologized short story "The Rain Came" questions the veracity of traditional beliefs by depicting the plight of a young girl who is sacrificed by her community to appease some cosmological forces, which are believed to be behind a devastating drought. In addition to depicting rural life and its tenuous relation to urbanity, Ogot's novels are informed by strong motifs relating to medicine and ailment. *The Promised Land* is about a man, Ochola, who, against the wishes of his father and wife, emigrates from Kenya to colonial Tanganyika in pursuit of economic advancement. Ochola is bewitched and contracts a strange skin disease.

Although her writing seems to avoid the self-conscious feminism associated with younger East African writers, Ogot's fiction functions as an important medium for reclaiming repressed subjectivities and identities. While novels such as *The Promised Land* focus on the institution of marriage, Ogot represents women as having more agency than men, and the novel revolves around a woman, Nyapol, who has an immense potential to subvert patriarchal structures. This search for a voice for the repressed is exemplified in the short story "Elizabeth" in *Land Without Thunder*, an allegory of all that has gone wrong in postindependence East Africa, where the men who have taken over from the colonialists are as abusive and exploitative as their colonial predecessors. The story is about Elizabeth's rape by her boss and her eventual suicide because of the trauma she experiences. Elizabeth's story is derived from her notebook, which the omniscient narrative voice lays bare, although it is a private document to which only the man who raped her, Mr. Jimbo, and Mother Hellena have access. This makes Elizabeth the origin of her own story, the privileged source of the narrative.

The most salient feature of Grace Ogot's narrative structures is the way she uses myth and narrative voice to retell old stories through gendered lenses. In *Miaha*, written in Luo in 1968 (translated as *The Strange Bride*), Ogot creates an Adamic myth about the origin of labor in the Luo community. Borrowed from Luo oral traditions, the narrative portrays the power of women to transform Got Owaga from a deprived village highly dependent on preternatural powers to an agricultural and fishing entity where people shape and control their own destinies. In the same stroke, the narrative celebrates the women's power not only to determine their destiny in a male-dominated society, but also to transform the nation's economy and politics. While in the original Luo myth Nyawir is reviled for condemning society to having to work for its survival, instead of sitting back as the farmlands till themselves, Ogot's narrative celebrates Nyawir's rebellious nature, which leads her to steal the magic hoe and work on the farm. Her activity leads to a revolutionary change in which people start farming more aggressively for their betterment. In addition to *Miaha*, Ogot has published a second novel in Luo, *Simbi Nyaima*.

PRIMARY TEXTS (IN ENGLISH)

Ogot, Grace. *The Promised Land.* Nairobi: East African Publishing House, 1966; Repr. Nairobi: East African Educational Publishers, 1990.

——. *Land Without Thunder.* Nairobi: East African Publishing House, 1968. Repr. Nairobi: East African Educational Publishers, 1988.

——. *The Other Woman.* Nairobi: TransAfrica Publishers, 1976; Repr. Nairobi: East African Educational Publishers, 1990.

——. *The Strange Bride.* Translated from the Luo by Okoth Okombo. Nairobi: Heinemann, 1989.

——. *The Island of Tears.* N.p.: Uzima Press, 1990.

REFERENCES

Achufusi, Ify. "Problems of Nationhood in Grace Ogot's Fiction." *Journal of Commonwealth Literature* 26, no. 1 (1991): 179–188.

Bardolph, Jacqueline. "The Literature of Kenya." In *The Writing of East and Central Africa*, edited by G. D. Killam, 36–53. Nairobi: Heinemann, 1984.

Chesaina, Ciarunji. "Grace Ogot: A Creative Writer's Contribution to Cultural Development and Women's Emancipation." *Writers' Forum: A Journal of Writer's Association of Kenya* 1 (1992): 73–80.

Kurtz, J. Roger. *Urban Obsessions, Urban Fears: The Postcolonial Kenyan Novel.* Lawrenceville, N.J.: Africa World Press; Oxford: James Currey Publishers, 1998.

Lindfors, Bernth. "Interview with Grace Ogot." *World Literature Written in English* 18, no. 1 (1979): 56–68.

Matzke, Christine. "Embodying the Self: Aspects of the Body and Female Identity in Kenyan Women's Writing." Diss., School of English, University of Leeds, 1996.

Nazareth, Peter. "The True Fantasies of Grace Ogot, Storyteller." In *Meditations on African Literature*, edited by Dubem Okafor, 101–117. Westport, Conn.: Greenwood Press, 2001.

[Mwangi]

Okurut, Mary Karooro (b. 1954) Ugandan woman novelist, playwright, and newspaper columnist. Okurut attended Makerere University, receiving a BA in literature in 1977 and an MA in drama in 1981, and taught for some years at the college. She later served in the administration of Yoweri Museveni as presidential press secretary and also held senior government appointments. Okurut's works criticize the social conditions in Uganda through satire and parody. Women's education and self-realization under a patriarchal system are central issues in her works, the most ambitious of which is her novel *Invisible Weevil* (1998), in which she makes subtle comparisons between Ugandan politics and the AIDS scourge, weaving history into issues of gender and commenting on the political transitions in Uganda. *The Official Wife* explores the contradictions of the practice of polygamy in a Christian context and criticizes the misrepresentation of Africa in the global media. Narrated from the perspective of Liz, one of the wives, the novel expresses the trauma facing a husband's sexual promiscuity in the era of HIV/AIDS. Her other works include a play, *The Curse of the Sacred Cow* (1993); the testimony of a street child prostitute, *Child of a Delegate*; and the collection *Milking a Lioness and Other Stories*. Okurut has also edited *A Woman's Voice*, a collection of new women's writing from Uganda, and has written a work of children's literature, *The Adventurous Sisters*.

PRIMARY TEXTS

Okurut, Mary Karooro. *The Adventurous Sisters*. Kampala: Fountain Publishers, 1993.

——. *The Curse of the Sacred Cow*. Kampala: Fountain Publishers, 1994.

——. *Child of a Delegate*. Kampala: Monitor Publications, 1997.

——. *The Invisible Weevil*. Kampala: Femrite Publications, 1998.

——. *Milking a Lioness and Other Stories*. Kampala: Monitor Publications, 1999.

——. *The Official Wife*. Kampala: Fountain Publishers, 2003.

Okurut, Mary Karooro., ed. *Woman's Voice*. Kampala: Femrite Publications, 1998.

REFERENCES

Simatei, T. P. *The Novel and the Politics of Nation Building in East Africa*. Bayreuth: Bayreuth University Press, 2001.

[Mwangi]

Oral Literature and Performance (Orature) Although East African oral literature is as old as the communities that have produced it, it did not become an important subject of study in the literature curriculum until the late 1970s. It has since then become the subject of continuing debate revolving around issues of definition and method. Jane Nandwa and Austin Bukenya define oral literature as "those utterances, whether spoken, recited or sung, whose composition and performance exhibit to an appreciable degree the artistic characteristics of accurate observation, vivid imagination and ingenious expression" (*African Oral Literature for Schools*, 49). It is called "oral" because it is composed, performed, and transmitted from one generation to another, and from one geographical space to the other, through word of mouth. It is "literature" because it uses language creatively to apprehend the reality about which the artist is commenting. However, the expression "oral literature" appears to be a contradiction in terms, and to designate this highly flexible art some scholars prefer the word *orature*, coined by Ugandan linguist and literary critic Pio Zirimu in the 1970s.

Oral literature has three main ingredients: First, it has a performer who enacts and sometimes creates the oral literary item. Second, each item has its ideal performer, and there are pieces that one cannot perform because they fall outside one's purview. Third, it has an audience that listens and participates in the performance. The audience that the performer has in mind is often specific, and there are items that cannot be allowed into the performance because of age, gender, and social status. The occasion of performance is also specific: one cannot perform a poem to celebrate a wedding at a circumcision ceremony, for example.

Because East African orature is dynamic, the nature of the performance will reflect the rhetorical situation, which, in turn, is governed by the performer, the audience, and the occasion. For example, the words of an initiation song can be changed to be performed at a modern graduation ceremony. The genres of orature are also flexible. These genres include riddles (puzzles involving a formulaic verbal challenge and response), tongue-twisters (statements that pun on words to enhance children's fluency), proverbs (pithy sayings expressing communal philosophy), oral poetry, various types of narratives (legends about historical characters and myths about the religious origins of the community and the actions of supernatural beings), etiological stories (stories about the origin of phenomena such as mountains and characteristics of animals—why the leopard has spots, for example), and folk tales (about animals, but essentially typifying human characteristics). Of course, these genres interact; there are proverbs and songs in oral narrative, and a proverb can be extended into a song or an oral narrative.

East African oral literature is essentially a product of preliterate societies. As the major genre of oral literature, the oral narrative continues to exert an influence on the literary culture of East Africa, and children continue to be introduced to the storytelling tradition at an early age, both at home and at school. Thus while it draws from the traditional cultures of different communities, oral literature is also dynamic, incorporat-

ing features from other cultures and countries. In fact, genres performed by young people such as riddles, play songs, and oral narratives display influences from English. For example, Wanjiku Mukabi Kabira's study of oral narrators in the Gikuyu community of Kenya details the retelling of European stories such as *Cinderella*.

Language and performance are crucial elements in the discussion of oral literature. Each East African community prides itself on the richness of its language, and this richness is revealed in the oral literature. Similarly, oral literature enhances linguistic skills. Thus, riddling sessions are meant to improve the proper use of language; similarly, the ability to speak in proverbs is respected as a mark of linguistic accomplishment. Some oral narratives treat the theme of inarticulateness and incoherence to demonstrate the importance of good narrative and rhetorical skills; other narratives associate the origin of death to the inarticulateness of messengers such as the Chameleon.

But what is the status of oral literature in contemporary East African society? With the imposition of colonialism and the culture of modernity, traditional performers were replaced by a new generation of artists who not only performed songs occasionally but also recorded them for sale. In the circumstances, despite rapid social change, oral literature has survived into modernity, but in a different form. Technological changes have quite often enhanced oral literature. Since the 1980s, for example, rapid globalization has generated new genres and styles and a new breed of urban storytellers. The old generation of singers such as Joseph Kamaru (Kenya), who sang in a language deeply rooted in the idioms of his Gikuyu people, or Fadhili Williams (Kenya), who sang in Kiswahili *sanifu* (untainted, pure Swahili), are fast being replaced by a new generation of song artists whose works reflect international influences. This new generation of artists consists of young people whose medium of communication is Swahili and English. When these performers use vernacular languages, they are often mixed with English and Swahili. In Tanzania, Mr. Nice, T.I.D., and Jay Dee, among others, perform their songs largely in Swahili (their national language), adding touches of their local Bantu dialects. In Uganda, artists such as Chameleone, Bebe Cool, Ambassador, and Peter Myles present their songs in a mixture of English, Baganda (the local language), and a little Swahili. Kenyan song artists such as Nameless, Amani, E-Sir, and Necessary Noise mostly perform in Sheng (a mixture of English, Swahili, and local languages).

These new oral forms have not grown in a vacuum. The language "revolution" in East African oral poetry has been actively propagated by a generation brought up in the cities, where they have not been exposed to traditional storytelling sessions, have not interacted with elderly people because the older generations live in the countryside, and have little or no competency in indigenous African languages. This generation of oral artists has been compelled by circumstances to fashion a new language in which they disavow any fixed ethnicity; in fact, their names and language choices indicate a sense of rebellion against ethnic belonging.

Finally, modern writing in East Africa has drawn heavily from oral literature. Okot p'Bitek's *Song of Lawino* not only treats oral literature as a primary theme, but also presents itself as an oral song. Oral literature has also been deployed in modern social movements, such as the campaign against HIV/AIDS, and has even been used in political rallies. Modern clothes such as the Kanga, the colorful, message-bearing cloths worn by women of the East African coast, are imprinted with Swahili proverbs. Finally, studies on oral literature in East Africa have

reflected a variety of approaches. Many critical studies are focused on sociocultural perspectives; others adopt narrator-based approaches. Gender stereotypes in oral literatures have attracted the interest of scholars, and performance-based approaches are gaining popularity in East African academies.

REFERENCES

Bukenya, Austin, Wanjiku Mukabi Kabira, and Okoth Okombo. *Understanding Oral Literature.* Nairobi: Nairobi University Press, 1994.

Finnegan, Ruth. *Oral Literature in Africa.* Nairobi: Oxford University Press, 1970.

Linnebuhr, Elisabeth. "Kanga: Popular Cloths with Messages." In *Readings in African Popular Culture,* edited by Karin Barber, 138–141. Oxford: James Currey, 1997.

Masinjila, Masheti, and Okoth Okombo. *Teaching Oral Literature.* Nairobi: Kola, 1997.

Miruka, Simon Okumba. *Encounter with Oral Literature.* Nairobi: East African Educational Publishers, 1994.

Nandwa, Jane, and Austin Bukenya. *African Oral Literature for Schools.* Nairobi: Longman Kenya Ltd., 1983.

Okpewho, Isidore. *African Oral Literature: Backgrounds, Character, and Continuity.* Bloomington: Indiana University Press, 1992.

[Mwangi]

Palangyo, Peter (1939–1993)   Tanzanian novelist and diplomat. Palangyo was born in Nkoaranga in the Arusha region of Tanzania. After finishing high school at Old Moshi Secondary School, he studied at St.

Olaf College in Minnesota, where he majored in biology. It was when he was in graduate school at the University of Minnesota that he decided to abandon the sciences and focus on literature. He later graduated with a diploma in education from Makerere University College and taught in several high schools. In 1968, he returned to the United States to join the famous writers' workshop at the University of Iowa, where he earned an MFA degree in creative writing. On his return to Tanzania in 1972, he taught at the University of Dar es Salaam and later spent many years in the country's diplomatic corps, at one point serving as ambassador to France. He died in a car accident in 1993.

Palangyo's reputation as a writer rests on his single novel, *Dying in the Sun*, published in 1969 and considered by many to be one of the most compelling works of modernism in African writing from this period. In this novel, the story of Ntanya's haunting return to his home in a bid to reconcile with his dying father, Palangyo simultaneously captured the sense of disillusionment and revolt that characterized East African literature at the end of the first decade of independence and vividly appropriated modernist forms to represent the sense of failure and betrayal that was endemic at the time. A remarkable aspect of the novel was its systematic and subtle critique of the traditionalism that had defined the narrative of independence, the belief that decolonization was enabled and legitimized by a return to African roots. Through his representation of Ntanya's alienation from his father and family, Palangyo deconstructed some of the most sacred themes of African cultural nationalism, including the ideal of the family and of collectivity as the foundation of identity. He plotted Ntanya's journey not as the proverbial nationalist return to the native land, but as a hallucinatory voyage into an empty self, one bereft of ideals, of tradition and home, cast into a state of perpetual internal exile, only able to speak the language of social death and decay.

Palangyo also consciously adopted the ideologies and forms of European modernism to explore tropes of failure and betrayal. In addition to focusing on a rhetoric of failure and fragmentation, in which the individual's ability to command the world was precarious and perhaps impossible, the author fell back on familiar modernist techniques such as stream of consciousness, fragmented temporality, and abstract symbolism to depict the condition of the new African subject, who was homeless in the decolonized polity. Although *Dying in the Sun* was a novel that celebrated the interiorized world of the character at the expense of its social milieu, it did present a powerful and haunting image of the postcolonial landscape, its shadows of death, its deracination, and occasionally its aspirations. Unfortunately, it was the only novel to come from Palangyo's pen.

PRIMARY TEXTS

Palangyo, Peter. *Dying in the Sun*. London: Heinemann, 1969.

REFERENCES

Ishmael Mbise, "Writing in English from Tanzania," in *The Writing of East and Central Africa*, edited by G. D. Killam, 54–69. London: Heinemann, 1984.

[Gikandi]

Poetry and Poetics Poetry in East Africa is one of the region's oldest genres, with traditions of poetic performance rooted in every community. Poetry and theories of poetic performance have been important components of East African culture and literary production for longer than any other literary form. Nevertheless, poetry in English, and theories about the mechanics of poetic creation and the ways of responding to modern poetry, are relatively new. The production of written poetry has been handicapped by low rates of literacy and its association by readers with difficulty and obscurantism. Much of the analysis of East African poetry has concentrated mainly on the themes, values, and concerns of the poet as reflected in the poetry, the relation of the work to the historical and social conditions of the society, and the study of allusions and references to other poets, but rarely to the technical aspects of prosody.

In thematic terms, East African poetry is marked with urgency and protest against inequality, with the poets questioning the importance of creating beautiful melodies while the populace suffers from hunger, official corruption, and various forms of discrimination. Tanzanian poet Freddy Macha's "An Artist and a Wailing Mother" expresses the painful dilemma of the poet who taps into the realities of his communities without changing the squalor in which the people live. Macha uses his poetry to evoke a poetic experience in which the people on whose lives his poetry is based can only raise disturbing questions:

> "What shall I eat my son?"
> She can't cry-she can't laugh
> she watches my poetry
> and she is hungry
> seeing nothing in it
> and I continue to write verses
> haunted by her poor voice.

> (Ojaide and Sallah, eds.,
> *The New African Poetry*, 41)

This dilemma, the tension between political commitment and aesthetic value, has shaped the discourse on the nature of poetry in East Africa. More often, however, the poets try to balance the two opposed positions in a way that makes the content inform the form as much as possible.

The 1960s and 1970s witnessed the rise of a poetic tradition that located its themes and techniques in the East African region while also drawing from Western sources. Critics have called the poetry from this period "domesticated African poetry in English." This poetry, according to D. I. Nwoga, is one which, though written in a foreign language, "talks to as many Africans as possible about issues of greatest relevance in Africa's ongoing development, both in the public management of affairs and in the maturation of human persons through emotions and values of life: love, laughter and sorrow, spiritual growth" (53). This poetry borrows from oral literature and explores issues that immediately affect the East African communities in a way that make it impossible for the poetry to be analyzed meaningfully without paying attention to sociocultural and political circumstances in the region. Forming a continuum with traditional oral poetry, the modern poetry in English is didactic and contains political and moral lessons to the reader. Pioneer poets in English such as Okot p'Bitek praised the traditions of their communities and lamented the cultural loss that accompanied the modernization of East Africa. In one such instance in *Song of Lawino*, the poetic speaker urges the audience to recognize the richness of African culture and to keep it vibrant:

> Let me dance before you
> My love,
> Let me show you
> The wealth in your house
> Ocol my husband,
> Son of the Bull
> Let no one uproot the Pumpkin.

> (120)

Okot p'Bitek's long poem is rendered as an oral performance by Lawino, a rural African woman, addressing her Westernized husband, Ocol, and his peers. Throughout the poem, Lawino engages in dances as a form of excavating and performing the values that colonialism has erased.

Okot p'Bitek's poem is the benchmark for poetic verse dealing with the conflict between colonial modernity and African traditions, and many poets from the region have responded to its main claims. "Letter to a Friend," by Marjorie Oludhe Macgoye, a Kenyan poet of European ancestry, is written for Okot p' Bitek and criticizes him for his tendency to present blacks versus whites in a simple and rigid dichotomy. It claims that there is nothing to be ashamed of in being both non-black and African, and it insists that polemics of Africanness will not help marginalized Africans improve their social situation. The speaker, like the writer, is a white woman with mixed-race children:

> Why should I be ashamed
> not to be black, when you, who are so
>   proud
> empty your years thinking of Africa
> and leave Lawino weeping?
>
> (Macgoye, *Make It Sing*, 5–7)

John Ruganda's "Reply to Okot P'Bitek's 'Lawino'" presents a cynical urbanite deconstructing the ethos of home evoked in *Song of Lawino*. In Okot p'Bitek's "song," Lawino laments the destruction of the homestead by Western influences; in contrast, the speaker in Ruganda's poem declares that he would not want to return to the "home" that Lawino appeals to:

> I can't return to the village
> I own no homestead there
> I own no homestead at all
> I have got no roots
> In any homestead
> Rats from distant homesteads
> Gnawed my roots
> Entirely.   (Luvai, ed., *Boundless Voices*, 173)

Although he rejects going back to the village "home," the speaker does not claim to have any home in the urban place either. Ruganda's poem expresses—without celebrat-

ing—the alienation of the postcolonial subject.

Thus, a significant aspect of poetics in East Africa is its contribution to the debate on African culture, which evocatively attempts to reassert African cultural heritage with a powerful critique of foreign influences. Muthoni Likimani raises the question of gender in her examination of the collapsing traditional society. In her collection of free verse *What Does a Man Want?*, she explores the relationship between the sexes. Taking different perspectives in each of the thirteen narrative poems that make up the collection, the speakers each try to comprehend her relational circumstances: intraracial and interracial marriages are examined alongside the themes of male cruelties to women and poverty in postcolonial Africa. While valorizing African traditional mores, the poetry from East Africa avoids romanticizing the past and even invites criticism of its own poetic engagement. Indeed, it has been a misinterpretation to take Lawino to be Okot p'Bitek's mouthpiece, because the poet does not always support the speaker: she is given ideas and words that would make us question her position.

The uniqueness of East African poetry resides in its attention to social and political issues in the region by employing stylistic techniques that tap into oral traditions of the region while also borrowing from modern Western poetry. In general, the most significant poems express the conflict between Western culture and African traditions, the political condition in the region, and personal relationships. Since the 1980s, gender has become a major issue in the poetry, and in the 1990s, the poetry began to self-consciously present poetic creation and readers' responses as major themes in their works. Marjorie O. Macgoye's *Make It Sing and Other Poems* (1998) is a collection of her oldest and newest poetry, selected as representing her best work. Covered are such themes as the place of poetry in society, freedom, identity, violence, displacement, and the place of the arts in life. Ugandan Susan N. Kiguli's *The African Saga* (1999) decries the use of complicated metaphors in a society that is suffering intense human degradation. Now anthologized in several publications, Kiguli's poem "I Am Tired of Speaking in Metaphors" raises the question of what role poetic form can play in moments of social crisis and personal anxiety. The woman speaker in the poem says she can ill-afford to speak in the indirectness of poetry, given the intensity of her suffering under patriarchy: "I will talk plainly / Because I am moved to abandon riddles." She further claims to have abandoned imagery in favor of direct statements to the powerful male who dominates her: "No! I will not use images / I will just talk to you."

Like Kiguli, Micere Githae Mugo draws from oral literature and attempts to reproduce the simplicity of verbal conversation in her poetry. In *Daughter of My People Sing*, the persona calls for simple aesthetics based on concrete social experiences. The poetry is rendered in clear language, as opposed to the obscurantism that informs modern poetics:

> Observe
> Listen
> Absorb
> soak yourself
> bathe
> in the stream of life
> and then sing
> sing
> simple songs
> for the people
> for all to hear
> and learn
> and sing
> with you.   (4)

If East African poetry has, of necessity, to be political and utilitarian, direct political statements are rendered with aesthetic distance, with such a degree of separation between the poet and the material presented that the statement does not appear to emanate directly from the poet. Okot p'Bitek gives his songs to personas who cannot be mistaken for him. Micere Githae Mugo uses a naïve voice to articulate the most politically direct statements. In "I Took My Son by the Hand," for example, she ridicules the nationalistic rhetoric with which the postindependence leaders hoodwink the public. The poetic situation is narrated by a woman reporting her naïve son's questions about *matunda ya uhuru* (the "fruits of independence") that the politicians are mentioning in a rally. The child innocently asks:

> Do we have
> *Matunda ya uhuru*
> In our hut?   (*Daughter of My People*
>   *Sing*, 55)

The question is left unanswered, but the poet suggests that "*matunda ya uhuru*" is just an empty expression in the grand politics of nationalism. If early East African poetry was politically engaged and served as an expression of cultural nationalism against colonial modernity, poetry since the late 1960s has contained satirical commentary on the direction of the region's political management. Henry Barlow's "Building the Nation" particularly captures the collapsing morality of the postcolonial state. Kundi Faraja in "Saluting Ujamaa," in Luvai and Makokha's *Echoes Across the Valley*, criticizes the Ujamaa (socialist) policies initiated by Julius Nyerere, the first Tanzanian president. The ideology is sarcastically figured as all-powerful, emasculating buffaloes and rhinos, and the memories of colonialism and slavery are evoked to criticize Ujamaa, which is itself a form of enslavement, because the poetic speaker cannot own a private house:

I've got houses to rent
And lodging rooms
In the town centre

    . . .

Do I hear you say
Cooperate
With other wajamaa?   (153–154)

National and international poetry competitions have been important in giving voice to East African verse. The annual school drama festivals—in which political commentary is discouraged unless it is in support of the government—have incorporated poetic recitations that have given rise to a new generation of writers who use the simple and direct language of oral performance. Pursuing aesthetics and practices that defy the dichotomy between popular and serious art, and sometimes rebelling against political commitment and the semantic opacity associated with academic poetry, this generation of poets has gained prominence in the public culture. An excellent case in point is the Kenyan poet Carolyn Nderitu, whose poetry, although superficial in its use of rhyme, repetition, and meter, uses dance and performance profusely, which has helped cultivate her following among a younger generation of readers brought up on rap music. An actor and poet since 1996, when she was twenty years old, Nderitu has performed dance, theater, and poetry on stages and art institutions in Europe and in a large number of African countries.

The BBC poetry competitions, and the anthologies that have emerged from it, have witnessed the rise of younger poets. *The Fate of the Vultures* (1989), edited by Musaemura Zimunya, Peter Porter, and Kofi Anyidoho, contains important new voices from East Africa. Gichora Mwangi's poems in the collection—"If," "Untitled," and "Waiting (for S)"—use ellipses and notions of erasure and suppression to address the hidden identities and fears of postcolonial East Africa.

In "If," he expresses the utopian wishes of a postcolonial poet in the 1980s, an era of political and sexual intolerance:

If he could have his way the artist
    might
change the hues of the sky and make
    it blue
at night

If she could have her way the
    songstress might
change the tune of the sad song and
    make fears
obsolete   (4)

The poet suggests that these poetic desires are unrealizable because of the demagoguery and political arrangements that structure expression in the region. Despite the pessimism in the poem, its very existence is evidence that poetry and poetics in East Africa have remained dynamic.

PRIMARY WORKS

Amateshe, A. D., ed. *An Anthology of East African Poetry*. Harlow: Longman, 1988.

Barlow, Henry. *Building the Nation and Other Poems*. Kampala: Fountain, 2000.

Benge, Okot, and Alex Bangirana. *Uganda Poetry Anthology*. Kampala: Fountain Publishers, 2000.

p'Bitek, Okot. *Song of Lawino*. Nairobi: East African Publishing House, 1966.

Cook, David, and David Rubadiri, eds. *Poems from East Africa*. London: Heinemann Educational, 1971.

Kariara, Jonathan, and Ellen Kitonga, eds. *An Introduction to East African Poetry*. Nairobi: Oxford University Press, 1976.

Kemoli, Arthur. *Pulsations: An East African Anthology of Poetry*. Nairobi: East African Literature Bureau, 1969.

Kiguli, Susan N. *The African Saga*. Kampala: Femrite, 1999.

Likimani, Muthoni. *What Does a Man Want?* Nairobi: Kenya Literature Bureau, 1974.

Luvai, Arthur, ed. *Boundless Voices: Poems from Kenya.* Nairobi: East African Educational Publishers, 1988.

Luvai, Arthur, and Kwamchetsi Makokha, eds. *Echoes Across the Valley.* Nairobi: East African Educational Publishers, 2000.

Macgoye, Marjorie Oludhe. *Make It Sing and Other Poems.* Nairobi: East African Educational Publishers, 1998.

Mugo, Githae Micere. *Daughter of My People Sing.* Nairobi: East Africa Literature Bureau, 1976.

Nderitu, Caroline. *Caroline Verses.* Nairobi: C. Nderitu, 2001.

——. *Play Your Drum: Selected Poems.* Nairobi: Phoenix, 2002.

Ojaide, Tanure, and Tijan M. Sallah. *The New African Poetry: An Anthology.* Boulder, Colo.: Lynne Rienner Publishers, 1999.

Okola, Lennard, ed. *Drum Beat: East African Poems.* Nairobi: East African Publishing House, 1967.

Wanjala, Chris., ed. *Singing with the Night: A Collection of East African Verse.* Kampala: East African Literature Bureau, 1974.

Zimunya, Musaemura, Peter Porter, and Kofi Anyidoho, eds. *The Fate of the Vultures: New Poetry from Africa.* Oxford: Heinemann, 1989.

REFERENCES

Dorsey, David. "Critical Perceptions of African Poetry." *African Literature Today* 16 (1988): 26–38.

Goodwin, K. L. *Understanding African Poetry: A Study of Ten Poets.* London: Heinemann, 1982.

Ojaide, Tanure. *Poetic Imagination in Black Africa: Essays on African Poetry.* Durham, N.C.: Carolina Academic Press, 1996.

Nwoga, D. I. "Modern African Poetry: The Domestication of a Tradition." *African Literature Today* 10 (1979): 32–56.

[Mwangi]

Popular Culture   The production of East African popular culture is part of a vibrant industry that draws its inspiration and methods from oral culture and borrows heavily from other African countries and global cultures in general. So critical is popular cultural expression in the region that proponents of development and political activists have, since the 1980s, been compelled to employ popular forms in their efforts to change attitudes and behavior among East African communities. Important in this area is local-language radio theater. Kimani Njogu is one of the development practitioners who has used soap operas and comic strips in Kiswahili to entertain audiences while educating them on issues such as HIV/AIDS, the protection of the environment, and gender equality. Tanzanian cartoonist Godfrey Mwampembwa is a leading satirist whose works broke political tradition by ridiculing East African dictators in visual representations that displayed their greed for power and contempt for democracy. *Democrazy!* (2000), his book of cartoons, is an absorbing analysis of the abuse of the term "democracy" in Africa, where ballot boxes are "bullet boxes," by-elections are "buy-elections," stakeholders are "steak holders," and freedom of expression is "freedom of oppression."

In East African popular culture, the boundary between tradition and modernity is blurred, because the two inform each other in fundamental ways. This is noted in the earliest East African text to directly present and discuss popular culture as an academic discipline. In *Popular Culture of East Africa,* which contains entries from different East African communities translated into English, Taban Lo Liyong reconceived oral literature by inserting into it issues emerging from the social, political, and economic arenas. He redefined culture, which informs and shapes the way we see and identify ourselves, as "a way of life as lived by a people in a particular moment in history in response to social, political and economic challenges" (ix). Thus, East Africa's diverse traditional values and cultural practices, which had been previously represented as moribund after the onslaught of modernity, were shown to have permeated modern society. For Taban Lo Liyong, then, popular culture was a living organism and not a museum piece; it was a mirror through which readers could examine their past and present actions, learn lessons, and chart a way forward into the future.

Music is an important genre in East African cultural production, and it is often appropriated by other genres. Similarly, proverbs are popularized through music to illustrate the veracity of philosophical statements. Narratives also use song interludes to relieve monotony and invite the audience to participate in the performance. This music reverberates with social relevance, and old songs are often reworked to express new realities. For example, James Ogude and Joyce Nyairo have shown how *Jamraimbo*, a Luo folk song that satirizes village idlers as rumormongers who move from one house to the next, has been reconceived as a warning to the community against the possible spread of HIV/AIDS.

Taarab music has been used in the Tanzanian and Kenyan coastal region to contest gender roles. In Swahili, *taarab* is a word borrowed from Arabic that implies delight, entertainment, enchantment, and aesthetically satisfying bodily and emotional movement. Its development goes back to the sixteenth century, but it has changed over time to adapt to new social climates. Performed mainly by women at weddings and usually focused on love themes, taarab songs are easily manipulated by the performer and audience to dispute and reinterpret important social issues and political positions. In analyzing this popular genre, Mwenda Ntarangwi says that the performance of taarab has little to do specifically with the bride and groom at the wedding in which it is performed; rather, "taarab performance is a social space in which local values, concerns, and relations are mobilized, discussed, evaluated, and reconfigured."

The younger generation of artists borrows from indigenous traditions and Western modernity to fashion their own unique hybrid forms of expression. Thanks to a marked increase in the number of recording studios, advertising sponsorship by local business communities, and the growth of FM stations in the 1990s, these artists fuse local languages and English to express political ideas. In Tanzania, this hybrid style is called "Bongo Flava," and in Kenya, the trend is called *Mahewa* ("air waves"). It is characterized by a blend of melodies, rhyming, and emulation of African-American hip-hop. Tanzania's Mr. Nice, Uganda's Chameleone, and Kenya's E-Sir are artists who use English vocabulary in Bantu-language songs to fashion a localized postmodernity. While these musicians are seen as alienated from their rural roots and languages, they see themselves as redefining themselves in relation to global artists and imported music. In the process, they reveal the anxieties of their generation.

E-Sir, whose death in March 2003 in a car accident at the age of twenty-one caused mourning throughout the region, used a hybrid language to address urbanized youths. The name E-Sir is an Anglicized version of the artist's real Muslim name, Issa, and points to his brash appropriation of English. His name is also suggestive of globalization, for the "E-" is a sign of the grammar of Web communication. E-Sir was among the pioneering young musicians behind the emergence of Kenyan hip-hop. His rhymes in English, Swahili, Kenyan languages, and Sheng (a mixture of English and African languages) were seen by his fans as evidence that Kenyan music could compete with imported pop music. What is remarkable about E-Sir's music was his use of elements of English to establish links between various languages from the region. In the first two lines of his song "Boomba Train," for example, the artist uses three words borrowed from English that establish the mood of the rest of the song. These are *kuparty* (partying), *tracky* (track record), and *heppy* (happy, or fun). The choices involve imaginative linguistic function shiftings: the adjective *happy* becomes a noun designating having fun.

In other instances, the Africanization of English has become an important means of domesticating it to African spaces. This is what happens when the artist invites his audience to have a feel of "*hizi floor za Afrika*" (these African [dance] floors). When the artist asks the DJ to "*weka* together" (put together), the expression articulates his own action of suturing languages; the meaning and feel of the English verb or noun depends on its relation to the Swahili words. Some of the lyrics are crude, treating women as objects of male desire, but the images of overt sexuality express the hypermasculinity of the generation that consumes this kind of music.

Pop culture is an important ingredient in both popular and serious novels, which deploy many scenes and motifs drawn from the world of radio, disco halls, popular magazines, television, and pubs. For example, John Kiriamiti's *Dangerous Trophy* pays tribute to the music of Congolese pop musician Koffi Olominde. But the use of popular culture in East African literature is not an act of passive reproduction; the writer changes the original utterance to refocus the text. A case in point is Ngugi wa Thiong'o and Ngugi wa Mirii's popular play *Ngaahika Ndeenda* (*I Will Marry When I Want*). It borrows its title from a popular song of the same title by musician Daniel Kamau, which was quite popular at the time

the play was first performed in the late 1970s. While the song mocks those who do not respect marriage, it is also registers a protest against the institution of marriage and its connection to class inequalities. In the play *Ngaahika Ndeenda*, the dramatists' goal is to inspire their audiences to fight social injustice. Kamaru's song is simultaneously appropriated to articulate communal protest and to transform the gender and ethnic chauvinism of the original. Popular culture in East Africa is full of such moments of transformation.

REFERENCES

Askew, Kelly Michelle. *Performing the Nation: Swahili Music and Cultural Politics in Tanzania*. Chicago: University of Chicago Press, 2002.

Lo Liyong, Taban. *Popular Culture of East Africa: Oral Literature*. Nairobi: Longman Kenya, 1972.

Ntarangwi, Mwenda G. *Gender, Performance, and Identity: Understanding Swahili Cultural Realities Through Songs*. Trenton, N.J.: Africa World Press, 2003.

Ranger, Terence O. *Dance and Society in Eastern Africa, 1890–1970: The Beni Ngoma*. London: Heinemann, 1975.

[Mwangi]

Popular Literature   To term any literature in East Africa popular is an overstatement, because the reading public is limited, largely because of low literacy rates, difficult economic conditions, and an educational curriculum that emphasizes specialization in subjects for examination. In addition, the term "popular literature" has been used to designate a type of writing that is not often taken seriously. Elizabeth Knight identifies some of the characteristics of popular literature in East Africa as the inclusion of stereotypical and predictable characters, worn-out themes, and uneven language.

The texts are mostly potboilers about urban exploits, with a particular focus on sex and crime. Few are set in rural areas. Nevertheless, the notion of popular literature in East Africa is not so straightforward. In fact, the term "popular literature" entered East African literary discourse in 1945, when the colonial governors in the region commissioned Elspeth Huxley, the white Kenyan novelist, to examine the need for books geared toward a general readership. At her recommendation, the East African Literature Bureau was formed to produce "popular literature" consisting of "books and other publications for the East African population of Kenya, Uganda and Tanganyika and Zanzibar." The texts would be in both English and local languages. This was the policy that came to govern the culture of reading in East Africa. Indeed, up to the 1970s, "popular literature" referred to adapted novels, original narratives, plays, and poetry that dealt with serious issues but that would appeal to general readers. These could be in either local languages or in simple English, preferably with an African setting. Most of the books published during this period dealt with explorers' adventures, biographies, politics, health, and history. They were mainly published by the East African Literature Bureau.

The East African Publishing House, which was established in 1966, initially focused on popular texts dealing with the Mau Mau war of liberation. These included a Swahili language translation of J. M. Kariuki's *Mau Mau Detainee*, General China's *Mau Mau General*, Godwin Wachira's *Ordeal in the Forest*, and Charity Waciuma's *Daughter of Mumbi*. Other popular texts focused on the cultural conflict occasioned by the colonial infiltration of the region and stories based on traditional beliefs. But in the early period of publishing in East Africa, what made certain works popular was not always clear. Some works were popular be-

cause of their themes and language, others because of their ability to stimulate debate on the issues troubling readers. For example, Okot p'Bitek's *Song of Lawino* (1966) was the first text in English to gain widespread popularity in and outside the academy in East Africa. A long poem in free verse incorporating African idioms in its celebration of African mores and its critique of modernity, *Song of Lawino* was not targeted at a mass audience, but by the mid-1970s it had sold 150,000 copies.

In contrast, Charles Mangua's *Son of Woman* (1971) was written for a mass audience used to American thrillers, and it sold over ten thousand copies in the first few weeks after its publication. However, what made Mangua's novel popular was not simply its mastery of an American idiom. For local readers, Dodge Kiunyu, the central character and narrator in *Son of Woman*, epitomized the promise and frustrations of the postindependence intelligentsia. As he made his way through the postcolonial city and remembered his days in school and jail, he persuaded new urban readers to examine the values of education and modernity and the relation of their colonial past to the present. The novel's popularity lay in its deployment of simple but heavily sarcastic language to invoke the lives of ordinary Africans who had been uprooted from their rural lives but could not fit into the new urban world.

The publication and popularity of *Son of Woman* led to a significant shift in East African popular literature. Imitations of *Son of Woman* flowed thick and fast from self-publishing authors. David G. Maillu, a graphic artist and illustrator, started Comb Books in 1972 to publish his writings, which local publishers had rejected. These included *Unfit for Human Consumption* (1972), *My Dear Bottle* (1973), *After 4:30* (1974), and *The Kommon Man* (1975). Maillu's texts were roundly condemned because of their explicit description of sex, urban depravity, and debauchery. His Comb Books brought out Maina Allan's *One by One* (1975) and Jasinta Mote's *The Flesh* (1975), but rejected Muli Mutiso's *Sugar Babies* (published by Transafrica Publishers, 1975) for being too sexually explicit. There was a proliferation of similar texts that took on an openly irrelevant attitude towards social problems. Usually told in the first-person narrative voice, these texts used derelicts, alcoholics, and social outcasts as characters, narrators, or poetic speakers. From that point on, the term "popular literature" took on a new inflection, suggesting writing by writers based outside university literature departments and dealing with the seedier aspects of life, such as slum existence and prostitution. The term almost became synonymous with pornographic or nonserious literature. In Kenya, Mang'ua, Meja Mwangi, and David Maillu were lumped together as popular artists and, generally, their works were excluded from high literary society. Euphrase Kezilahabi's Kiswahili novel *Rosa Mistika* (1970) and the works of David Maillu were banned by the Tanzanian government.

By the mid-1970s, the dichotomy between popular and serious literature had been firmly established. When he realized that Heinemann, the main publisher of serious African fiction, was rejecting novels about romance and crime, which would be termed "popular" and therefore nonserious, Henry Chakava, the manager of their East African branch, started the Spear Books series. Texts in this series include Rosemary Owino's *Sugar Daddy's Lover*, Sam Kahiga's *Lover in the Sky*, John Kiriamiti's *My Life in Crime*, David Maillu's *Operation DXT*, and John Kiggia Kimani's *Life and Times of a Bank Robber*. The series provided a contrast against which literariness could and would be judged, but it also opened up a new market and the popular mass consumption of

books. Other publishers followed Chakava's example: Macmillan, for example, responded with its Pacesetter series. Targeting teenagers and young adults, Pacesetter titles dealt with romance, espionage, danger, intrigue, and mystery. Longman also published popular works such as Muli wa Kyendo's *Whispers* and Omunjakho Nakibimbiri's *The Sobbing Sounds*. Transafrica, established in 1974, published popular works such as *Hesitant Love* and *First Love*.

The critical response to this kind of literature was mixed. Academic critics such as Chris Wanjala dismissed "popular literature" as a scabrous reproduction of city filth that would fuel crime and sexual depravity, but for critics such as Francis Imbuga, himself a popular playwright, this literature was "closer to the reality experienced by a majority of East Africans than the so-called serious literature." Imbuga's argument was that "it is in popular literature that ordinary men and women are tempted in one way or another by basic human desires for financial, physical and even spiritual fulfillment. And this is the life that most East Africans know." Unfortunately, most of the publishing firms specializing in popular literature collapsed in the late 1970s after the end of the coffee boom, and the focus of the remaining publishers since then has been on textbooks or literary works that are likely to be used in schools, which constitute the major market for books in the region.

REFERENCES

Arnold, Stephen H. "Popular Literature in Tanzania: Its Background and Relation to East African Literature." In *When the Drumbeat Changes*, edited by Carolyn A. Parker et al., 88–118. Washington, D.C.: Three Continents Press, 1981.

Imbuga, Francis. "East African Literature in the 1980s." In *Matatu*, edited by Dieter Riemenschneider and Frank Schulze-

Engler, 121–135. Amsterdam: Rodopi, 1993.

Knight, Elizabeth. "Popular Literature in East Africa." *African Literature Today* 10 (1979): 177–190.

Lindfors, Bernth. "A Basic Anatomy of East African Literature in English." *New Literature Review* 8 (1980): 8–14.

——. "East African Popular Literature." *Journal of Popular Culture* 13 (1979): 106–115.

——. *Popular Literature in Africa.* Trenton, N.J.: Africa World Press, 1991.

Wanjala, Chris L. *For Home and Freedom.* Nairobi: East African Publishing House, 1980.

——. "The Growth of a Literary Tradition in East Africa." Inaugural Lecture, University of Nairobi, 2003.

——. *The Season of Harvest: Some Notes on East African Literature.* Nairobi: Kenya Literature Bureau, 1978.

[Mwangi]

Precolonial Society One of the central concepts in East African literatures is that tradition is often presented as the essence of precolonial African societies and as the opposite of colonialism and modernity. The preponderance of powerful images and notions of an African culture at odds with the social processes triggered by colonialism is now so well established that it is easy to forget that African cultures were, before colonialism, diverse and disconnected from one another. While congruent cultures and communities shared a common set of values and belonged to related linguistic families, the idea of a uniform precolonial culture was the invention of colonial anthropologists and their native informants. It was during the colonial and nationalist periods that both European and African writers produced narratives that sought to establish the commonality of cultural groups

and to minimize their differences. However, to argue that the idea of a unanimous or unified precolonial African culture emerged in the crucible of colonialism is not to negate the existence of powerful social systems that predated colonialism.

Indeed, in East Africa, as elsewhere on the continent, precolonial systems of social organization were closely connected to the physical environment, which in turn determined the relationship between different polities and the outside world. On the East African coast, for example, a Swahili civilization mixing Arabic and Bantu cultures had been in existence since the fifteenth century. It was built around the religion and culture of Islam, commercial links with the Persian Gulf states and India, and trade connections to the interior of central and eastern Africa. In the plains behind the coastal strip, communities such as the Akamba of eastern Kenya and the Nyamwezi of central Tanzania dominated the trade routes between the coast and the East African interior. In the highland regions around Mt. Kenya and Mt. Kilimanjaro, the Bantu-speaking communities were primarily agricultural and were organized around small decentralized administrative units. Their neighbors in the Rift Valley plains were pastoralists. In the Great Lakes region of Uganda were the large centralized kingdoms of Buganda, Bunyoro, Toro, and Ankole.

The specific features of all these polities have been the subject of extensive histories by historians of East Africa. In addition, both historians and creative writers have turned to them for a usable past in their efforts to imagine the structure and social organization of precolonial African societies. Indeed, the historiography of East Africa in the late colonial and postcolonial period was essentially the ethnography of specific ethnic groups that had shaped or reshaped their identities in response to the colonial experience or in the aftermath of nationalism.

Conversely, the idea of precolonial societies with distinct histories and traditions came into being through elaborate processes of writing; it was then that colonial and native intellectuals began to document the customs and practices of different ethnic groups. It was in the process of writing and institutionalizing custom that tradition was, to paraphrase Terence Ranger's words, invented.

In the circumstances, what came to be known as precolonial society was the result or effect of four traditions of writing: First, there were the writings of colonial ethnographers, missionaries, and administrators, who were the first to systematize or codify the social practices of specific African groups. It was in the writings of these ethnographers that the everyday experiences of African cultures entered the intellectual traditions as unified systems of culture. It is in the works of these ethnographers that knowledge of precolonial societies was first disseminated. For example, our knowledge of precolonial Gikuyu culture owes much to the works of C. W. Hobley and William Scoresby Routledge, both colonial administrators who also produced ethnographies. Similarly, the first authoritative source of the precolonial beliefs of the Baganda and their social organization were the works of John Roscoe, the Anglican missionary, and Sir Apolo Kagwa, his most important native informant. This pattern was to continue for other groups well into the 1960s.

Second, educated Africans were quick to recognize the significance of writing their own histories of precolonial society, either to complement those produced by missionaries and colonial administrators or to oppose it. Sir Apolo Kagwa's *The Customs of the Baganda* is an example of an ethnography produced to compliment the missionaries' library, while Jomo Kenyatta's *Facing Mount Kenya* was a deliberate effort to counter the colonial production of African subjects. Third, in the 1960s and 1970s, the first serious historical studies of precolonial

societies were undertaken in the new University of East Africa and its constituent colleges. This period witnessed the emergence of oral history as an important medium for recovering the African past.

Fourth, creative writers would draw on the other three traditions to provide images of how precolonial society might have looked like and functioned and to discuss how they could be imagined as part of the national imaginary. Colonial and nationalist ethnographies and postcolonial histories of the precolonial past provided the key terms that creative writers would rehearse and popularize in their works. The idea of a precolonial African past thus came to revolve around a certain set of categories, which remained consistent from the 1938 publication of Kenyatta's *Facing Mount Kenya* to John Mbiti's *African Religions and Philosophy*, first published in 1969.

Irrespective of the traditions to which they belonged or subscribed, East African writers and intellectuals shared certain paradigms concerning the idea of a precolonial society. They conceived precolonial African societies as unified by myths of origin and characterized by a social life that emphasized the power of the communal over the individual. They portrayed precolonial society as a polity defined by a close relationship between Africans and their land, a primarily agrarian structure of life, strong kinship ties, and a system of education built around rites of passage and the mastery of oral culture. Obviously, these paradigms were placed in radical opposition to the world of colonial modernity, which was often seen as disregardful of tradition and obsessed with rationality, capitalist production, and excessive individualism. Indeed, the idea of a precolonial culture was intended to perform the foremost task in the project of cultural nationalism: namely, to show that Africans had a valid culture before colonialism and that there was no truth to the claim that the African was, to use Kenyatta's words, "a clean slate on which anything could be written" (*Facing Mount Kenya*, 259). The best defense of an African cultural system that predated colonialism was to insist on its integrity, unity, and totality. This was the point made by Kenyatta at the end of *Facing Mount Kenya* in 1938:

> In concluding this study we cannot too strongly emphasise that the various sides of Gikuyu life here described are the parts of an integrated culture. No single part is detachable; each has its context and is fully understandable only in relation to the whole. The reader who has begun at the beginning and read through will appreciate this for himself, but it is worth while to point out briefly some of the implications.   (297)

The unanimous opinion was that what ensured the integrity of this culture was the essential nature of Africans as a religious people. This point was succinctly made by Mbiti in *African Religion and Philosophy*: "Africans are notoriously religious, and each people has its own religious system with a set of beliefs and practices. Religion permeates into all the departments of life so fully that it is not easy or possible always to isolate it. A study of these religious systems is, therefore, ultimately a study of the peoples themselves in all the complexities of both traditional and modern life" (1).

These powerful ideas of a precolonial culture affected literary production in East Africa in three broad ways. First, beginning in the 1950s and continuing into the early 1960s, writers began to search for images and symbols that could represent what African cultures might have looked like before colonialism. Quite often, as in the poems of Jonathan Kariara and the early stories of Ngugi wa Thiong'o published in *Penpoint*, there was an attempt to recover the precolonial landscape, a world of the hearth and the ridges and plains, as the essential background to African life. It is not incidental that in some of these works the intrusive world of colonialism was absent. Second, and perhaps more powerfully, a precolonial order of things was posited as the counterpoint to the destructive forces of colonialism. Ngugi's first novel, *The River Between*, opens with a powerful image of an African community isolated from the rest of the world, moving according to its own rhythms. It then goes on to narrate the traumatic events that take place as colonialism, through the Christian mission, transforms the landscape. Finally, during the 1960s, a group of writers, many of them associated with Okot p'Bitek's "song" tradition, used their poetry to deploy a set of images that pleaded for the adoption of precolonial traditions as the basis of a postcolonial polity.

After the late 1970s, however, the role and place of precolonial cultures in the East African political landscape became much more complicated, because the idea of traditionalism was itself often used by the postcolonial states in the region to justify their rejection of democracy and other values deemed Western. In this situation, writers made the ambivalence of a precolonial culture a central preoccupation in their works. For example, the early novels of Nurrudin Farah are preoccupied with the use of Islamic and Somali cultural traditions by the Siad Barre dictatorship, while at the same time, the novels acknowledge these cultures as the basis of a contested Somaliness. Ngugi's later novels, *Petals of Blood*, *Devil on the Cross*, *I Will Marry When I Want*, and *Matigari* are both narrative accounts of the state's misuse of traditionalism and attempts to recover African identity as the basis of a new socialist order.

REFERENCES

Kagwa, Apolo. *The Customs of the Baganda.* Translated by Ernest B. Kalibala, edited by May Mandelbaum. New York: Columbia University Press, 1934.

Kenyatta, Jomo. *Facing Mount Kenya*. New York: Vintage Books, 1965. First published in 1938 in London by Secker and Warburg.

Mbiti, John. *African Religion and Philosophy*. 2nd ed. London: Heinemann, 1990.

[Gikandi]

Publishing The East African region has one of the oldest publishing industries in the world. In Ethiopia, publishing in Geez, the main language of literature in ancient times, reached its zenith between the fourth and the seventh centuries. All of the steps in the production of a book—writing, copying, illustration, and distribution—were usually performed by the same person, most often in Christian monasteries. Despite this early start, printing and publishing did not become widespread in the region until the colonial period in the nineteenth and early twentieth centuries, when Christian missionaries set up presses to print the Bible and publish religious literature. Some of the earliest presses, such as the Vuga Mission Press, Ndanda Missionary Press, and Highway Press, were affiliated with missionaries.

The example set by missionaries quickly inspired the colonial governments, which established presses in the early twentieth century to publish newspapers in local languages and materials for adult-education classes. In the 1950s, the rise in literacy rates in the region, though modest, attracted multinational publishing firms. Major British educational publishing firms such as Oxford University Press, Nelson, and Longman entered the regional book trade in the early 1950s, eager to provide educational materials for the expanding school system. They appointed local representatives, whose duties included selling books published in Britain and scouting for manuscripts. Other companies, including Macmillan, Evans, Heinemann, Pitman, and Cambridge University Press, followed suit. According to Henry Chakava, by the middle of the 1970s, approximately ninety publishing companies, mainly British ones, had a presence in the region.

The East African Literature Bureau (EALB) was established in 1948 by the colonial government at the recommendation of a commission chaired by the novelist Elspeth Huxley. Charles Granston Richards (1908–1996), a British missionary who had gone to East Africa with the goal of promoting literacy, became its first director. The EALB published texts in African languages. It was based in Nairobi, Kenya, with sales offices in Uganda and Tanzania. When the East African Community formally broke up in 1977, Kenya, Uganda, and Tanzania were compelled to run separate national literature bureaus. Since there were no publishing structures in Tanzania and Uganda, these countries founded publishing firms partly owned by the government. The Uganda Literature Bureau became the main publisher of texts in indigenous languages in Uganda, while the Kenya Literature Bureau supplemented the Jomo Kenyatta Foundation as the major supplier of textbooks in Kenya.

However, even before the breakup of the EALB, individual governments in the region continued to have a stake in publishing interests. Tanzania Publishing House was established in 1966 as a government-owned organization in partnership with Macmillan UK, leading to complaints from other multinational companies, who were concerned that the new entity would be privileged in the lucrative schoolbook market. Kenya established the Kenya Institute of Education in 1964 to develop the curriculum for primary and secondary schools and to provide materials to educational institutions. The Jomo Kenyatta Foundation was started in 1965 to publish primary (elementary) school textbooks developed by the

Kenya Institute of Education. These East African presses concentrated on publishing textbooks recommended by the government for use in schools. This meant that books critical of the government or that offered an alternative to the government's vision were rarely published by these presses.

After political independence in the 1960s, private, local publishing ventures were started, and they began competing with both the multinationals and the government presses. In Kenya alone, according to Chakava, about ten publishers attempted to set up firms between 1963 and 1977. The East African Publishing House was established in 1965 with the aim of providing a venue for intellectuals and creative writers whose works might have been rejected by multinational outlets because of differences in aesthetic taste or ideological interest. Academic and creative publishing thrived because of the flourishing, vibrant intellectual culture of the 1960s and 1970s. This period saw the rise of major writers including Ngugi wa Thiong'o, Okot p'Bitek, Taban Lo Liyong, Micere Mugo, Jared Angira, and Francis Imbuga. Except for Ngugi, who was published by Heinemann in London, all the other writers named above were published by local presses. The 1970s witnessed the emergence of popular writers like David Maillu, Sam Kahiga, and Charles Mangua. Indigenous firms such as Comb Books, started by David Maillu, were important printers of popular literature. By the end of the 1970s, however, most of them had gone bankrupt.

In the 1980s, some multinational companies began to indigenize, and local branches evolved into full-fledged companies and broke with their overseas parent companies. In 1983, the local branch of Heinemann was incorporated locally as East African Educational Publishers, with branches in Nairobi, Dar es Salaam, and Kampala. In Kampala, Fountain Publishers was founded in 1988, and it soon became Uganda's largest indigenous publishing house. Furthermore, new companies developed from the ashes of collapsed ones. For example, Phoenix Publishers, founded by Gacheche Waruingi, then a lecturer at the University of Nairobi, grew out of the collapse of the East African Publishing House (EAPH). It adopted a host of authors who had been orphaned by the collapse of EAPH and reprinted old titles from the latter's defunct list. In fact, Phoenix opened its operations in 1988 with a reissue of the popular EAPH readers for primary schools.

Competition among publishers characterized the East African publishing scene in the 1990s. In Kenya, the government issued a book policy whose goal was to liberalize, privatize, and commercialize the provision of textbooks. This would replace the monopoly that the government had held on the production and sale of textbooks. While books had previously been seen as purely intellectual products with little commercial value, the liberalization of the publishing industry in the 1980s and 1990s changed the publishing landscape in East Africa considerably. Now even the most conservative of publishers started seeing books as commercial commodities to be aggressively marketed. The period also saw the appearance of new companies. Sasa Sema, which focused on children's books and comics, was founded in 1996, and brought out fictional biographies of regional leaders in the Lions Books Series. This category included books on the politicians Jomo Kenyatta and Ronald Ngara, the traditional religious leader Elijah Masinde, Mau Mau guerilla leader Dedan Kimathi, international photojournalist Mohamed Amin, and woman poet Mwana Kupona. The Uganda Printing and Publishing Corporation, a state corporation, was established in 1992. Uganda's Monitor was started in 1997, initially publishing primary school textbooks before bringing out novels by leading writers like Goretti Kyomuhendo.

The 1990s also witnessed the rise of publishing by nongovernmental organizations. The Kenya Oral Literature Association published texts on oral literature, usually based on workshop and conference proceedings and fieldwork. Femrite, the organization of Ugandan women writers, was established in 1996, publishing novels and collections of poetry and short stories by its members. It also started publishing *New Era*, a quarterly publication whose sections include "Children's World," "Culture," "Gender Wars," "Growing Up," "Parenting," and "Relationships." To encourage indigenous publishing, the African Publishers Network was established in 1992, bringing together national publishers' associations and publishing communities throughout Africa.

In spite of these developments, commercial publishing in East Africa faces numerous difficulties. Distribution networks remain poor, and the market is limited both by low literacy rates and by the general crisis in educational institutions. The publishing industry in general and the book market in particular continues to be dominated by Western firms, which have a better infrastructure and can produce books of higher quality. Online publishing is limited mainly because of the lack of a widespread electricity grid and poor telecommunications infrastructure. Finally, there is a lack of diversification in book publishing. Companies duplicate one another's successful projects, which has led to a glut of school literary guidebooks and popular literature series.

REFERENCES

Altbach, Philip G. "Perspectives on Privatization in African Publishing." In *The Challenge of the Market: Privatization and Publishing in Africa*, edited by Philip G. Altbach, 3–8. Oxford: Bellagio Publishing Network, 1996.

Chakava, Henry. *Publishing in Africa: One Man's Perspective*. Oxford: Bellagio Publishing Network; Nairobi: East African Educational Publishers, 1996.

Kanuya, Albert. "Marketing Books: The Tanzanian Experience." In *Indaba 2000: Millennium Market Place*, 88–92. Harare: Zimbabwe International Book Fair Trust, 2000.

Makotsi, Ruth. "Regional Economic Policies and the Intra-African Book Trade." In *Indaba 2000: Millennium Market Place*, 234–244. Harare: Zimbabwe International Book Fair Trust, 2000.

Makotsi, Ruth, and Lily Nyariki. *Publishing and Book Trade in Kenya*. Nairobi: East African Educational Publishers, 1997.

Mcharazo, Alli A. S. "The Book Chain in Tanzania." Available online at http://www.inasp.info/pubs/bookchain/profiles/Tanzania.html.

Okonkwo, Lawrence U. "Marketing African Books." In *Indaba 2000: Millennium Market Place*, 51–64. Harare: Zimbabwe International Book Fair Trust, 2000.

Saiwaad, Abdullah. "An Informal History of Publishing in Tanzania." *African Publishing Review* 6, no. 2 (1997): 15.

Wassie, Atnafu. "Privatization and the Challenges for Publishing in Ethiopia." In *The Challenge of the Market: Privatization and Publishing in Africa*, edited by Philip G. Altbach, 47–61. Oxford: Bellagio Publishing Network, 1996.

[Mwangi]

R

Rubadiri, David (b. 1930) Malawian poet, novelist, critic, educator, and diplomat. Although he is a Malawian by nationality and birth, Rubadiri has had a long and close relationship with the East African literary scene and he is considered one of the major architects of literature in the region, especially in the "renaissance" of art and culture that followed independence in the early 1960s. Born in what was the British colony of Nyasaland, Rubadiri attended the elite King's College, Budo, in Uganda, an institution initially established by Anglican missionaries to educate the African aristocracy. He then attended University College, Makerere, and Cambridge University, where he read English. Returning to central Africa in the late 1950s, Rubadiri became principal of Soche College in Nyasaland; it was during this time that he also became active in nationalist politics. In 1959, he was briefly imprisoned in what was then the British colony of Southern Rhodesia. When Malawi became independent in 1964, Rubadiri was appointed ambassador to the United States and the United Nations, but he soon fell out of favor with President Kamuzu Banda, whose increasingly autocratic rule he opposed; he resigned his diplomatic appointment and returned to Uganda, where he took up a teaching appointment in the English department at Makerere.

From the mid-1960s to the late 1970s, Rubadiri was closely associated with the Makerere School of English, which was heavily influenced by the literary criticism of F. R. Leavis. Rubadiri was influential in shaping the literary careers of some of the most important writers from the region, many whom he published in the collections *Origin East Africa* and *Poems from East Africa*, coedited with David Cook. In 1978, fleeing the ruthless rule of Idi Amin, Rubadiri took an appointment at the University of Nairobi, where he was active in the theater. He later taught at the University of Botswana, where he was a professor of English. When Banda fell from power in the 1990s, Rubadiri was again appointed Malawi's ambassador to the United Nations

and later became vice chancellor of the University of Malawi.

In East Africa, Rubadiri is mainly known as a poet. Some of his poems—an "An African Thunderstorm," "Stanley Meets Mutesa," and "Negro Laborer"—have been anthologized in many major editions of East African verse. Generally, Rubadiri's verse can be categorized into two categories, which reflect the general nature of poetic production in the East African region from the 1960s and 1970s. In the early poems collected in *Origin East Africa*, we see one of the most skillful deployments of English prosody, the aesthetic of modernism associated especially with T. S. Eliot, and some of the most pressing themes of African literature in the age of decolonization, the colonial encounter being most prominent among them. In "An African Thunderstorm," for example, Rubadiri borrows heavily from the conventions of English prosody, carefully balancing meter and rhythm. At the same time, however, his poem derives its visual imagery from its reference to a unique African event, a tropical thunderstorm "Tossing things up on its tail / —hurrying / Like a madman chasing nothing" (*Origin East Africa*, 77).

Like many poets of the Makerere school, Rubadiri's early poetry can be seen as an attempt to bridge the gap between forms of modern prosody and the African landscape. In these works, the display of African historical, cultural, and natural references was intended to make this verse more than a mere imitation of the "Great Tradition." The marriage of English style and an African referent is most evident in "Stanley Meets Mutesa," arguably Rubadiri's most famous poem. On a formal level, "Stanley Meets Mutesa" uses a prosodic style reminiscent of T. S. Eliot's "The Journey of the Magi": "Such a time of it they had / The heat of the day / The chill of the night" (*Origin East Africa*, 78). On a thematic level, however, the poem is far removed from Eliot's mythical journey. On the contrary, it functions as a powerful commentary on the colonial encounter, providing a vivid representation of the meeting between the imperial agent, Henry Morton Stanley, and Kabaka (King) Mutesa of Buganda, the moment when "The reed gate is flung open / . . . And the west is let in" (80).

One of the major complaints levied against the Makerere School of writing, of which Rubadiri was both product and patron, is that while it sought to make inherited English conventions the conduit through which African subjects could enter the canon of modern writing, it was so obsessed with formal achievement that, in the end, its local themes seemed subservient to the forms of English verse or prose. This complaint applies to Rubadiri's early poetry where, as in "Stanley Meets Mutesa," the great theme of the fatal colonial encounter is overshadowed by echoes of Eliot. Rubadiri seems to have been aware of this criticism because in his later verse, collected in *Poems from East Africa*, there is less attention devoted to the technical aspects of prosody, especially meter and rhythm, as Rubadiri deploys free verse to accommodate the less-ordered world of postcolonial Africa. In addition, Rubadiri shifts his focus from elevated themes to quotidian experiences—death in a hospital, the world of prostitutes, and objects in the landscape. In 2004, Rubadiri published his long-awaited collection of poetry, *An African Thunderstorm and Other Poems*.

Rubadiri is less known as a prose writer, but *No Bride Price*, his only novel, belongs to the cluster of works that have come to be associated with the failure of decolonization in Africa. Based largely on Rubadiri's early experiences as a diplomat and civil servant in Malawi in the early 1960s, the novel is the story of Lombe, a hard-working administrator, who strives to rise through the ranks and believes in the promise of independence as the gateway to a modern identity, only to discover that the old colonial order holds sway over most matters of state and that the new political configuration has yet to be born. Rubadiri uses Lombe's rise and fall to narrate the agonized and troubled nature of decolonization, the now familiar story in which the euphoria of independence is followed by the ascendancy of corrupt politicians, the abuse of power, and the inevitable coup d'etat. This is a story told powerfully in other African novels of the same period, most notably Chinua Achebe's *A Man of the People* and Ayi Kwei Armah's *The Beautyful Ones Are Not Yet Born*. Nevertheless, because of the poetic sensibility he brings to Lombe's struggle to survive in the new postcolonial climate, and because of his keen sense of the interplay of the larger public themes—political ambition and corruption—and the vulnerability of individuals struggling to survive and come to terms with failed love, desire, and the vagaries of the everyday world, Rubadiri's *No Bride Price* holds a unique place in East African letters.

PRIMARY TEXTS

Rubadiri, David. "An African Thunderstorm," "Stanley Meets Mutesa," and "A Negro Labourer in Liverpool." In *Origin East Africa: A Makerere Anthology*, edited by David Cook and David Rubadiri. London: Heinemann, 1965.

———. *No Bride Price*. Nairobi: East African Publishing House, 1967.

———. "Death at Mulago," "Paraa Lodge," "The Prostitute," "Two Epitaphs," and "Witch Tree at Mubende." In *Poems from East Africa*, edited by David Cook and David Rubadiri. London: Heinemann, 1971.

———. *An African Thunderstorm and Other Poems*. Nairobi: East African Educational Publishers, 2004.

EDITED COLLECTIONS

Rubadiri, David, ed. *Growing up with Poetry: An Anthology for Secondary Schools.* Oxford: Heinemann International, 1989.

Rubadiri, David, and David Cook, eds. *Origin East Africa: A Makerere Anthology.* London: Heinemann, 1965.

——, eds. *Poems from East Africa.* London: Heinemann, 1971.

REFERENCES

Sicherman, Carol. "Ngugi's Colonial Education: The Subversion . . . of the African Mind." *African Studies Review* 38, no. 3 (1995): 11–41.

Wipper, Audrey. "African Women, Fashion, and Scapegoating." *Canadian Journal of African Studies* 6, no. 2 (1972): 329–349.

Zeleza, Paul Tiyambe. "The Democratic Transition in Africa and the Anglophone Writer." *Canadian Journal of African Studies* 28, no. 3 (1994): 472–497.

[Gikandi]

Ruganda, John (b. 1941)   Ugandan playwright and director. Considered the most important playwright to have come from East Africa, Ruganda's career as a writer and theater director began when he was a student at Makerere University College in the 1960s. Born near Fort Portal in western Uganda into a Catholic family, Ruganda was educated at St. Leo's College, Ntare, before studying English at Makerere. It was while at the college that he started writing plays, two of which won the Inter-Hall Competition in 1966 and 1967. After graduating with an honors degree from Makerere in 1967, Ruganda worked as the editorial and sales representative for the Kampala branch of Oxford University Press and later held a senior fellowship in creative writing at the college. Ruganda moved to Kenya in 1972 and joined the department of literature at the University of Nairobi where, in 1973, he founded the Free Traveling Theatre. For most of the 1970s and 1980s, he was deeply involved in the teaching and promotion of drama in Kenya, and most of his major plays were performed at the National Theater. He studied for a PhD at the University of New Brunswick in Canada and later taught drama at the University of the North in South Africa, where he was instrumental in the formation of student theater groups.

As a playwright and director, Ruganda has been linked with the tradition of minimalist theater, associated with writers such as Athol Fugard and Wole Soyinka, rather than the grandiose, ritualistic projects of many of his East African contemporaries, most notably Ebrahim Hussein and Ngugi wa Thiong'o. In general, however, his works are defined by a continuous tension between his focus on the experiences of ordinary bourgeois life and the need to comment on the political and social problems of the postcolonial experience. While most of his works derive their dramatic power from the conflicts generated by individuals caught up in intricate and subjective relationships or torn between their duty to self and community, Ruganda's goal has always been to turn subjective conflict into the source of larger moral and political claims. His plays are thus caught between their detailed focus on personal relationships and the need to elevate the ordinary into a large allegorical matrix.

This tendency is perhaps represented best in two of Ruganda's earliest plays, *Black Mamba* and *Covenant with Death.* The first play focuses on very personal, social, and sexual relations between a white anthropologist, his black male servant, and the anthropologist's mistress, who is also the servant's wife. Set in a typical drawing room, the dramatic conflict in the play is generated by questions of class, race, and prejudice, but it is remarkable for its refusal to make such issues visible and direct, preferring to represent them as they emerge from the characters' belated discovery that what they thought were narcissistic acts had larger social meanings. In *Covenant with Death*, on the other hand, Ruganda starts with a set of characters with overt allegorical functions and explores their relationships in terms of larger, almost ritualistic moments, rather than with inner, more personal conflicts.

Ruganda's subsequent career has oscillated between these two forms of drama—the intensely personal and the allegorical. In *The Burdens*, clearly one of his most famous and most often produced plays, he adopted the form of bourgeois drama as represented by Ibsen and combined it with the anger motif of John Osborne and the generation of British playwrights known as the "angry young men," producing one of the most devastating portraits of postcolonial failure. In this play, Ruganda's goal was clearly political—to represent postcolonial failure as embodied by a politician who had been reduced from absolute power to self-pity and, as Ruganda put it in the preface to the play, "to diagnose the symptoms and damage of this modern cancer—empty-headed ambition and its attendant spirit, self-pity." But such political issues are approached indirectly in a play whose minimalism eschews the larger social canvas that has made and unmade its characters. The politics of postcolonialism are refracted through the main character's failure as a father in the most mundane of tasks, such as providing a bed for his son or taking his daughter to a hospital. It is only at the end of the play that the audience makes a direct link between domestic and political tragedy.

Although he has rarely issued manifestos to account for his preference for certain kind of plays, Ruganda's works are often self-referential with respect to their scenes of cultural production, staking out the author's own position in relation to debates about art and politics in East Africa. Indeed,

in the plays written in the late 1970s, when the politicization of the dramatic scene heralded by the publication of Ngugi's and Mugo's *The Trial of Dedan Kimathi* divided writers in Kenya between those who espoused a doctrine of art as an instrument of political engagement and those who preferred a more autonomous aesthetic, Ruganda's works became attempts to justify his own project. Indeed, at the heart of *The Floods*, arguably Ruganda's most powerful play, is an ongoing debate on the role of art in society, which is the bone of contention between Nankya, "the pseudo-intellectual," and Bwogo, "the executive." Nankya advocates art as part of the worker's revolution, while Bwogo's artistic work is authorized by detachment—"he looks at the external environment with directness; at women with fascination; at men with sympathy, although in the final analysis, he is a cynic" (23).

Bwogo's creed would seem to echo that of the author's, for Ruganda seems to prefer the invocation of liberal sympathy rather than revolutionary fervor. His sympathy is with the human subjects who struggle to free themselves from the entrapments of culture, society, politics, and the environment, rather than with the advocates of particular ideological projects. His characters struggle in a world defined by politics, but the playwright often seeks to make art, or the aesthetic, the medium that will enable them to transcend the political. Still, the opposition between art and politics in his work is also subject to his keen ironic sense, for, as it turns out, the liberal Bwogo in *The Floods* is also the head of the infamous State Research Bureau, the security agency that was responsible for torturing and killing people during the Idi Amin era in Uganda. But the play stands out ultimately as the one in which Ruganda's focus on the personal as the setting in which political drama is played out and his interest in where personal conflict meshes with the politics of death and violence were brought together most neatly. *The Floods* was first performed in 1979 in Nairobi to great acclaim. In the same year it was performed, with equal success, at the Festival of Small and Experimental Scenes in Yugoslavia.

If the success of *The Floods* depended on its ability to turn what might appear to be subjective, interpersonal conflicts into a forum for commenting of the politics of dictatorship and death, the plays that followed it, *Music Without Tears* and *Echoes of Silence*, did not achieve a successful balance between the interpersonal and the allegorical. In these plays, the personal drama tended to either be overtly allegorized, or the larger social canvas ended up subsumed by what appeared to be moments of pure solipsism. Ruganda might have become increasingly aware of the limits of his minimalist drama and the economy of anger, for in his later works, especially *Igereka and Other African Narratives*, he started to experiment with more allegorical and communal forms, such as the epic and oral narrative.

PRIMARY TEXTS

Ruganda, John. *Black Mamba; Covenant with Death*. Nairobi: East African Publishing House, 1971.

——. *The Burdens*. Nairobi: Oxford University Press, 1972.

——. *The Floods*. Nairobi: East African Educational Publishers, 1980.

——. *Music Without Tears*. Nairobi: Bookwise, 1982.

——. *Echoes of Silence*. Nairobi: Heinemann Kenya, 1986.

——. *Igereka and Other African Narratives*. Nairobi: East African Educational Publishers, 2002.

REFERENCES

Breitinger, Eckhard. *Uganda, the Cultural Landscape*. Bayreuth African Studies Series. Bayreuth: Bayreuth University Press, 1999.

Dusaidi, Claude Baingana. *East African Drama: A Critical Study of the Plays of Elvania Zirimu, John Ruganda, Francis Imbuga, and Ngugi Wa Thiong'o*. Ottawa: National Library of Canada, 1983.

Imbuga, F. D. *Thematic Trends and Circumstance in John Ruganda's Drama*. Nairobi: East African Educational Publishers, 1991.

[Gikandi]

Rugyendo, Mukotani (b. 1949) Ugandan playwright, editor, and communications officer. Rugyendo was educated at the University of Dar es Salaam, where, in the 1960s and 1970s, he studied theater arts. His three-play collection *The Barbed Wire and Other Plays* (1977) deploys popular theater techniques to address social problems in Africa. The title play revolves around Ugandan peasants who revolt to get back their land, which has been annexed by Rwambura, the village's rich man, who is supported in his suppression of the majority by the police and the courts, and he uses technology to enforce his will on the people. The playwright is influenced by the socialist ideology of Tanzania's founding father Julius Nyerere. In the play, barbed wire is a symbol of degenerate capitalism, which selfishly seizes communal property and prevents its rightful owners from utilizing it. The second play, *The Contest*, uses oral literary devices from communities in eastern and central Africa to present various interpretations of development. The third play, *The Storm Gathers*, dramatizes the consequences of a military coup. Rugyendo's poetry has appeared in *An Introduction to East African Poetry*, edited by Jonathan Kariara and Ellen Kitonga (1976), and in *Singing with the Night*, edited by Chris Wanjala (1974). The poetry is humorous in its presentation of the daily anxieties of ordinary people.

PRIMARY TEXTS

Rugyendo, Mukotani. *The Barbed Wire.* Kampala: Crane Publishers, 1989.

——. *The Barbed Wire and Other Plays.* London: Heinemann, 1977.

——. "My Husband Is Gone." In *An Introduction to East African Poetry*, edited by Jonathan Kariara and Ellen Kitonga, 25–26. Nairobi: Oxford University Press, 1976.

——. "The Rose," "The Poet," "Terminus," and "Drowning." In *Singing with the Night*, edited by Chris Wanjala, 69–72. Nairobi: East African Literature Bureau, 1974.

[Mwangi]

Ruheni, Mwangi (b. 1934) Mwangi Ruheni is the pseudonym of Nicholas Muraguri, a Kenyan popular novelist and scientist. Until he retired in 1990, Ruheni had been a Kenyan government scientist for twenty-two years, during which time he criticized the civil service, prudently using a penname. One of the few scientists in East Africa to engage in creative writing, Ruheni was educated at Makerere University College, from where he graduated with a BC, and later did advanced postgraduate work in chemistry at the University of Strathclyde, Scotland. Ruheni's novels draw on his experiences as both a student in Uganda and Scotland and as a civil servant in Kenya. His first novel, *What a Life!* (1972), is the story of Willie, a Kenyan who goes to study in England after a long struggle to get an education in Kenya. When he returns, he finds that life is as difficult as it was before he left, and he can hardly make ends meet. *The Future Leaders* (1973) is a satirical examination of the failures of Western-educated intellectuals to adjust to positions of leadership in Africa. It follows the misadventures of Ruben Ruoro as he struggles, in spite of his Makerere education, to find a niche in postindependence Kenya. *What a Husband!* (1974) revolves around the marriage of Kinyua, where the chaos of the urban life of Nairobi threatens relationships at the most fundamental level. Ruheni's novels are often structured by an absolute contrast between rural harmony and urban disarray. *The Minister's Daughter* (1975) is a moralistic tale about a Christian girl who is easily lured into sex, and subsequently, pregnancy, when she moves to the city. She reforms and settles in rural Kenya. *The Mystery Smugglers* (1975) is the story of Michael Magana, who finds himself part of a transnational gang of uranium smugglers, while *Love Root* (1976) examines modern medicine and traditional witchcraft. *The Diamond Lady* (2005) interweaves romance with the themes of government administration, prison, and capital punishment to reveal the selfishness, dehumanization, corruption, and hypocrisy eating away at East African institutions. As Nicholas Muraguri, he self-published *Random Thoughts* (1995), a collection of humorous commentaries on an array of topics including religion and soccer. *In Search of Their Parents* (1973) is a children's story about the adventures of two boys, and it discusses crime as one of the myriad problems facing the emergent East African urban centers in the 1970s.

PRIMARY TEXTS

Muraguri, Nicholas. *Random Thoughts I.* Nairobi: Nicholas Muraguri, 1995.

Ruheni, Mwangi. *What a Life!* Nairobi: Longman, 1972.

——. *The Future Leaders.* London: Heinemann, 1973.

——. *What a Husband!* Nairobi: Longman, 1974.

——. *The Minister's Daughter.* London: Heinemann, 1975.

——. *The Mystery Smugglers.* Nairobi: Spear Books, 1975.

——. *The Love Root.* Nairobi: Spear Books, 1976.

——. *The Diamond Lady*. Nairobi: Mvule Africa, 2005.

[Mwangi]

Ruhumbika, Gabriel (b. 1938) Tanzanian novelist, short-story writer, critic, and translator. Ruhumbika was born in the Sukuma region and was educated at Makerere University College, from where he graduated with a BA degree in 1964, before proceeding to France, where he earned a PhD at the Sorbonne. From 1970 to 1985, Ruhumbika was a lecturer at the University of Dar es Salaam. In 1985, he moved to the United States and taught English at Hampton University in Virginia until 1992, when he received an appointment as a professor of comparative literature at the University of Georgia.

Ruhumbika's first and only novel in English, *Village in Uhuru* (1969), reflects the political climate in Tanzania during the period of the Arusha Declaration, when the government sought to modernize Tanzanian society under the slogan of African socialism. In keeping with this creed, Ruhumbika's novel represented a community wedded to its old, precolonial traditions, and described its painful transition from the old way of life to the modern world of President Julius Nyerere and his ruling party, the Tanganyika African Union (TANU). On the surface, *Village in Uhuru* was one of the few novels published in East Africa in the late 1960s that did not advocate the separation of the writer from the political class. At the same time, however, the novel was not merely an instrument for promoting the cultural interests of the state. In his intimate portrait of a community struggling with the process of change, caught between the need to hold on to a stable set of ancestral values while coming to terms with the new order, Ruhumbika was able to present a powerful allegory of the politics of nationhood and change in Tanzania. More importantly, Ruhumbika's English novel struggled with a question that has been crucial to his critical and intellectual work: What language is better suited to representing the process of change in Africa? In terms of language, *Village in Uhuru* represented a compromise between English and Swahili, the language favored by Nyerere and TANU, in the sense that it used a form of English weighed with the rhythms of African languages and punctuated by the regular use of non-English, mostly Swahili, words.

Later in his career, Ruhumbika gave up writing in English, and two of his most influential works are novels in Swahili, *Miradi Bubu ya Wazalendo* (*The Invisible Enterprises of the Patriots*, 1992) and *Janga Sugu la Wazawa* (*Everlasting Doom for the Children of the Land*, 2002). He has also published *Uwike Usiwike Kutakucha* (*Whether the Cock Crows or Not It Dawns*), a collection of Swahili short stories. In addition to translating works from French to Swahili, he is the editor and translation from Kikerewe to English of Aniceti Kitereza's epic novel *Myombekere and His Wife Bugonoka, Their Son Ntulanalwo, and Daughter Bulihwali: The Story of an Ancient African Community*, first published in 1945.

PRIMARY TEXTS (IN ENGLISH)

Ruhumbika, Gabriel. *Village in Uhuru*. London: Longman, 1969.

TRANSLATIONS

Myombekere and His Wife Bugonoka, Their Son Ntulanalwo, and Daughter Bulihwali: The Story of an Ancient African Community. Translation, with an introduction and notes, of Aniceti Kitereza's 1945 Kikerewe novel. Dar es Salaam: Muki na Nyota Publishers, 2002.

[Gikandi]

S

Sahle-Sellassie, Berhane Mariam (b. 1936)
Ethiopian novelist and translator. Sahle-Sellassie was educated in Ethiopian schools and graduated from the University of Addis Ababa before pursuing graduate studies at the University of Marseille in France and the University of California, Los Angeles. Returning to Ethiopia in 1973, he worked for the British embassy as a translator and started writing stories in English and Amharic for local newspapers and periodicals. His first novel, *Shinega's Village*, was published in the Chaha language, while a second novel, *Wotat Yifredew*, was written in Amharic. Sahle-Sellassie's first novel in English, *The Afersata*, is the story of a man who attempts to find out who burned his house using the Afersata, a gathering of villagers in which no one is allowed to leave until the criminal has been exposed. In his novel, Sahle-Sellassie used this traditional means of investigating crime to create a site for examining class and social relationships in the old Ethiopian feudal order; for this reason, his novel has a strong didactic element, with the telling of the story often interspersed with social commentary.

In his second novel in English, *The Warrior King*, he turned his attention to the historical past, retelling the epic story of Kassa Hailu, who united the provinces of Ethiopia in the nineteenth century and remade himself as the famous Emperor Tewodros II. While Sahle-Sellassie relied heavily on historical chronicles and legends for his rewriting of the Tewodros story, he brought a fresh perspective to this period of Ethiopian history by portraying it through the perspective of a peasant boy. In *Firebrands*, published when he was already in exile in the United States, Sahle-Sellassie's concern was the consequences, on both the personal and communal level, of the Ethiopian Revolution of 1974, the event that overthrew the feudal order represented in his earlier novels and promised a new beginning for the country but ended up unleashing an unprecedented reign of terror.

PRIMARY TEXTS

Sahle-Sellassie, Berhane Mariam. *Shinega's Village; Scenes of Ethiopian Life*, translated from the Chaha by Wolf Leslau. Berkeley: University of California Press, 1964.
——. *The Afersata: An Ethiopian Novel.* London: Heinemann Educational, 1969.
——. *The Warrior King.* London: Heinemann Educational, 1974.
——. *Firebrands.* London: Longmans, 1975.

REFERENCES

Molvaer, R. K. *Black Lions: The Creative Lives of Modern Ethiopia's Literary Giants and Pioneers.* Lawrenceville, N.J.: Red Sea Press, 1997.

[Gikandi]

Seruma, Eneriko (Henry Kimbugwe) (b. 1944) Ugandan poet and novelist. Educated in Uganda and the United States, Seruma was active in the East African literary scene in the late 1960s and early 1970s and is best known for his novel *The Experience* (1970), which presents the challenges of life in America for black people. It is the story of Tom Miti, who, through his benefactor Ian Turner, travels to New Hampshire on a scholarship. He encounters the works of Hemingway, Fitzgerald, and Orwell, and, in the process, becomes sensitive to the images that emerge from literature and popular culture in the United States in the works of Richard Wright and others. As he acquires a literary education, Miti also becomes aware of the racial tensions in a community where he is the only black man and the target of racist jokes. He does not appear to have learned much, though, because he returns to Uganda a happy-go-lucky black boy who, together with his white friends and fellow educated Africans, looks down upon blacks who have not, in their mind, been Westernized. The novel articulates the ironies of the educated Africans who are barely different from the racists and colonialists Miti likes to criticize. Seruma also published a collection of short stories, *The Heart Seller* (1971), drawing on his experiences in both East Africa and America.

PRIMARY TEXTS

Seruma, Eneriko. *The Experience*. Nairobi: East African Publishing House, 1970.

——. *The Heart Seller*. Nairobi: East African Publishing House, 1971.

[Mwangi]

Serumaga, Robert (1939–1980) Ugandan playwright, novelist, and theater director. For most of the 1960s and 1970s, Serumaga was one of the most distinguished figures on the East African theater scene, the writer and producer of several powerful plays, the founder of successful theater companies, and an innovator on the stage. Born into an impoverished Buganda Catholic family, Serumaga was raised by his mother, Geraldine Namatovu, and won scholarships to some of the best schools in the country, acquiring his secondary education at St. Mary's College, Kisubi, and St. Henry's College, Kitovu. After high school, Serumaga studied economics at Trinity College, Dublin. Upon his return to Uganda in the mid-1960s, Serumaga was employed as a government economist, but his interests quickly shifted to the theater. He founded the National Theater Company in 1967, and later cofounded Theater Limited, a private theater production company later renamed Abafumbi. It was with Abafumbi that he took his plays to many theater festivals in Europe and Asia throughout the 1970s. During this period, Serumaga also held a creative writing fellowship at Makerere University.

After the cultural renaissance of the 1960s, the Ugandan cultural scene was put under extreme political pressure after Idi Amin came to power in 1972. Between 1972 and 1979, when Amin was driven out of the country by a group of Ugandan exiles and Tanzanian troops, many artists were killed or forced into exile, but Serumaga was able to stay in Uganda until the final years of the Amin regime. He developed modes of drama—based mostly on ritual and mime—that could represent the climate of violence and death that dominated this period without drawing the unwanted attention of the ruthless military class. Serumaga eventually went into exile in the late 1970s, but he returned to the country in 1979, after Amin was ousted; he was central to the formation of a new coalition government, serving briefly as minister of commerce under President Yusuf Lule. Serumaga died under mysterious circumstances in Nairobi in 1980.

Although Serumaga was the author of one successful novel, *Return to the Shadows*, his reputation as a major East African writer rests on his plays, starting with the experimental *A Play*, first performed in 1967, and ending with his great "silent" dramas *Renga Moi* and *Amanyirikiti*, produced at the height of the Amin regime in the late 1970s. *A Play* was first performed at the National Theater in Kampala under the direction of Elizabeth Keeble, with a cast that included Robert Serumaga and two other major figures of the Ugandan theater, David Rubadiri and the late Rose Mbowa.

A Play is very much the work of an apprentice playwright, but it also contains some of the most salient aspects of Serumaga's work. It is set in the contemporary period—indeed, its central actions take place in 1967, the year of its production—and its initial audience had no doubts that the events narrated in the story emerged out of their own cultural, social, and political concerns. Moreover, like most African works from this period, Serumaga's central concern in this play was the sense of disenchantment that had developed in the country after the euphoria of independence. Mutimukulu, the main character of the play, is an old intellectual who sees himself increasingly losing his grip on reality, often confusing the stressful present with a more blissful past or vice versa.

On a formal level, Serumaga's tactic, later repeated in his major dramatic works, was to focus on a small set of characters and to use their personal or domestic conflicts to touch on larger social issues. While the immediate source of tension in *A Play* is between Mutimukulu and his wife Rose as they struggle to reconcile their competing senses of reality (and, by implication, their relationship), the private drama is shown to be larger than the couple's concerns. What they echo in their private encounters with themselves and their friends and acquaintances are the larger conflicts defining Ugandan society of the late 1960s, a time when the reality of postcolonialism had to be separated from the fantasy of decolonization. Finally, it was in *A Play* that the theme of death, one of the most persistent concerns in Serumaga's oeuvre, emerged. Here, the reflection on the nature of reality and the meaning of life is also an attempt to confront the inevitability of death, what one of the characters in the play calls the "turning point" of life.

The theme of death is also a central concern in *Return to the Shadows*, Serumaga's only published novel. The novel was published four years before Amin's coup, and although it is not as innovative as Serumaga's drama, or indeed as memorable as other great African novels of postcolonial failure,

it captured the culture of violence that defined politics in the period following the exile of the Kabaka (king) of Buganda and the mood of despair that defined the larger Ugandan culture of the time. The novel revolves around a government economist named Joe Musisi, a man driven by idealism who returns from school abroad to serve his country but finds it more and more difficult to reconcile his dreams with the failed political culture of Uganda. After a coup d'etat, Musisi flees the city with his servant Simon, hoping to seek refuge in his mother's house in the countryside, but he is disabused of his belief that the rural countryside might be immune to violence and death when he arrives home to find that members of his family have been slaughtered and his mother, though alive, has been sexually assaulted. Like Mutimukulu in *A Play*, Musisi finds himself in a world of conflicted perspectives—one in which reality and phantasm have been conjoined. At the end of the novel, he struggles with what Serumaga considered to be the central questions facing his generation: What is the use of practical action or commitment in a world defined by extreme contradictions? And is not passivity, silence, and withdrawal preferable to involvement?

These were the questions that Serumaga addressed in *The Elephants*, his most famous published play. While this play was rarely performed on stage during Serumaga's lifetime, it represented the clearest and most profound articulation of his central concerns: the effect of political violence on human relationships, the tension between the imperative to remember and the compulsion to forget, and the role of death as the final arbiter of fate. As in Serumaga's earlier plays, *The Elephants* opens with what initially appears to be a simple social and cultural conflict between a group of intellectuals. David is a research fellow who has adopted Maurice, an artist and refugee from another African country. The play takes place on the Sunday morning when the stable relationship David has established with Maurice, a kind of surrogate parenthood, begins to unravel. Maurice is about to marry Jenny, an American expatriate, and wants to return home to inform his parents. The trouble is that Maurice's parents were killed during a political pogrom and, to protect his protégé from the bitter truth, David has been maintaining the illusion that they are still alive. What appears to be a conflict between two friends is thus elevated into an allegory of the crisis of politics in Africa; in the end, both David and Maurice are orphaned through cruel acts that mirror one another across national and cultural boundaries.

But if intellectuals like David, Maurice, and the others who populate Serumaga's earlier works define their vocations by reflecting on such abstract notions as free will or by engaging with postcoloniality as an existential condition, the playwright's more mature works focus on the response of ordinary people to the strange world ushered in by decolonization, a world caught between truncated native traditions, atrophied colonial culture, and stillborn postcolonial modernity. This is the world explored in *Majangwa*, without doubt one of the most important plays to come out of East Africa.

Majangwa is unique in East African theater for three main reasons: For one, it was the first play from the region to have ordinary people, rather than intellectuals, occupy the center of the stage, and thus it provides a perspective on the nature of postcolonial society from the vantage point of those involved in the business of daily struggle. The themes here are the same ones as in the previous plays: the failure of love, betrayal, and the inevitability of death, but Serumaga presents them with an intensity well beyond the domestic drama of his earlier works. Second, there is a significant shift from a dramatic structure built on conversation, irony, and reversal to a more performance-oriented approach. On the surface, *Majangwa* appears minimalistic, the action and dialogue focused on the struggle between an aging Baganda street performer and his wife. But the play is remarkable in its painful ability to open up the most private feelings and grievances of the couple to the whole world. At one point, Majangwa and his wife are forced to have sex in public in order to earn a living, and their private debasement is a dramatic indictment of the spectators who derive pleasure from the painful life of others. Third, in this play Serumaga made the first strides away from bourgeois theater, drawing on elements of ritual, myth, and legend to expand his repertoire. In his final works, *Renga Moi* and *Amanyirikiti*, produced during the Amin years, Serumaga abandoned dialogue altogether, exploring the themes of violence and death through mime, dance, and ritualistic choreography.

PRIMARY TEXTS

Serumaga, Robert. *Return to the Shadows.* London: Heinemann, 1969.

——. *The Elephants.* Nairobi: Oxford University Press, 1971.

——. *Majangwa: A Promise of Rains and a Play.* Nairobi: East African Publishing House, 1974.

REFERENCES

Bukenya, Austin. "An Idiom of Blood: Pragmatic Interpretation of Terror and Violence in the Modern Ugandan Novel." *The Uganda Journal* 46 (2000): 17–37.

Nazareth, Peter. "The Social Responsibility of the East African Writer." *Callaloo* 8, no. 10 (1980): 87–105.

Obi, Joe E., Jr. "A Critical Reading of the Disillusionment Novel." *Journal of Black Studies* 20, no. 4 (1990): 399–413.

[Gikandi]

Tejani, Bahadur (b. 1942)   Kenyan poet, dramatist, and literary critic. Born in Kenya of Gujarati parents, Tejani was educated at Makerere University College and Cambridge University. He later completed a PhD in literature at the University of Nairobi, where he was also a lecturer. Tejani was a major contributor of short stories and poems to the major East African journals of the 1960s and 1970s, but is best known for his novel *Day After Tomorrow* (1971), considered to be the first novel by an Asian from East Africa. The novel's major concern is the racism meted on the Asian minority in East Africa, which finds itself discriminated against both by the indigenous African majority and by the Europeans, who use them as the buffer between whites and blacks. Through its young protagonist Samsher, the novel explores the implications of the racist balkanization of communities for economic gain. Although the novel presents an idealistic solution to the racial and colonial problems, it does not hesitate to criticize the Asian community for being responsible for its own problems, especially its isolation. Set in postindependence Uganda, the novel supports Tejani's later criticism of the Asian community in "Farewell Uganda," an essay published in the journal *Transition*, in which he remarked that the Asians were being self-destructive in their idealistic view of the postcolonial African governments and in their self-isolation from indigenous communities. Tejani's short stories and plays are also preoccupied with the theme of race and community. The short story "Alice in Yankeeland" is a parody of racism in the West.

Most of his poetry discusses the individual connection or disconnection from the cultural, natural, and national environment and the problems of marginalized peoples. The poem "In the Orthopedic Ward" envisions communities of human subjects who stand above dominant notions of race. Another poem, "On Top of Africa," examines the deep fears of a person conceived to be a foreigner and his attempt to locate himself in relation to the natural environment and his native companions. Most of Tejani's poems, collected in *The Rape of Literature* (1969), were written between 1967 and 1968, when the poet visited Asia for the first time; they reflect his shock at discovering the real, as opposed to the imagined, India of his ancestors. The poems also critically examine the Asians' attitude toward other communities and are intended to serve as an appeal for a common humanity, regardless of race, gender, and class. Like his prose and poetry, Tejani's literary criticism engages with the place of the critic in the shaping of critical tastes in an ethnically variegated society. In his critical essays, he argues that despite the presence of colonialism as the discursive reference point in writing, African literature is marked by diversity as a result of the internal differences embedded in the local cultures from which writers draw their materials and techniques.

PRIMARY TEXTS

Tejani, Bahadur. *The Rape of Literature and Other Poems.* Delhi: Falcon Poetry Society, 1969.

——. *Day After Tomorrow.* Nairobi: East African Literature Bureau, 1971.

REFERENCES

Elder, Arlene A. "Indian Writing in East Africa: Multiple Approaches to Colonialism and Apartheid." In *Reworlding: The Literature of the Asian Diaspora*, edited by Emmanuel S. Nelson, 115–139. Westport, Conn.: Greenwood Press, 1992.

Kosh, Annie. "The Afro-Asian and American Dreams of Race Relations in Ba-

hadur Tejani's *Day After Tomorrow.*"
Wasafiri 3 (1991): 11–13.

Tejani, Bahadur. "Culture Versus Literature." In *Writers in East Africa*, edited by
Andrew Gurr and Angus Calder, 131–149.
Nairobi: East African Literature Bureau,
1974.

——. "Farewell Uganda." *Transition* 45
(1974): 64–66.

[Mwangi]

Theater and Performance Modern East African drama emerges from traditional theater based on rituals and related forms of
performance. Traditionally, in Africa, religious activities and healing exercises have
been accompanied by dramatic enactment.
For example, during the Mudimu initiation
ceremony among the Wamakonde community of Tanzania, as documented by Fran-
coise Grund-Khaznader, "masked dancers
represent spirits and express the solidarity
of the ancestors with the young initiates."
The people playing the role of "spirits" join
human beings in celebrating the initiates'
entry into adulthood. In precolonial East
African societies in general, drama was not
produced for its own sake, but served ritualistic imperatives. Modern theater activities,
too, are anchored in the many social demands made on individuals and communities in the region. There are different theatrical institutions in the region, but many
have had to struggle to meet the imperatives
expected of theater in the postcolonial period, and this struggle has shaped the direction of the dramatic arts in East Africa.

East African governments, both colonial
and postcolonial, have been involved in the
development of drama as part of the mandate for education and social development.
The Kenya National Theatre was opened on
November 6, 1952, and remained the hub of
theater activities in the country for a long
time. The history of Kenyan theater is

closely tied to the politics surrounding that
institution. In addition, the Kenya Schools
Drama Festival, an initiative of the British
Council and East African Theatre Guild, influenced Kenyan theater strongly. The first
national annual festival was held in 1959 at
the Kenya National Theatre, and it hosted
the event annually until 1982, when the
event began being hosted by the eight
provinces of the country in rotation.

The funding for the Kenya National Theatre came from government grants, but financial assistance was also provided by the
Nairobi City Council. In spite of these resources, there was a feeling that the Kenya
National Theatre was not advancing national interests. The majority of Kenyans
could not access the theater because the
colonial authorities, who had founded it
with the entertainment needs of the white
community in mind, had built it in an ex-
clusive area of Nairobi. High performance
fees made it difficult, if not impossible, for
African theater groups to use the facility.
The history of theater in Kenya for most of
the 1970s thus became a struggle between
expatriate and local communities for the
control of the Kenyan National Theatre.

In Uganda, theater and drama has been
encouraged by national competitions since
1946 and with intramural contests at Makerere University College. In 1959, the
British colonial government built a national
theater in Kampala, and in 1962, it was in
this institution that the first East African
play in English, Ngugi's *The Black Hermit*,
was first performed.

The story of theater in Tanzania is different. Here, the government's involvement in
cultural matters was more direct. The
Arusha Declaration of 1967 became the organizing principle of political, social, and
cultural life in the country. A central tenet of
the Arusha Declaration was the role of culture in the building of the new Tanzanian
nation. In this postindependence socialist

disposition, the artists' role was to pass the message of the government to the people. Under the aegis of the National Arts Group (NAG), locally based theater groups and school theaters were formed and nurtured to serve the socialist state. Traditional art forms were adapted to serve the government's developmental agenda. In 1972, the National Theatre Troupe was established. This was an urban-based traveling theater that was set up to challenge the colonialist notion that theater did not exist in precolonial Tanzania. While using Western dramaturgical strategies and receiving training from actors and directors from the Soviet Union and Britain, the group also incorporated traditional dance and mime. Although the group faced formidable challenges and eventually disbanded in 1979, artists learned from their failures and continued experimenting with traditional theater in other institutions.

In the late 1980s and 1990s, a discourse of development emerged in response to the failure of state institutions, placing culture at the center of the debates over national transformation. The impetus for this change was UNESCO's declaration making the 1980s the United Nations' Decade for Cultural Development. At this time, in response to the failure of the formal theater, Theatre for Development (TFD) emerged as a formidable movement in East Africa. It was during this time that East African scholars of theater came to distinguish between "community theater" and "popular theater." Community theater involved locally based actors working or performing for a particular community. In this kind of theater, members of the community would also perform among themselves for entertainment and education.

The products of community theater were mainly elements of folk culture transmitted through song, myth, and dance. These plays, which had no individual authors, were presented in oral, aural, and visual modes. The community theaters rarely left the performers' area of residence. On the other hand, popular theater involved the participation of amateur actors in collaboration with a community. In this tradition, communal problems—and their possible solutions—could be analyzed in groups and then enacted on stage.

Unlike popular theater, TFD is facilitated by theater professionals and is more theoretically grounded. According to Opiyo Mumma, TFD recognizes indigenous performances and incorporates them in the play or dance in order to address modern themes such as literacy, health, sanitation, corruption, communication, and environmental education. The most famous representative of this kind of theater is Ngugi wa Thiong'o's Kamirithu experiment in the late 1970s, in which the theater practitioners engaged the community in producing their own plays, *Ngaahika Ndeenda* (*I Will Marry When I Want*) and *Maitu Njugira* (*Mother Sing for Me*).

The 1980s and 1990s saw the entrenchment of TFD practices in formal institutions. For example, in 1993, the University of Dar es Salaam engaged in TFD projects across Tanzania. Through the activities of the Bagamoyo College of Arts, the city of Bagamoyo in Tanzania became one of the most important centers for the exchange of traditional knowledge in the region. It hosted artists from other eastern and central African countries. In Uganda, the Small World Theatre brought together roughly 180 participants from six secondary schools in Kampala to research and develop for their school a performance about children's rights. Around the same time, Ugandan actor, academic, and producer Rose Mbowa produced *Mother Uganda and Her Children*, based on Bertolt Brecht's *Mother Courage and Her Children*. It chronicled the resilience of Ugandans over a decade of social strife and civil wars. In Kenya, Kimani Njogu scripted a 206-episode radio drama series on reproductive health, "Ushikwapo Shikamana" ("When You Are Helped, Pitch In, Too") and "Kuelewana ni Kuzungumza" ("Dialogue Is the Basis of Understanding").

Critics such as Mike Kuria and Mercy Mirembe Nitangaare have noted that the United Nations' Decade for Women (1976–1985), whose summit took place in Nairobi, inspired drama and performances on women's issues. Swahili play *Mama Ee* by Kenyan writer Ari Katini Mwachofi exploits the traditional *shairi* verse form to discuss the victimization of women in patriarchal societies, while Alakie Akinyi Mboya, in her English play *Otongolia*, uses mythology to depict patriarchal power struggles and to contest the idea of a monolithic nation.

The most accomplished playwrights from East Africa, John Ruganda, Francis Imbuga, Robert Serumaga, and Ebrahim Hussein, have often fused traditional theater with modernist experimentation to produce plays of varying levels of sophistication. They tackle the themes of dictatorship, tradition and modernity, and the struggle to survive in a fragmented world. Although relatively unknown outside the region, East Africa has a host of other fine dramatists and playwrights involved in experimenting with and transforming the form of drama. The Ugandan writer Byron Kawadwa authored the satirical *Oluyimba lwa Wankoko* (*Song of Wankoko*) and *St. Lwanga* and was a major figure in East African theater before he was dragged from the Ugandan National Theater in Kampala in 1977 and murdered by Idi Amin's security agents. In *Oluyimba lwa Wankoko*, Kawadwa used a local fairy tale about the infighting between Wankoko (the cock) and Nkwale (the quail) to comment on the power struggles between the modern government of Milton Obote and the traditional kingdom of Buganda. Wycliffe Kiyingi-Kagwe also wrote experimental plays in Luganda, and Eli Kyeyune, Pio Zirimu, and Cliff Lubwa-p'Chong created dramas in English based on traditional forms of theater. John Katunde's *The Dollar* attacks excessive materialism, and *The Inspector*, fashioned after Gogol's *The Government Inspector*, criticizes hospital mismanagement. In Tanzania, Emanuel Mbogo's *Giza Limeingia* (*The Dawn of Darkness*) explores the advantages of Ujamaa (socialist) policies, while the works of Penina Muhando Mlama and Amandina Lihamba deal with the problems of freedom, liberation, and women's rights. Despite the problems facing it, including a lack of funding, poor infrastructure, and censorship, theater has been one of the most dynamic areas of artistic production in East Africa.

REFERENCES

Kerr, David. *African Popular Theatre*. London: James Currey, 1995.

Kuria, Mike. "Contextualizing Women's Theatre in Kenya: Alakie-Akinyi Mboya's *Otongolia* and Ari Katini Mwachofi's *Mama Ee*." In *African Theatre: Women*, edited by Martin Banham, James Gibbs, and Femi Osofisan, 47–57. Oxford: James Currey, 2002.

Lang-Peralta, Linda. "Cultural Renaissance Through Performing Arts in Kenya." In *Modern Kenya: Social Issues and Perspectives*, edited by Mary Ann Watson, 152–161. Lanham, Md.: University Press of America, 2000.

Lihamba, Amandina. "Politics and Theatre in Tanzania After the Arusha Declaration: 1967–1984." PhD diss. University of Leeds, 1985.

Maule, Annabel. *Theatre Near the Equator: The Donovan Maule Story*. Nairobi: Kenway, 2004.

Mlama, Penina Muhando. *Culture and Development: The Popular Theatre Approach in Africa*. Oslo: Nordiska Africainstitutet, 1991.

Mumma, Opiyo. "Concepts and Terms." In *Drama and Theatre, Communication in Development*, edited by Opiyo Mumma and Loukie Levert, 7–13. Nairobi: KDEA, 1997.

Nitangaare, Mercy Mirembe. "Portraits of Women in Contemporary Ugandan Theatre." In *African Theatre: Women*, edited by Martin Banham, James Gibbs, and Femi Osofisan, 58–65. Oxford: James Currey, 2002.

Ntangaare, Mercy Mirembe. "Democracy and the Proletariat's Dream in Byron Kawadwa's *The Song of Wankoko*." In *African Languages Literature in the Political Context of the 1990s*, edited by Charles Bodunde, 63–89. Bayreuth: Bayreuth University Press, 2001.

Riccio, Thomas. "Tanzanian Theatre: From Marx to the Marketplace." *The Drama Review* 45, no. 1 (2001): 128–152.

[Mwangi]

Thuku, Harry (1895–1970) Kenyan nationalist politician and autobiographer. Although not well known as a writer, Thuku was one of the first major nationalists in East Africa and the leader of the first regional movement against oppressive colonial policies. His legendary early work in defense of African interests was to become part of the mythology of cultural nationalism and its literature, especially in Kenya, for most of the 1930s and 1940s. Born at Kambui in central Kenya, Thuku was educated at an American Protestant mission near his home until 1911, when he left for Nairobi to seek employment. After briefly working with the Nairobi branch of the Standard Bank, he joined the main white newspaper, the *Leader of British East Africa*, where he worked as a typesetter. It was during this period that Thuku became interested in nationalist politics. He founded the East African Association in 1921 and was also active in the Kikuyu Central Association (KCA). In 1922, he led the legendary march outside the Norfolk Hotel in Nairobi to protest the mandatory requirement that Africans wear the *kipande*, a metal identity card, which he considered demeaning and restrictive. For his role in organizing the march, Thuku was arrested by the colonial government and detained in the remote parts of the coastal and northern provinces of Kenya from 1922 to 1930. After his release, he continued working within the organs of the nationalist movement and represented the KCA before several colonial commissions investigating land grievances in Kenya. However, by the 1940s, it was apparent that Thuku's gradualist approach to reform fell far short of the demands of a new generation of radical nationalists and that his reputation as a symbol of the revolt against colonial policies, though symbolic, was no longer considered relevant to the issues of the day. This view was confirmed in the 1950s, when at the height of the armed Mau Mau revolt against the British colonial government, Thuku solidly aligned himself with so-called Gikuyu loyalists, a group of chiefs and landowners pledged to fighting, in the name of the British crown, what they saw as the terror of Mau Mau.

With the release of Jomo Kenyatta from prison in 1960 and his ascendancy to the premiership in 1963, it was not clear where the future of former loyalists lay, but by 1964, it had become apparent that they were indeed the major custodians of the postcolonial order. By the time Thuku published his autobiography in 1970, former loyalists or their descendants controlled the key organs of the Kenyan state, a fact reflected in Thuku's self-congratulations not so much regarding his legendary role in early nationalism, but with respect to his work as a beacon of modernity and morality in the "dark" days of Mau Mau. In this context, the autobiography is an important record of the transformation of the narrative of nationalism in Kenya from its nascent phase in the

1920s through the radical and troubled periods in the 1940s and 1950s and its unexpected apotheosis in the 1960s and 1970s.

PRIMARY TEXTS

Thuku, Harry, with Kenneth King. *Harry Thuku: An Autobiography*. Nairobi: Oxford University Press, 1970.

[Gikandi]

Tuma, Hama (b. 1950) Ethiopian lawyer, poet, satirist, and short-story writer. Born Iyassu Allemayehu in Addis Ababa, Tuma became involved in radical politics when he was a law student at the then-named Haile Selassie University. He was a leading member of the Ethiopian Peoples' Revolutionary Party, an organization of militant students opposed to the absolute reign of Emperor Haile Selassie. After the overthrow of the emperor in 1974, Huma continued to fight for democracy in Ethiopia and was one of the most prominent opponents of the military dictatorship (the Dergue) of Mengistu Haile-Mariam and of the Tigrina regime that succeeded it. Tuma was arrested by all three regimes and his works were banned. It was out of this experience with dictatorship and his opposition toward it that he horned his skills as a master of political satire, first evident in *The Case of the Socialist Witchdoctor and Other Stories*. In this collection of short stories, Tuma approached the subject of political failure in Ethiopia—the rise of totalitarianism, duplicity, and terror—with a mixture of parody and dark irony, satire and comedy. Working with the conviction that the line between fiction and reality in African politics was so thin that it could only be represented through parody, Tuma also published a series of satirical commentaries on the contemporary African scene, published as *African Absurdities* in two volumes. Satire also permeates his two collection of poems in English, *Of Spades and Ethiopians* and *Eating an American*.

As a writer and critic, Tuma's project has been driven by the belief that the failure of the nation-state in Africa and what he calls "the assault of ethnicity on the unity aspirations of Africans" had forced intellectuals to "re-question facile theories and conclusions." In these circumstances, he argued in a 2003 lecture at Columbia University, New York, the task and priority of the African writer was "to write stories that expose and shame the real enemies of Africa, to pen stories against the tyrants and their systems" ("The Role and Ordeal of the African Writer," 6). Although he is better known for his writings in English, Tuma is an accomplished writer in Amharic, with two collections of poetry and a novel in that important Ethiopian language.

PRIMARY TEXTS

Tuma, Hama. *Of Spades and Ethiopians*. N.p.: Free Ethiopian Press, 1991.
———. *The Case of the Socialist Witchdoctor and Other Stories*. N.p.: Heinemann, 1993.
———. *African Absurdities: Politically Incorrect Articles*. 2002.
———. *Give Me a Dog's Life Any Day: African Absurdities II*. N.p.: Trafford, 2004.

REFERENCES

Booker, M. Keith. "African Literature and the World System: Dystopian Fiction, Collective Experience, and the Postcolonial Condition." *Research in African Literatures* 26, no. 4 (1995): 58–75. ·

[Gikandi]

Urbanization and the Rural The city and Anglophone literature in East Africa are intricately connected because they are both new phenomena and depend on each other for sustenance. Much of the literature in the region is published in the city, and because most of the writing has colonialism as its reference point, the urban space figures in the literature as a symbol of the modernity that European imperialism brought in its wake. Urbanization is not, of course, a new phenomenon in East Africa. The major cities of the region were founded as early as the fifteenth century, mainly in response to the emergence of trade relations with both the Eastern and Western world. Major coastal towns such as Lamu, Mombasa, Bagamoyo, Zanzibar, and Lindi predate colonialism. Nevertheless, as in the rest of Africa, urbanization in East Africa was closely tied to the colonial project; it was after contact with the West that urban centers developed most rapidly. Indeed, most literary texts present towns and cities as expressions of Westernization counterpoised against the traditional culture of the villages. Even major cities that had a precolonial origin came to be represented in literature as sites of Westernization.

However, the dominance of the city as a theme in East African writing does not mean that it has been privileged by writers. In the 1960s, canonical writers set their works in rural areas to evoke the past that colonialism erased and replaced with modernity, and they often represented the city as an alien and alienating space. In his early novels *The River Between* (1964) and *Weep Not, Child* (1965), Ngugi wa Thiong'o used the village as his primary setting in order to portray the African's deep connection to the landscape and to show the alienation of the peasants by settler colonialism, which displaced the Africans from their ancestral land. In Tanzania, Gabriel Ruhumbika uses a rural setting in *Village in Uhuru* (1969) to crystallize the tension between traditional identities and the exigencies of a national culture.

During the first decade of independence, East African poets and playwrights were even more lyrical in celebrating an innocent past. In Henry Barlow's poem "The Village Well," the speaking persona conflates his childhood with images of a pure village well, which ends up desecrated by undescribed developments:

> This spot,
> Which has rung with the purity of
>   childhood laughter;
> This spot,
> Where eyes spoke secretly to
>   responding eye;
> This spot,
> Where hearts pounded madly in
>   many a breast. . . .

In John Ruganda's play *The Floods*, a rural setting is used to accentuate the destruction of innocent people by a military government. Here, the character of Kyeyune brings into the drama overtones of age and responsibility, while similar overtones in *The Headman* indicate that even traditional power and responsibility have not been spared abuse by the military regime, which has no respect for African traditions.

Quite often in East African literature, modern life is represented as lacking in humanity, and the individual is presented as a victim of developments beyond his or her control. Characters are presented as being vulnerable for having been inserted into modern society, which is represented by the city and all its problems. Thus village and traditional mores and urbanization and modernity are seen as diametrically opposed. In figuring the rural, the writers attempt to render into English the speech rhythms of the traditional Africa. In *Song of Lawino*, for example, Okot p'Bitek draws on the idiom of the rural Acholi community to enrich the long poem with images of a threatened lifestyle of immense beauty and philosophical resourcefulness. Overall, texts such as *Song of Lawino* are haunted by a desire to valorize a fading culture and idiom while guardedly embracing the new possibilities offered by modernization.

The history of urbanization is, however, more complex than the dominant rural/urban dichotomy suggests. While colonialism and postcolonial modernity forced some rural dwellers to move to the city, this was because urban areas were associated with new lifestyles, which were attractive to rural people dispossessed by colonial settlers. Having no land to cultivate, the landless opted to move into the cities, where they had a means of earning a living. In addition, colonialism had created a new class of educated Africans who sought white-collar jobs that could only be found in the new urban centers. The shifts from the rural to the urban caused congestion in the urban places, a rise in the crime rate, and impoverishment of both the rural areas and the city. The literature of the 1970s and afterward captures the alienation of the rural African who comes to the city to look for a job and ends up as a derelict on the city streets. Particularly predominant in the poetry of the period is the motif of the beggar at the city street corners. Novels by Meja Mwangi (*Kill Me Quick, Cockroach Dance,* and *Going Down River Road*) and Leonard Kibera (*Voices in the Dark*) also represent the decrepitude of the city in a variety of ways. Without engaging in a direct critique of nationalism, Mwangi describes city life down to the most minute details, and his stories do not spare anyone, not even the social "vermin" that infest urban places. In contrast, Kibera contrasts the disillusionment of the beggars to the promises made during the fight for independence in order to express the pitfalls of a nationalism that leaves the majority of the population in abject poverty.

Life in the city slums and rampant prostitution form the background against which the city is drawn by a majority of popular writers. Popular East African potboilers are set in the city, and lack of employment leads the protagonists into crime. Told mainly by male narrators, these novels depict life in the prisons, daring robberies, and smuggling. The "prostitute novel" is usually narrated by a prostitute who offers an insider's perspective of her trade. The novels employ colloquial language and the code-switching common among urban dwellers, which enhances the narrative's rapport with the reader. Although often mundane, these novels are popular and riveting in their cynical reproduction of the seedier aspects of urban life. Charles Mangua's *Son of Woman,* perhaps the most popular of these novels, tells the story of the son of a prostitute who is educated by the missionaries in the rural areas and proceeds to study for a degree in Makerere. Now hard-bitten and cynical, he narrates his misadventures through the city's poverty, crime, and dilapidated civil service. In a single paragraph in his novel, Mangua is able to catalogue the problems of the city: "This is Eastleigh. Most famous place in Nairobi for advanced prostitution. Ninety percent of kids are fatherless. They are bastards. . . . That's what we are. Bastards."

More than any other setting, the urban space enables the artists to depict the socioeconomic gap dividing the rich and the poor, because it is in the cities where the exploitation of the poor is at its most intense. Abuse of power, especially by the police, is a prominent theme. Ngugi's later novels and short stories depict the exploitation of women (symbolizing the nation) by a male minority. Ben Mutobwa's *Dar es Salaam by Night* depicts, in graphic detail, the vicious circle of prostitution in the city: its main character, Rukia, becomes a prostitute, like her mother did, barely after entering puberty. Though not sophisticated in its presentation, the novel blames government policies that have concentrated resources in the city at the expense of the rural areas. The writer seems to argue that the problems of the city can only be eased by developing alternative economies in the rural areas. Other writers decry the difficulties of going back to the rural areas. Tanzanian poet Jwani Mwaikusa presents, in "Back Home," an uprooted African who returns to the village only to discover that his grandfather, the cherished symbol of old traditions, is dead and can no longer pass on the wisdom of the past.

While much of the literature associates the city with the rottenness of modern life and decries the loss of traditional values, women's writing celebrates the liberating potentials offered by the city. Margaret Ogola's feminist texts see the city as a site where traditional patriarchy can most energetically be deconstructed. In Marjorie Oludhe Macgoye's *Coming to Birth* (1986), Paulina starts to mature as a woman when she reaches the city. When she arrives in the city she is naïve, but her stay in Nairobi helps her realize her economic and political potential in a male-dominated society. As in the literature, the popular music up to the 1980s used proverbs and traditional oral forms to decry the problems of the city and the loss of cultural values, but the 1990s witnessed the rise of an urban popular culture in which the younger artists, perhaps because they do not have a firm rural background, celebrated the freedom offered to them by the city. In this music, migration is no longer from the rural to the urban, but from one area of the city to another, as the young protagonists move around in search of city pleasures.

REFERENCES

Anderson, David M., and Richard Rathbone. *Africa's Urban Past.* Oxford: James Currey; Portsmouth, N.H.: Heinemann, 2000.

Kurtz, J. Roger. *Urban Obsessions, Urban Fears: The Postcolonial Kenyan Novel.* Trenton, N.J.: Africa World Press, 1998.

O'Connor, Anthony. *The African City.* New York: Africana Publishing Company, 1983.

Stren, Richard E., and Rodney R. White., eds. *African Cities in Crisis: Managing Urban Growth.* Boulder, Colo.: Westview Press, 1989.

[Mwangi]

Vassanji, M. G. (b. 1950) The novelist M. G. Vassanji is hard to categorize because of his hybrid background and origins. Born in Kenya of parents of Indian background, Vassanji grew up in Tanzania. After a short stint at the University of Nairobi, he was awarded a scholarship to study physics at the Massachusetts Institute of Technology and later graduated with a PhD in nuclear engineering from the University of Pennsylvania. In 1978, he moved to Canada, where he was employed at a power plant and also taught at the University of Toronto. It was while he was working as an engineer that Vassanji started writing fiction, as part of his attempt to establish connections between his Indian and East African backgrounds and to account for the process of migration that had created the Indian diaspora in Africa, Europe, and North America. His first novel, *The Gunny Sack,* was published in 1989 and won the 1990 Commonwealth Writers Prize for the African Region. Vassanji followed the success of *The Gunny Sack* with a quick succession of novels published in the first half of the 1990s: *Uhuru Street, No New Land,* and *The Book of Secrets,* which was awarded the Giller Literary Prize for the best fictional work in English published by a Canadian writer.

Vassanji has been fairly consistent in terms of the issues he has taken up in his novels. His novels elaborate themes first introduced in *The Gunny Sack*, focusing on the author's representation of the struggle by Indians in Africa, and later North America, to come to terms with their multiple histories of displacement while rebuilding their communities in exile. It is when he moved to North America that Vassanji first recognized the significance of Indian culture in the diaspora; he has been quoted as saying that one of the central functions of his novels is "to understand the roots of India that we have inside us."

Reflections on Indianness in Vassanji's works are also attempts to mediate the connection or disconnection between a distinctive East African Indian experience, one defined by the complex relationship between native Africans and migrants from the Indian subcontinent, against the background of the historical movement from colonialism to independence. In his treatment of the past, clearly a major theme in his works, Vassanji sets out to complicate linear histories of migration, colonization, and independence by making the past "deliberately murky." These themes get their fullest expression in *Amriika*, the story of an East African Indian who finds himself caught in the civil strife in the United States in the 1960s and 1970s, and *The In-Between World of Vikram Lall*, the story of interracial relationships played out against the background of the Mau Mau conflict in Kenya and the aftermath of decolonization. *The In-Between World of Vikram Lall* won the Giller Prize for 2004, an acknowledgement of both Vassanji's role as a chronicler of Africa and the Asian diaspora and his status as a major Canadian writer.

PRIMARY TEXTS

Vassanji, M. G. *The Gunny Sack*. London: Heinemann International, 1989.

——. *No New Land*. Toronto: McClelland & Stewart, 1991.

——. *Uhuru Street*. London: Heinemann International, 1991.

——. *The Book of Secrets*. New York: Picador, 1994.

——. *Amriika*. Toronto: McClelland & Stewart, 2000.

——. *The In-Between World of Vikram Lall*. New York: Knopf, 2004.

REFERENCES

Kanaganayakam, Chelva, " 'Broadening the Substrata': An Interview with M. G. Vassanji." *World Literature Written in English* 31, no. 2 (1991): 19–35.

Malak, Amin. "Ambivalent Afflictions and the Post-Colonial Condition: The Fiction of M. G. Vassanji." *World Literature Today* 67, no. 2 (Spring 1993): 279–282.

[Gikandi]

Waciuma, Charity (b. 1936) Kenyan novelist and children's writer. Born in the then Fort Hall (Murang'a) district of Kenya, Waciuma was trained as a teacher and was one of the first women writers in East Africa. Her numerous children's books include *Mweru and the Ostrich Girl* (1966), *The Golden Feather* (1966), *Who's Calling* (1972), and *Merry-Making* (1972). She is, however, best known for *Daughter of Mumbi* (1969), an ethnographic description of life among the Gikuyu people of central Kenya. Autobiographical in nature, *Daughter of Mumbi* is one of the most powerful testimonies on the effect on individuals and families of the state of emergency imposed on Kenya by the colonial government in 1952. Waciuma uses her family's story to give a historical account of colonial occupation in East Africa. She condemns the separation of families by colonial administrators, who put the local population in segregated concentration camps. The book is also ethnographic in nature, exploring the Gikuyu rites of passage from childhood to adulthood. At the same time, it captures the tension between traditional culture and settler colonialism. Also covered are the themes of polygamy and gender. In its combination of autobiographical and ethnographic registers, the novel invites its readers to condemn colonialism and the strand of Christian evangelism that condoned it.

PRIMARY TEXTS

Waciuma, Charity. *Daughter of Mumbi.* Nairobi: East African Publishing House, 1969.

[Mwangi]

Wainaina, Binyavanga (b. 1971) Kenyan essayist, editor, short-story writer, and food consultant. Wainaina attended Mang'u High School and Lenana School before studying commerce at the University of Transkei, South Africa, in 1991. In 1996, he relocated to Cape Town, where he wrote "Encounters," a weekly interview column for the *Weekend Argus,* and feature articles on African cuisine and travel for various publications. He is perhaps best known for his short story "Discovering Home" (2001), which won the Caine Prize in 2002. First published online in the Web magazine *Generator 21* (at http://www.gen21.net), the story examines the fluidity of identities. The narrative is delivered in an autobiographical voice that slides into the author's own, aligning itself more with travelogue than fiction. Further transgressing the conventions of both short story and travelogue, "Discovering Home" traverses different societies and discusses its relation with earlier African literature such as Okot p'Bitek's poetry and Negritude art. It supports a more unanchored sense of identity than the one celebrated in earlier East African writing. The story emphasizes the intersection of different cultures as a blending of

one's own multiple senses of belonging. The more the narrator moves away from what he considers to be his home and roots, the more he discovers strands of his identity in other cultures. "Ships in High Transit" subverts travel narratives by mockingly presenting travelers, especially know-it-all foreign tourists who base their understanding on mediated constructions. Collapsing the dichotomy between fiction and reality, the story grapples with the concept of "magical realism," about which its character Matano meditates as he refers to the work of Gabriel Garcia Marquez while making love.

"An Affair to Dismember" (2002) is a more sophisticated narrative. Referring to Wole Soyinka's play *The Road* and attempting to emulating the complexity of Soyinka's drama, the short story presents the divided psyche of Geoff Mwangi, an intellectual. Pushing the frontiers of stylistic and generic imperatives, the story tackles the theme of the reluctance of intellectuals to challenge conventions. *Beyond the River Yei: Life in the Land Where Sleeping Is a Disease* (2004) combines an essay, stark photography by Sven Torfinn, and poetry to depict the problems and potentials of the Kakwa ethnic community, who inhabit tsetse fly–infested and war-torn southern Sudan.

Wainaina is the founding editor of *Kwani?,* a journal of creative writing launched in 2003. It sees itself as a "socially committed miscellany of eclectic and exciting works of prose, poetry and eccentric in-betweenery." The journal gained immediate international interest upon its appearance: one of its stories, "Weight of Whispers" by Yvonne Adhiambo Owuor, won Africa's most important writing prize, the Caine Prize for Writing, in 2003.

PRIMARY TEXTS

Wainaina, Binyavanga. "An Affair to Dismember." *Wasafiri* 37 (Winter 2002): 20–25.

——. "Discovering Home" and "Ships in High Transit." In *Discovering Home: A Selection of Writings from the 2002 Caine Prize for African Writing*, 9–26. Bellevue, South Africa: Jacana, 2003.

——. *Beyond the River Yei: Life in the Land Where Sleeping Is a Disease*. Nairobi: Kwani Trust, 2004.

[Mwangi]

Wangusa, Timothy (b. 1942) Ugandan poet and novelist. Born in rural Uganda and educated in English at Makerere University and the University of Leeds in the United Kingdom, Wangusa has taught at Makerere University since the 1970s, with short stints in the Ugandan government, where at one point he served as minister of education. His work is influenced both by folklore and Western poetic forms. He has written in both English and his native Lumasaba language. The poems in his *Salutations: Poems 1965–1975* reflect the poet's folkloric influences and his affinity for the poetry of high modernism. In "Song to Mukokoteni," the speaker uses oral techniques to eulogize the urban handcart, setting it against more sophisticated forms of transportation unaffordable by the urban poor and the technologically challenged postcolonial nations:

> O my legs of vegetable and metal
> My perennial Mercedes Benz
> My ever-ready cargo plane
> My sputnik to brand new planets.

The praise of "Song to Mukokoteni" is a commentary on the relations of power between the rich and the poor, a recurrent motif in Wangusa's verse. In "Mother Teresa's Wish," published in *A Pattern of Dust: Selected Poems, 1965–1990*, he satirizes the rich West's habits of honoring Third World icons with expensive banquets instead of using the money to alleviate poverty in less developed nations. Wangusa's novel *Upon This Mountain* (1989) uses African folktale techniques and proverbs to tell the story of a young Ugandan coming of age after World War II. The conflict of Western culture and traditional values is poignantly drawn and the hypocrisy of colonialists and missionaries exposed even as the novel retains rich Christian symbolism.

MAJOR TEXTS

Wangusa, Timothy. *Salutations: Poems 1965–1975*. Nairobi: East African Literature Bureau, 1977.

——. *Upon This Mountain*. Oxford: Heinemann International, 1989.

——. *A Pattern of Dust: Selected Poems, 1965–1990*. Kampala: Fountain Publishers, 1994.

[Mwangi]

Watene, Kenneth (b. 1944) Kenyan playwright and theater critic. One of the earliest graduates of the National Theatre Drama School, Watene was active in the Kenyan literary scene in the late 1960s and early 1970s, writing short stories, poems, and plays for various journals and newspapers. He attracted literary attention and notoriety with his controversial presentation of Dedan Kimathi, the legendary hero of the Mau Mau struggle, in two of his plays, *My Son for My Freedom* (1973) and *Dedan Kimathi* (1974). His portrayal of Kimathi and the Mau Mau liberation movement was seen in certain critical circles as negative, and the conflicted Kimathi figure in his drama provoked Ngugi wa Thiong'o and Micere Mugo to write *The Trial of Dedan Kimathi* as a corrective to what they considered a misrepresentation of the history of Kenya's revolution. *My Son for My Freedom* dramatizes the dilemma faced by Kikuyu Christian families of whether to participate in nationalist violence. Published in the same volume are the one-act plays *The Haunting Past*, which, weaving dance into verse drama, presents conflicts between different generations, and *The Pot*, about the consequences of drunkenness, modernity, and disrespect for women. Watene's novel *Sunset on the Manyatta* (1974) examines the theme of individual freedom in a society whose traditions have been disrupted by colonial education and modernity. It is the story of Harry Nylo ole Kantai ole Syambu, who visits Germany and makes friends in a community radically different from his own. The story follows a familiar line of presentation—alienation abroad, culture shock, and sexual discovery. Watene stopped writing after 1974, preferring business ventures to the theater.

MAJOR TEXTS

Watene, Kenneth. *My Son For My Freedom and Other Plays*. Nairobi: East African Publishing House, 1972.

——. *Dedan Kimathi*. Nairobi: Transafrica Publishers, 1974.

——. *Sunset on the Manyatta*. Nairobi: East African Publishing House, 1974.

[Mwangi]

Worku, Daniachew (1944–2003?) Ethiopian short-story writer, poet, and novelist. Worku was born near Dubre Sina in the North Shoa Region and was educated at Koletebe High School. After training as a teacher, he joined the University of Addis Ababa and after graduation served as a lecturer at the university before studying for an MFA degree at the prestigious writers' workshop at the University of Iowa. Upon his return to Ethiopia from the United States, Worku worked as an editor and translator for the Ethiopian Standards Institution and Industrial Projects Services. It was while he was working for the government that Worku began to produce literary works that sought to merge the influence of both his Amhara culture and the ancient Geez traditions of Ethiopia. He was also in-

fluenced by leading Amharic writers including Mengistu Lemma, Kebede Mikael, and Makonnen Endalkachew.

Although Worku was the author of a single novel in English, *The Thirteenth Sun*, he is considered one of the most important figures in modern Ethiopian literature because of his use of experimental prose forms, his combination of techniques borrowed from Amhara traditions, and his modernist fictional techniques. *The Thirteenth Sun* reflects all these influences. It has a simple plot, based on the quest motif common in most African oral traditions: a son takes his ailing father on a pilgrimage to a monastery seeking a cure. But this story is the only simple feature of the novel, for the characters involved in the pilgrimage are allegorical representations of the generational conflict that defined Ethiopian society in the troubled decades leading to the revolution of 1974. Worku, the ailing father, is a barely disguised portrait of Emperor Haile Selassie, caught in the rigid mentality of a feudal order whose dreams of grandeur are cut off from the harsh reality of life in the empire, while the son, Goytom, is a symbol of the intellectual class that opposed the imperial order but led impractical lives themselves, investing in abstract notions of change and imagined, impotent notions of revolution.

The conflict between father and son was thus represented as the competing notions of what the reality of Ethiopian life in the late imperial period was like, and it discussed the inability of both sides in this divide to come to terms with reality. Worku's novel predicted the tragic events that were to overtake Ethiopia in the revolutionary period of the late 1970s, when the old imperial order was replaced by a dictatorship built on the unbending yet imaginary idea of revolution. Upon its publication in 1973, however, *The Thirteenth Sun* stood out not for its prophetic political sense but for the novelist's ability to combine the allegorical structure of a folk motif with some of the most common techniques of modernism, including the use of stream of consciousness, a fragmented and obscure plotline, and its breakdown of linguistic conventions.

PRIMARY TEXTS (IN ENGLISH)

Worku, Daniachew. *The Thirteenth Sun.* London: Heinemann, 1963.

REFERENCES

Bardolph, Jacqueline. "La Littérature Éthiopienne de Langue Anglaise." *Bulletin des Études Africaines* 6, no. 11 (1986): 83–111.

Molvaer, R. K. *Black Lions: The Creative Lives of Modern Ethiopia's Literary Giants and Pioneers.* Lawrenceville, N.J.: Red Sea Press, 1997.

[Gikandi]

Z

Zirimu, Elvania Namukwaya (1938–1979) Ugandan short-story writer, playwright, and actress. Born in a Buganda family near Entebbe, Zirimu was educated at King's College, Budo, and Makerere University College, where she trained as a teacher. She later went to Leeds University, where she graduated with a degree in English. She then returned to Uganda, where she was heavily involved in the development of the theater. Her first play, *Family Spear*, was first performed by Ngoma Players in Kampala. It is a one-act play that deals with gender and generational tensions in a family where the man is expected to be the provider but the woman still must work extremely hard to provide for her husband. *Snoring Strangers*, also first produced by Ngoma Players in 1973, is a one-act play based on village rituals. Zirimu's best-known play, *When the Hunchback Made Rain*, was first produced in 1970 and dramatizes the interaction of human beings and supernatural powers. In the play, based on a Baganda folktale, humans are threatened by a drought and are required to sacrifice to God to avert disaster. The hunchback serves as the intermediary between the people and God. The playwright uses the play to comment on power hierarchies in postcolonial East Africa, where the poor may not be allowed to engage God without powerful mediators. The play also celebrates the cunning ability of underdogs to master their destiny without relying on the goodwill of "supernatural" elites.

PRIMARY TEXTS

Zirimu, Elvania Namukwaya. *When the Hunchback Made Rain, and Snoring Strangers.* Nairobi: East African Publishing House, 1975.

[Mwangi]

Zirimu, Pio (?–1977) Ugandan linguist and literary theorist. Zirimu is credited with coining the word "orature" as an alternative to the self-contradictory term "oral literature" used to refer to the nonwritten expressive traditions of Africa. Zirimu was also central in reforming the literature syllabus at Makerere University to focus on African literature and culture instead of the English canon. Born in Buganda and educated at King's College, Budo, Zirimu attended Makerere University College and the University of Leeds, where he was a contemporary of Ngugi wa Thiong'o. He later taught at the Institute of Language Studies at Makerere, where he was involved in the formulation of standards for judging the emergent African literature of the 1960s. He defined "orature" as the use of the spoken word as a means of aesthetic expression. In 1977, he coauthored an essay with Austin Bukenya, "Oracy as a

Tool of Development," in which the two researchers showed the centrality of orature to participatory development. In "An Approach to Black Aesthetics," he set out to distinguish black aesthetics from other systems of artistic practice and appreciation. He argued that despite internal differences, "it can be stated categorically that the dominant aesthetic values of all black people are more similar to one another than to white ones and vice versa" (60). For Zirimu, the distinguishing characteristics of a black aesthetic resided in the rhythm of African life, the communal production of art, and its special perception of nature and beauty.

REFERENCES

Gurr, Andrew, and Pio Zirimu, eds. *Black Aesthetics: Papers from a Colloquium Held at the University of Nairobi, June 1971*. Nairobi : East African Literature Bureau, 1973.

Zirimu, Pio. "An Approach to Black Aesthetics." In *Black Aesthetics: Papers from a Colloquium Held at the University of Nairobi, June 1971*, edited by Andrew Gurr and Pio Zirimu, 58–68. Nairobi: East African Literature Bureau, 1973.

Zirimu, Pio, and Austin Bukenya. "Oracy as a Tool of Development." Paper presented at the Festival of African Arts and Culture (Festac '77), Lagos, Nigeria, January 15, 1977.

[Mwangi]

Selected Bibliography

HISTORY AND CULTURE

Alpers, Edward A. *Ivory and Slaves: The Changing Pattern of International Trade in East Central Africa to the Later Nineteenth Century.* Berkeley: University of California Press, 1975.

Anderson, David, and Douglas Hamilton Johnson. *Revealing Prophets: Prophecy in Eastern African History.* London: James Curry, 1995.

Ayot, H. Okello. *Topics in East African History, 1000–1970.* Kampala: East African Literature Bureau, 1976.

Barz, Gregory F. *Music in East Africa: Experiencing Music, Expressing Culture.* Global Music Series. New York: Oxford University Press, 2004.

Beachey, R. W. *A Collection of Documents on the Slave Trade of Eastern Africa.* New York: Barnes and Noble, 1976.

———. *A History of East Africa, 1592–1902.* Vol. 3 of *The International Library of African Studies.* London and New York, 1996.

———. *The Slave Trade of Eastern Africa.* New York: Barnes and Noble, 1976.

Boxer, C. R., and Carlos de Azevedo. *Fort Jesus and the Portuguese in Mombasa, 1593–1729.* London: Hollis & Carter, 1960.

Brett, E. A. *Colonialism and Underdevelopment in East Africa: The Politics of Economic Change, 1919–1939.* London: Heinemann, 1973.

Cameron, John. *The Development of Education in East Africa.* New York: Teachers College Press, 1970.

Chittick, H. Neville, and Robert I. Rotberg. *East Africa and the Orient: Cultural Syntheses in Pre-Colonial Times.* New York: Africana Publishing Co., 1975.

Cooper, Frederick. *From Slaves to Squatters: Plantation Labor and Agriculture in Zanzibar and Coastal Kenya, 1890–1925.* New Haven, Conn.: Yale University Press, 1980.

———. *Plantation Slavery on the East Coast of Africa.* Portsmouth, N.H.: Heinemann, 1997.

Coupland, Reginald. *East Africa and Its Invaders.* Oxford: The Clarendon Press, 1938.

——. *The Exploitation of East Africa, 1856–1890: The Slave Trade and the Scramble.* London: Faber and Faber, 1939.

Davidson, Basil, and J. E. F. Mhina. *East and Central Africa to the Late Nineteenth Century.* London: Longmans, 1967.

De Vere Allen, James, and John Middleton. *Swahili Origins: Swahili Culture and the Shungwaya Phenomenon.* Eastern African Studies Series. London: James Currey, 1993.

Ehret, Christopher. *An African Classical Age: Eastern and Southern Africa in World History, 1000 BC To AD 400.* Charlottesville: University Press of Virginia, 1998.

——. *Ethiopians and East Africans: The Problem of Contacts.* Nairobi Historical Studies 3. Nairobi: East African Pub. House, 1974.

Freeman-Grenville, G. S. P. *The East African Coast: Select Documents from the First to the Earlier Nineteenth Century.* 2nd ed. London: Collings, 1975.

——. *The Swahili Coast, Second to Nineteenth Centuries: Islam, Christianity, and Commerce.* London: Variorum Reprints, 1988.

Ghai, Yash P. *Constitutions and the Political Order in East Africa.* Dar es Salaam: University College, 1970.

Historical Association of Kenya, and Bethwell A. Ogot. *Ecology and History in East Africa: Proceedings of the 1975 Conference of the Historical Association of Kenya.* Nairobi: Kenya Literature Bureau, 1979.

——. *History and Social Change in East Africa: Proceedings of the 1974 Conference of the Historical Association of Kenya.* Nairobi: East African Literature Bureau, 1976.

Horton, Mark, and John Middleton. *The Swahili: The Social Landscape of a Mercantile Society.* Malden, Mass.: Blackwell, 2000.

Iliffe, John. *East African Doctors: A History of the Modern Profession.* African Studies Series. Cambridge: Cambridge University Press, 1998.

Ingham, Kenneth. *A History of East Africa.* Books That Matter. New York: Praeger, 1962.

Johnson Douglas, H., and David Anderson. *Revealing Prophets: Prophecy in Eastern African History.* Eastern African Studies. London: J. Currey, 1995.

Mangat, J. S. *A History of the Asians in East Africa, C. 1886 to 1945.* Oxford Studies in African Affairs. Oxford: Clarendon Press, 1969.

Muga, E. *African Response to Western Christian Religion: A Sociological Analysis of African Separatist Religious and Political Movements in East Africa.* Kampala: East African Literature Bureau, 1975.

Nabudere, D. Wadada. *Imperialism in East Africa.* London: Zed Press, 1981.

Ogot, Bethwell A. *Hadith 6: History and Social Change in East Africa: Proceedings of the 1974 Conference of the Historical Association of Kenya.* Nairobi: Published for the Historical Association of Kenya by the East African Literature Bureau, 1976.

——. *Zamani: A Survey of East African History.* New ed. Nairobi: East African Publishing House, 1974.

Oliver, Roland Anthony. *History of East Africa.* Oxford: Clarendon Press, 1963.

——. *The Missionary Factor in East Africa.* London: Longmans, Green, 1952.

Oyugi, Walter Ouma. *Politics and Administration in East Africa.* Nairobi: East African Educational Publishers, 1994.

Strayer, Robert W., Edward I. Steinhart, and Robert M. Maxon. *Protest Movements in Colonial East Africa: Aspects of Early African Response to European Rule.* Eastern African Studies 12. Syracuse, N.Y.: Program of Eastern African Studies, Syracuse University, 1973.

Sutton John, E. G. *A Thousand Years of East Africa.* Nairobi: British Institute in Eastern Africa, 1990.

Welbourn, Frederick Burkewood. *East African Rebels: A Study of Some Independent Churches.* World Mission Studies. London: SCM Press, 1961.

Were, Gideon S., and Derek Wilson. *East Africa Through a Thousand Years: A History of the Years A.D. 1000 to the Present Day.* 2nd ed. London: Evans, 1982.

LITERARY CRITICISM

Biersteker, A. "Language, Poetry, and Power: A Reconsideration of 'Utendi wa Mwana Kupona.' " In *Faces of Islam in African Literature*, edited by K. W. Harrow, 59–77. Portsmouth, N.H.: Heinemann, 1991.

p'Bitek, Okot. *Africa's Cultural Revolution.* Nairobi: Macmillan Books for Africa, 1973.

——. "The Future of Vernacular Literature." In *East African Literature: An Anthology*, edited by A. Zettersten, 198–206. New York: Longman, 1983.

Bukenya, A. "An Idiom of Blood: Pragmatic Interpretation of Terror and Violence in the Modern Ugandan Novel." *Uganda Journal* 46 (2000): 17–37.

Cook, David. *In Black and White: Writings from East Africa with Broadcast Discussions and Commentary.* Kampala: East African Literature Bureau, 1976.

Eastman, C. M. "An Ethnography of Swahili Expressive Culture." *Research in African Literatures* 15, no. 3 (1984): 313–340.

Gerard, Albert. *African Language Literatures: An Introduction to the Literary History of Sub-Saharan Africa.* Harlow: Longman, 1981.

Gikandi, Simon. *Ngugi wa Thiong'o.* Cambridge: Cambridge University Press, 2002.

——. *Reading the African Novel.* London: James Currey, 1987.

Graebner, Werner, ed. *Sokomoko: Popular Culture in East Africa.* Matatu 9. Amsterdam: Rodopi, 1992.

Griffiths, G. "Writing, Literacy, and History in Africa." In *Writing in Africa*, edited by Paul Hyland and Mpalive-Hangson Msiska, 139–158. London: Longman, 1996.

Gurnah, A., ed. *Essays on African Writing.* Vol. 1, *A Re-evaluation.* London: Heinemann, 1993.

——. *Essays on African Writing.* Vol. 2, *Contemporary Literature.* London: Heinemann, 1995.

Irele, Abiola. *The African Experience in Literature and Ideology.* London: Heinemann, 1981.

——, and Simon Gikandi, eds. *The Cambridge History of African and Caribbean Literature.* Cambridge: Cambridge University Press, 2004.

JanMohamed, Abdul. *Manichean Aesthetics: The Politics of Literature in Colonial Africa.* Amherst, Mass.: University of Massachusetts Press, 1983.

Killam, G. D., ed. *The Writing of East and Central Africa.* London: Heinemann, 1984.

Lazarus, Neil. *Resistance in Postcolonial African Fiction.* New Haven, Conn.: Yale University Press, 1990.

Lindfors, Bernth. *African Textualities: Texts, Pre-texts, and Contexts of African Literature.* Trenton, N.J.: Africa World Press, 1997.

——. *Mazungumzo: Interviews with East African Writers, Publishers, Editors, and Scholars.* Athens: Ohio University, Center for International Studies, 1980.

Lo Liyong, Taban. *Another Last Word.* Nairobi: Heinemann Kenya, 1990.

——. *Popular Culture of East Africa: Oral Literature.* Nairobi: Longman, 1972.

——. *The Last Word: Cultural Synthesism.* Nairobi: East African Publishing House, 1969.

Mugambi, J. N. K. *Critiques of Christianity in African Literature, with Particular Reference to the East African Context.* Nairobi: East African Educational Publishers, 1992.

Nazareth, Peter. "Africa Under Neo-Colonialism: New East African Writing." *Busara* 1 (1974).

Owomoyela, Oyekan, ed. *A History of Twentieth-Century African Literature.* Lincoln: University of Nebraska Press, 1993.

Schild, U. *The East African Experience: Essays on English and Swahili Literature: 2nd Janheinz Jahn-Symposium.* Berlin: D. Reimer Verlag, 1980.

Sicherman, C. *Ngugi wa Thiong'o: A Bibliography of Primary and Secondary Sources, 1957–1987.* London: Hans Zell, 1989.

——. *Ngugi wa Thiong'o, the Making of a Rebel: A Source Book in Kenyan Literature and Resistance.* London: Hans Zell, 1990.

——. "Revolutionizing the Literature Curriculum at the University of East Africa: Literature and the Soul of the Nation." *Research in African Literatures* 29, no. 3 (1998): 129–148.

Simatei, T. P. *The Novel and the Politics of Nation Building in East Africa.* Bayreuth: Bayreuth University Press, 2001.

Smith, Angela. *East African Writing in English.* London and New York: Macmillan, 1989.

Somjee, S. H. "Oral Traditions and Material Culture: An East African Experience." *Research in African Literatures* 31, no. 4 (2000): 97–103.

Wanjala, Chris. *The Season of Harvest: A Literary Discussion.* Nairobi: Kenya Literature Bureau, 1978.

——. *Standpoints on African Literature: A Critical Anthology.* Nairobi: East African Literature Bureau, 1973.

Zirimu, Pio, and Andrew Gurr, eds. *Black Aesthetics.* Nairobi: East African Literature Bureau, 1973.

——, eds. *Writers in East Africa.* Nairobi: East African Literature Bureau, 1974.

Index